Raising Ruby

Patricia Smith Wood

Aakenbaaken & Kent

Raising Ruby

aakenbaakeneditor@gmail.com

ISBN: 978-1-958022-07-8

Introduction

Why Write This Book?

I've been a student of history for as long as I can remember. As an only child in a large family of adults for my first six years, listening to their conversations intrigued me. They often talked about "old times", long-gone members of the family, events in the world prior to and after my arrival, and sometimes their hopes for the future.

We went to the movies most weeks when I was a child, and the newsreels gave us the latest film of the happenings in the world. The radio also brought news of World War II each day it raged. We listened to those newscasters to get the latest information.

My mother was a beautiful woman and wanted to instill in me a love for literature, music, history, and the finer things of life. She grew up in poverty during the Great Depression. Her family lived as tenant farmers on a variety of farms, and the children were expected to work as hard as the adults.

I believe the history of those times and the story of her life will help the reader better understand people from the previous two centuries. The context of their lives, the limitations they had, and the choices they made become more understandable—at least that is my wish.

$\mathcal{P}rologue$

Mother's Day, Sunday, May 10, 1936

Ruby stood on the sidewalk and watched her new friends drive away. On the trip to Fort Worth, her emotions had run the gamut between panic and relief. Now that she was here, she felt apprehension about her future. Would she be able to find a job? Would anyone hire a 16-year-old girl they didn't know? Maybe because she was tall, people would think she was older. She had to stop thinking this way. Her future could wait. At the moment, she felt intense gratitude just to be here.

She picked up her battered suitcase and turned toward the boarding house. She reached the front porch and rang the doorbell.

A short, plump lady answered the door. She smiled when she saw the tall young girl and her pitiful suitcase.

"Hello, child." The voice had the familiar, slow Texas drawl. The woman's warm smile crinkled her pleasant face. "Are you here 'bout rentin' the room?"

Ruby nodded. "Yes, Ma'am. I saw your ad."

"Well, come on in." The woman opened the screen door. "My name is Mrs. Murphy. I'll show you the room. If it suits you—and if you have $2 for the week's rent—we have a deal."

Ruby relaxed a bit. Mrs. Murphy seemed warm and welcoming. Maybe things wouldn't be so different from her small farming community.

The plump woman chatted as she climbed the stairs, but Ruby couldn't focus. She kept running over the events of the day. It didn't seem real that she got away.

She didn't feel safe yet and wouldn't until she found a job. Maybe tomorrow. For now, it was a hot, humid Sunday in May. She was exhausted from tension and fear. She only wanted to sleep.

Seeing her mother looking so old and tired this afternoon almost changed Ruby's mind. Then Mamma reached into the envelope she'd retrieved from the cupboard. She pulled out ten crumpled, one-dollar bills, put them in Ruby's hand, and wiped her eyes. "You'd best hurry. He'll be back soon. "

Ruby swallowed, nodded, and stuffed the money into her small, purse. How had Mamma saved it?

She turned to walk away and Mamma said, "Get word to me where you are. Let Aunt Ina know what happened."

"I will, Mamma."

But she knew she wouldn't. Eventually she'd contact her mother's sister, but she didn't want anybody to know why she left.

Ruby became aware Mrs. Murphy had spoken to her. "I'm sorry, Ma'am. Did you say something?"

Mrs. Murphy frowned. "Are you all right child? You look exhausted. You haven't told me your name."

Ruby smiled. "I'm Ruby Ellen Scott. I just arrived from a small farm in Erath County. I guess I'm tired, and I'm excited to be in the big city."

Mrs. Murphy unlocked the door to the small bedroom. It was sparsely furnished, but it looked comfortable and inviting. Mrs. Murphy said, "The bathroom is right down the hall."

Ruby nodded. "It's a nice room." She walked inside, put her suitcase on the bed, and looked around. Mrs. Murphy stood expectantly in the doorway.

When she turned back to the landlady, Ruby realized she needed to give the woman her rent in advance. "Oh," she said. "I don't know where my head is. You'll be needing my rent for the week." She reached in her purse and pulled out two of the crumpled one-dollar bills.

Mrs. Murphy smiled as she took the money and handed Ruby the room key. "Supper is at 6 p.m. on the dot. Don't be late."

And with that, Ruby Ellen Scott shut the door to her new home, locked it, and for the first time in months, felt the remaining fear and dread melting away.

Part One
April 8, 1896, to May 10, 1936
Chapter 1
1896 to 1918

Between April 6 and April 16, 1896, one amazing event (and a rather ordinary one) happened. The amazing event occurred in Athens, Greece on April 6, with the beginning of the Modern Olympic Games—the first in the 1,500 years since they had been banned by Roman Emperor Theodosius I.

The ordinary event happened on Wednesday, April 8, when Jimma Jane Palmer entered the world. Born in Somervell County, Texas, she became the third-born child and second daughter of J.R. and Ellen Palmer. The Palmer's first child had died at age three.

The Palmers couldn't have imagined the changes that would occur within a 100 years. The challenges and opportunities of the 20th century would unfold without many people noticing at first. The huge innovations, the wars, and the exploding immigration from Europe would dramatically change the United States. There were amazing improvements, heart-breaking losses, and new challenges.

Barely three months after the 20th century began, Jimma Jane Palmer celebrated her fourth birthday. Two more siblings (a boy and a girl) had arrived before the end of the 19th century, and the 20th century brought four more siblings: two girls and two boys.

In those days, especially in farming families, each child had their place in the family work force. Jimma was designated to take her place at her father's side as soon as she was old enough to help with planting, tending, and harvesting crops. Her older sister, Gena, was mother's helper inside. It was Gena who learned to cook, clean, wash clothes, and otherwise maintain a home for the family. She also helped her mother with the younger children. When sister Wilsie was old enough, she helped Gena. Jimma and the three boys worked with their father in the fields. Therefore, Jimma learned few homemaking skills, hated to cook, and had practically no childcare experience.

J.R. and Ellen Palmer were typical country folks in North Central Texas in the late 19th and early part of the 20th century. J.R. became a farmer and a veterinarian early on. Eventually he served as a deputy sheriff in his spare time, and during Prohibition, he became a Revenuer for the US Bureau of Prohibition. J.R. grew up with just his mother, his stepfather, and his younger half-brother. His wife Ellen grew up in a family with lots of children. She learned all about household chores and raising kids. Her mother died at Ellen's birth, and she was raised by the rest of her siblings and her stepmother. She was well suited for J.R. and for raising a large family. She was a gentle, loving soul, and J.R. was kind, strong and capable.

Jimma was never interested in household chores. She was an artist, loved the outdoors, and loved painting it. She was more interested in creating beautiful pictures than cooking, cleaning, and caring for children.

Jimma met her future husband, Thomas Lester Scott, early in 1918. By that time, she was almost twenty-two. Her older sister Gena had married in 1913, and J.R. and Ellen were beginning to worry about their second daughter. But the Great War had been raging in Europe since 1914, and young men in the U.S. were concerned about being drafted and shipped off to those far away battles. During that same time, the Spanish Flu Pandemic raged throughout the world. It had apparently started in the United States at a military training base where young soldiers trained for the war. With newly minted soldiers leaving that facility in droves to join the war effort in 1918, the virus spread like hungry ants at a picnic. The whole of Europe was engulfed in the pandemic although ironically, Spain had fewer infections than most countries.

Lester and Jimma married on September 12, 1918, in Bonham, Texas. They held off starting their family until Lester could be sure he wouldn't be drafted. He didn't want to leave his new wife pregnant.

On November 11, 1918, at 11:00 a.m. Paris, France time, the Armistice was signed. It ended the fighting, but Germany did not surrender. The armies involved in that war simply stopped fighting, put down their weapons, and went home.

Lester and Jimma Scott breathed a sigh of relief. That very night, in Red River County, Texas, the young couple initiated the conception of their first child—Ruby Ellen.

Chapter 2
Late 1918 to Mid 1919

De Leon, Texas came into being in 1881 when the railroad decided to lay tracks for the Missouri-Kansas-Texas (Katy) Railroad. In 1910, De Leon became the hub for the Katy between the Texas cities of Waco, Albany, and Cross Plains. Many railroad jobs were created, and the men and their families flocked to the little town.

Right after Christmas 1918, Lester and Jimma decided to move back to Iredell and live with his mother. That's where they were when Lester secured the job with the railroad in De Leon.

Travel in the backroads of Texas in 1918 was largely by horse and buggy. Most folks eked out a living farming or raising livestock. Some sought other jobs because farming was tough work and often didn't earn enough for the basics. Even though Henry Ford's one-millionth Model "T" automobile came off the assembly line in 1915 at a price of $250, most farmers could only dream of owning an automobile or truck, but it wouldn't be forthcoming without saving a lot of money.

Lester had a horse and buggy. On a good day, the horse traveled between five and eight miles an hour. De Leon was at least 33 miles from some relatives, and more than 40 from others. The only choice was moving to De Leon by the end of the year.

Lester found a suitable place in a rooming house in De Leon, and for the next eight months, he worked at the railroad, and made it back to De Leon at the end of each trip. Around the end of February, Jimma realized she was pregnant. She had made friends with the lady who owned the house. Her landlady had a daughter, who was just a baby at the time. This young woman understood Jimma's worries and trepidations about the birth.

For her part, Jimma worked most days at the De Leon Peanut Company to bring in extra money, but because of her condition, that became more and more difficult as the months went by. Eventually she had to quit the job when the heat of July turned into a sweltering August. She had gotten too big and too weary to be on her feet all day. When the evening of August 11, 1919, rolled around, Jimma was glad to have the help and support of her landlady. When labor started, the helpful woman summoned a midwife.

When Ruby Ellen Scott made her debut in the early morning hours of Tuesday, August 12, 1919, Jimma sighed in relief that her baby was healthy and perfect. Unfortunately, Jimma, herself, would shortly come down with a scary disease—Typhoid fever.

Chapter 3
1919 to 1921

Jimma's mother traveled to DeLeon to care for her daughter and new granddaughter. Being raised in a large family gave Ellen experience caring for sick people and comforting them when they hurt. Ellen insisted on taking her and the baby back to the Palmer home in Somervell.

Jimma recovered, Lester left the railroad, and moved his wife and child back to Iredell. Then J.R offered them the use of a small house and farmland he owned around Hico, so they moved again.

On Ruby's first birthday, the country waited for ratification of the 19th Amendment to the Constitution—giving women in the United States the right to vote. It finally happened on August 18, 1920, when by a margin of one vote, the Tennessee legislature became the 35th state to sign. Official ratification happened August 26, 1920 when the Governor of Tennessee signed the legislation. Ruby would be just short of her 85th birthday when the last state in the Union signed off on the 19th amendment on March 22, 1984.

In February 1921, Ruby's baby brother, James Lester Scott, arrived. The Scott family had a bright future ahead, if not a financially stable one. Fortunately, Jimma and Lester had family who loved them, friends and neighbors who cared about them, and the future always held the promise of something better.

For Ruby's second birthday in August 1921, her father had saved up a little money and bought her a beautiful doll. It had a leather body and a bisque head. Ruby wanted a doll so badly, and when she received it, she begged to take it down the road to show her playmate, Daisy. Jimma—somewhat reluctantly—agreed.

Daisy's mother sat at her ironing board in front of the open backdoor of the kitchen. In the heat of August, it helped when tackling such a chore. When Ruby arrived with her precious doll, she excitedly reached up and put the doll on the ironing board so Daisy's mother could admire it. Daisy's mother "oohed" and "aahed," telling Ruby how beautiful it was. Daisy, a few months older than Ruby, apparently felt left out. She reached up and knocked the doll to the floor, smashing the beautiful bisque head.

Ruby's shock and grief would be seared into her memory for the rest of her life. It was the earliest, detailed memory she had, and it was devastating for a little girl to lose the thing she had—only seconds earlier—been so excited to show her friend. Ruby dreaded what her mother would say.

She felt even worse when Jimma told her husband what had happened to the expensive gift. Ruby adored her daddy and didn't want him to be angry with her. But Lester didn't want her to feel even worse than she already did. He didn't scold her.

Jimma glued the bisque doll's head together the best she could. It sat high up on a shelf, and Ruby didn't understand why she couldn't play with it. Later, Ruby heard her mother telling her father he shouldn't have purchased such a breakable thing for a two-year old. It made Ruby feel even worse.

Chapter 4
Fall/Winter 1921

By fall 1921, the broken and glued bisque doll was permanently put out of sight. Ruby's grandmother Ellen made her a series of rag dolls, dressed in bright, happy colors, and Ruby's grief about the loss of the beautiful doll slowly receded. But her dislike of Daisy, the Doll Destroyer, had not. Ruby no longer wanted to play with her former friend.

By November 1921, the United States began to recover some of its economic losses caused by a recession after the Great War. That two-year recession hit farmers harder than anyone. But Lester Scott now had a better job, which brought in more money for the young family. Christmas would be upon them soon, and Lester wanted Ruby to have a nice gift.

When Christmas Eve arrived, the entire family attended services at their church. There was a small, plank bridge to cross between the road and the entrance to the church. The planks had spaces between them, and Ruby was afraid to walk across on her own. So, her daddy picked her up and carried her into the church.

All the parents had been asked to bring a gift for their child. After the service, Santa Claus arrived. He gathered up the gifts, placed them in his big bag, and started distributing them on the opposite side of the church. Ruby watched with rising anticipation.

As luck would have it, Daisy the Doll Destroyer and her family had scooted into the pew beside Ruby's family. Santa came closer to their pew, and Ruby spied something poking out of the gift bag that caused her eyes to light up. It was a little toy broom—just the right size for Ruby. She watched as the gifts were distributed. When Santa stopped at Ruby's pew, her heart almost leaped out of her chest. The toy broom would be hers!

She reached out to receive her prize, but instead, Santa handed the tiny, kid-sized broom to the unworthy Daisy. Ruby couldn't believe this treasure, obviously meant for her, was now in the hands of her sworn enemy. Anger enveloped her like a suffocating storm.

Then Santa reached in his bag again and withdrew a rubber baby doll. He handed it to the stunned Ruby. She looked at the ugly, squinty-faced baby doll, threw it on the floor, and burst into angry tears of disappointment. Daisy the Doll Destroyer had not only taken her beautiful bisque birthday doll from her, now she triumphantly and gleefully swept the aisle beside their pew with the lovely little toy broom Ruby so coveted.

Lester felt awful. He had agreed to Jimma's suggestion of the rubber doll since it might make up for the broken one and was certainly a better choice for a two-year-old. Jimma scolded Ruby for being so ungrateful for her gift. She pointed out that her father was disappointed because he thought she would like the rubber baby doll. Ruby hated to disappoint her daddy.

On the way home that Christmas Eve, Ruby fell asleep with her head on her father's shoulder. He carried her gently over the bridge with the cracks while she clutched the rejected rubber doll. The child's guilt feelings would only linger in memory if another, more traumatic memory became imprinted.

Ruby didn't have long to wait.

Chapter 5

January 1922

After Christmas came January—the worst month of the year for most kids and, in truth, for most adults. It was a new year, with a new set of worries, and challenges.

Lester now had a job driving a McConnon's Dry Goods Wagon. The new job required that he leave each Monday morning, driving his route, servicing his customers. He didn't return home until Saturday afternoons. There was no time for farming. He discussed it with Jimma, and they agreed they would leave the farm and rent a house down the road.

Lester felt confident his new job would allow them to easily meet the rent payments, and even pay off some debts they had accumulated over the past year.

On Monday, January 9, 1922, Lester readied the horse-drawn wagon to take on his weekly route, and discovered he needed to grease one of the wheels.

At age six years, Lester was riding horseback when he fell on the pommel of his saddle. Unknown to him or anyone else—it left him vulnerable.

Now, on this cold Monday, Lester went about fixing the wheel. He needed to lift the wagon to remove the wheel for greasing. When he did, his old injury ruptured, and his intestines were now being strangled. He fell to the ground in agony.

Jimma came outside and saw the situation. They had no car, no telephone, and no way to get help. It was about 10 a.m., and Jimma's father had planned to arrive there at noon. They had to wait for J.R. He arrived on horseback at noon and immediately returned home to get his car. By this time, Lester had been suffering for three hours. J.R. returned with his son Russ, and the two men lifted Lester into the car. They drove as fast as they could to a hospital in Waco, but it took more than an hour.

The doctors quickly took Lester into surgery and removed part of his intestine. Nevertheless, within a few days, gangrene set in. The young man, who by this time was mostly sedated, waited for the agony to end.

Jimma wanted to be with her husband. Her father took the children home with him so their grandmother could care for them. Jimma stayed with Lester as much as she could.

On Sunday afternoon, Lester was awake. Jimma sat with him through the evening, and they talked for hours into the night about things young parents would discuss when one of them was gravely injured.

At one point, very early in the morning, Lester turned to his wife and said, "Jimma, do you see those three angels at the foot of my bed? They're dressed in white and have the most beautiful wings."

Jimma saw the look of peace and awe on her husband's face. She sadly admitted to him she did not see what he saw. He insisted they were there and very real. They seemed to comfort him and ease his pain.

In the early morning hours of Monday, January 16, 1922, just a few weeks short of his 24th birthday, Thomas Lester Scott left his earthly body behind and followed his angels.

Chapter 6
The Funeral – January 1922

Young children notice things their parents don't realize. The days and nights have a pattern, giving life a rhythm.

Ruby understood, on one level, that her father was gone during the week. That was his pattern. He climbed up on the big wagon, took the horse's reins, and waved a cheery goodbye to Ruby and Jimma. When he returned on Saturdays, he would swing his little girl up in the air and make her giggle. Ruby loved those homecomings.

Now things were different in Ruby's world. She didn't understand the changed patterns. Her daddy didn't come home on Saturday, but his wagon was there. Her mother cried a lot, and Ruby and her baby brother were hauled off to her grandparents' farm. The days passed slowly for a little girl Ruby's age. She was far too young to understand the concept of time.

Then one day, her grandmother dressed her up in her nicest dress, and her grandparents took her to church in their big wagon. Everyone had been so sad, and Ruby hoped going to church meant things were okay now.

She walked in, clutching the hand of her tall grandfather. She saw a big old horse trough setting up in the front of the church, right where the Christmas tree had been. She wondered why it was there and what was in it.

They approached the front of the church and sat next to her mother. Mamma was crying, but she hugged Ruby real tight and cried harder. The preacher stood next to the horse trough and talked a long time.

After all the talking and singing hymns, people stood and walked toward the big old horse trough. Ruby's grandfather picked her up and carried her so she could see inside.

Ruby felt excited—just like when her daddy came home. But now, her daddy was in that trough, and he was asleep. She couldn't think why he would come to church to sleep in a horse trough.

A few days later, Grandma and Grandpa took Ruby and Bud back home. Her daddy still wasn't there, but Mamma hugged Ruby so hard it hurt.

Mamma explained that Daddy died. Ruby struggled to understand that because she knew the animals at the farm died all the time. Sometimes, she saw her mother, or her grandmother kill a chicken for Sunday dinner.

But the way Mamma explained it, Daddy was sleeping in that big old horse trough because he was dead. Mamma said he was inside that box, in the ground, and after some time passed, he would be a skeleton. Ruby had seen a skeleton hanging from a tree on Halloween last year. Mamma told her skeletons were people who had died.

That night, Ruby had a dream she remembered for a very long time. In her dream, she saw a skeleton dancing in the graveyard, and it waved to her. It comforted her because she knew it was her Daddy, and he still remembered her.

Maybe he would come back next Halloween and wave to her again.

Chapter 7

Late January 1922

In the days after the funeral, Jimma's grief left her numb. Even so, she faced some difficult decisions. Although Lester's job with McConnon's had been a promising one, he hadn't been with them long enough to pay off debts the family had incurred during the past year. Not only that, but Jimma knew they hadn't managed to build any savings in the short time Lester had worked for the company. With no other options, she decided to ask her parents for help.

The last thing Jimma wanted was to move herself and her kids into her parents' home. She loved them both, but she and her father had clashed frequently since she was a child. Jimma and J.R. were both stubborn, and the fact that J.R. was her father never seemed to keep her from arguing with him. Still, she was desperate and couldn't think of a better solution. She went to them and asked if she and the children could live there.

Jimma understood the household was already crowded with several of her siblings still at home. Two of her brothers, Russ, 24, and Dyer, 20, helped their father in the fields, as did brother Lillard, 15, when he wasn't in school. At 18, her sister Ina Mae hadn't yet married, and sister Margie was only 13. Jimma vowed that this time, she would avoid the impulse to engage in any arguments with her father—no matter what.

It turned out that *no-matter-what* came a lot sooner than she expected.

Chapter 8
February 1922

Jimma felt nervous about the move to her parent's farm, but Ruby was delighted. She basked in their attention and love.

Winters in Texas can be miserably cold. The dampness and cold northern winds make it hard to warm a home. The only heat in the entire house came from the wood stove in the kitchen.

Shortly after Jimma and her kids moved in, she awoke one morning, feeling colder than usual. She gathered up the children and took them into the kitchen. She put both kids close to the stove, and joined them.

Coffee was a big staple at the farm—especially in the dead cold of winter. Granny already had a huge gallon-sized enamel coffee pot on the burner, ready to warm the insides of the men working outdoors.

Jimma's tired, grieving brain didn't warn her of the danger. The three of them sat in front of the stove, absorbing the warmth of the burning wood. Granny was preparing breakfast, but Jimma and the two children were in the way.

Granny Palmer moved the coffee pot to the next burner. When she did, the coffee pot "caught" on one of the burner caps and caused the full pot to tip over, spilling hot, boiling coffee on Jimma, Buddy, and Ruby.

The hot mess barely touched Jimma and didn't reach Buddy at all. Ruby received most of the burning liquid, soaking the cotton stockings covering her legs. She screamed, and when Jimma ripped off the stockings, most of the skin along Ruby's shins came off.

Jimma screamed, Buddy cried, and Granny Palmer was horrified. Granny was angry because Jimma put herself and her kids in such a dangerous place.

Ruby would always remember the pain of that burn, and the tender, loving treatment she received.

Ruby's Aunt Ina Ruth was five years older than her sister Margie, who already planned to become a nurse. The two young ladies took on the task of daily removal of the old bandages on Ruby's legs, the application of burn salve, and applying new bandages. Ruby always cried when it was time to change the bandages. But either Ina or Margie would distract her with a song, or a long, interesting story, while the other aunt removed the old dressing and applied the salve and new dressing. Ruby stopped crying when they distracted her, and later admitted she hadn't felt any pain during the process.

When Ruby grew older, she'd learn many people had access to doctors during their childhood. But Ruby and her family never saw a doctor until they left home and were on their own. In the country, everyone knew basic first aid—how to set broken bones, and just about anything else that happened. If they were lucky, the women had the comfort of a midwife to help with childbirth, but if they didn't, a family member or a neighbor would deliver the child.

Ruby would always be grateful for her aunts. They took the time and energy to teach and entertain Ruby during those days living with the grandparents.

Chapter 9

Late February 1922

Not long after the burning incident, Jimma and her father had a huge argument. Father and daughter argued often, and rarely remembered why. For the rest of their lives they occasionally became engaged in heated arguments.

Ruby always felt nervous and jittery when her mother became angry. On that day, she and her brother had been playing outside when they heard loud voices coming from the barn. Grandpa Palmer rarely raised his voice, but when his next-to-the-oldest daughter went on a tirade, Grandpa vigorously let her know his opinion.

This time, coupled with Jimma's grief, fear of the future, and the horrible incident that had caused Ruby to be burned, Jimma's anger clouded any judgement she might have had. She only knew she had to take herself and her children someplace away from her parents.

All Ruby remembered was her angry mother coming into the house and throwing all their belongings into a burlap sack. She grabbed her children, and they left. Ruby walked down the road, clinging to her mother's skirt. Jimma used one arm to carry her baby son, and the other arm carried a burlap sack with all the clothes the little family owned. Jimma cried as she walked down the road, and Ruby wondered where they were going and how long it would take to get there.

After what seemed like a very long time, Jimma stopped and sat down beside the road. She told Ruby they would wait for the mailman to come along in his truck. Perhaps she could persuade him to take them to Iredell. And that's exactly what happened.

They arrived at Grandma Scott's little house in Iredell later that morning. Grandma Scott was always happy to see her daughter-in-law and her grandchildren. She assured them they could stay with her as long as they needed. But realistically, Jimma knew they couldn't live here more than a few weeks.

Gussie Allen Scott was a sweet, loving woman. Her husband, Thomas Pocus Scott, had left her just six weeks after their last child was born. Gussie, very poor and illiterate, worked the only way she knew how. She cleaned other people's houses and took in laundry. What she had in generous supply was love for her family.

Word came to Jimma in the 1940s that Thomas Pocus Scott had died in an accident at a hotel in Florida. The hotel needed large-scale fumigation. They warned all residents to leave the premises and not return for several days. The building needed to be completely vacant.

The chemical did its job obliterating all the vermin—including Thomas Pocus Scott.

Jimma understood Grandma Scott's situation. She couldn't help but see herself in the same position one day if she didn't come up with a way to earn a living for herself and her children.

She made the decision to contact her older sister, Gena. Gena and Tom Kemp had four sons and a daughter. Jimma wrote to her sister, who lived not far from J.R. and Ellen, and asked if she and the children could come stay with them for a while.

Time to move again.

Chapter 10
The Rest of 1922

One day toward the end of February, Gena arrived at Grandma Scott's house driving her two-seated surrey. To Ruby it looked like something out of a story book. The surrey was a four-wheeled carriage, pulled by two horses. The driver and one passenger could sit on the front seat, and two or three others could sit in the back seat. It even had a top overhead to shield the passengers from the sun or rain. Some surreys had fringe around the top. (In later years, Ruby would hear a song from the musical *Oklahoma* —"Surrey with The Fringe on Top." It always reminded her of Aunt Gena's surrey.)

Jimma and her children settled in at the Kemp house. Ruby was delighted. She loved playing with her cousins. The four boys seemed like brothers to Ruby, and their sister, Ina Mae, was a wonderful playmate close to Ruby's age. It was one of the best years Ruby would remember.

Jimma talked it over with her sister Gena, and decided she needed to go back to school and acquire certification to become a teacher. With her teaching certificate, she could support herself and her children. Gina welcomed Ruby and Buddy to stay with them for the year, while Jimma went back to school. The arrangement worked out well because Jimma could visit her children frequently. So off she went to acquire the certification.

At some point during this stay, Bud starting walking on his own. Mamma acted like it was the most amazing thing. Ruby didn't remember herself not walking, so she didn't understand all the attention Bud got for just taking some stumbling steps. He always fell right away, but Ruby noticed he was getting better at it. Then one day, her little brother was running. He wasn't as good a runner as Ruby, but she figured maybe he'd get better at it. After that, Bud followed Ruby wherever she went, and that sometimes annoyed her.

One hot summer day, the Kemp family were on their way to church in the surrey. Ruby sat on the floor in the back, watching one of the wheels turn. In her child's mind she wondered what would happen if she stuck her foot into the turning wheel. She proceeded to do that, and immediately found herself sitting in the middle of the road, crying. One of the boys yelled to Aunt Gena to stop, and someone retrieved the stunned Ruby, none the worse for wear.

On another occasion during that time, the family returned home from a nighttime church event. During the ride home, a wheel came off the surrey, and Uncle Tom hopped down to put it back on. Most of the kids were sound asleep in the back, so Uncle Tom unloaded the sleepers from the surrey and placed them in the weeds beside the road while he put the wheel back on. When they arrived at the farm, they unloaded the kids and discovered one missing. Uncle Tom had to go back down the road to the spot where he repaired the wheel. He retrieved the still sleeping boy. It was Rex, their third son. When they reached home, they put him to bed. He never knew anything happened. He slept through the entire episode.

Chapter 11
1922 and 1923

Jimma finally made up with her father, and just in time. Gena and Tom were moving to a distant town for his job. Jimma packed up their things and took Ruby and Bud back to the Palmer farm.

The Kemps loaded all their things onto a covered wagon and headed off to Wolf City, Texas, about 135 miles away. Covered wagons were common and the best way to move a household in those days.

Jimma borrowed a wagon to move her possessions back to the Palmer farm. The wagon had a spring-equipped seat where the driver sat. Jimma put her sleeping son on the floor of the wagon, and Ruby sat on the seat beside her mother. During the relatively short journey, they had to cross a creek. Jimma maneuvered the wagon down a large embankment, and back up on the other side. When they had almost finished the steep climb up the other side, the wagon hit a rut. Ruby bounced on the springy seat, lost her balance, and started falling. Jimma panicked and grabbed the child with one hand. She pulled Ruby close, guided the horses with the other hand, and held on tight until they were on level ground. Then she hugged Ruby, and said, "I was so afraid you were going to fall. I couldn't stand to have anything happen to my little girl."

Ruby felt a warm glow. Eventually she realized the feeling was surprise and a stab of gratitude for being loved. She never knew until that moment that she was important to her mother.

Ruby had good memories of her grandparents. She learned many things from both. She realized Granny was a patient person and was more likely to explain why they shouldn't do certain things, rather than yelling at them for doing it. One day, Ruby and Bud were playing in the yard, and Ruby decided to climb the tall windmill. As usual, Bud followed and climbed right behind her. They got to the top, but Bud continued and climbed onto the ledge. Ruby chickened out.

Granny Palmer saw where they were and went to the base of the windmill. She calmly urged them to come down, and when they reached the bottom, she scolded them. She told them how dangerous it was. Ruby always understood why Granny was upset with her, but she never made her feel bad.

Ruby also felt close to Grandpa Palmer. She would follow him everywhere, and he didn't seem to mind. J.R. had a big, bushy mustache, and he would swing Ruby up in the air over his head. She would giggle, then he would nuzzle her chin with his mustache. Ruby loved all the attention he gave her.

Time slipped by, and 1923 replaced 1922. Mamma came home for the summer, and she had her teaching certificate. Sooner than the adults expected, Ruby's fourth birthday arrived. There was an air of celebration, so Mamma and Granny made Ruby a beautiful birthday cake. It had four little pink candles on top, Granny lit them and told Ruby to make a wish, then blow out all the candles. If she did, her wish would come true.

Ruby blew as hard as she could. The candles were extinguished. She hoped that meant Mamma wouldn't go away again.

Chapter 12
Fall 1924 to Spring 1925

With her new teaching certificate in hand, Jimma set out to find a job. She found one at a very remote, one-room schoolhouse in Walnut Springs. Granny Palmer would hitch up her wagon on Fridays, and they would head over to Walnut Springs to bring Jimma back to the farm for the weekend.

It was a stressful assignment. The school hadn't had a full-term teacher in several years. The students were so rowdy and undisciplined that teachers refused to stay on more than a few weeks. In the past few years, none of the teachers hired by the school board stayed on even through the first term. Students believed Jimma would also be some creampuff to be maneuvered into leaving.

They were in for a rather bad shock.

As usual, the older children concocted a plan to scare off this new teacher. One little girl, who really liked Jimma, warned her about the planned attack. Jimma went outside, cut a big switch from a willow tree, and hid it under her desk.

When the older children started chanting and making a circle around her, Jimma wasn't the least bit intimidated. Instead, she pulled out the willow stick and laid into them. As a result, they did not run her off, and they showed her more respect thereafter. She finished the year but said she wouldn't be back. The trustees of the school offered her a substantial raise if she would sign up for another year. But Jimma refused, saying no amount of money would induce her to stay and teach those ruffians.

For her next teaching job, Jimma signed a two-year contract for 1924-1926 to teach at the Marthal Gap School in Erath County. It was a much better school, with children who wanted to learn and parents who disciplined them.

Ruby and Bud (as he was now called) stayed with their grandparents during the school year. During that first year, Ruby and Bud would see less of their mother because Marthal Gap was not close enough to come home every weekend as she had been doing.

But Ruby didn't mind. She would still be in her favorite place—with her grandparents on the farm.

Chapter 13
Spring/Summer 1925

In the spring of 1925, Jimma Scott had almost finished her first year of teaching at the Marthal Gap School in Erath County, Texas. She stayed with the Ewers family in that area, and Jenny Ewers had become her close friend. Ruby and Bud were with Grandma Ellen and Grandpa J.R. Palmer in Somervell.

That same spring a few miles away, Joe Parnell became restless. He had been a widower for close to eighteen months now. He and his two daughters, ages six and eight, lived on a rented farm in another part of the county of Erath. The previous season had brought in good money for the crops he grew. Still, a persistent melancholy settled around him. He wanted a better life for himself and his children, and the more he thought about it, his decision became firm: he needed a partner to help him raise his girls and end his loneliness.

The next time he traveled into town, he saw a young woman he'd never noticed before. She intrigued him, and he asked a friend in the community about her. His friend explained that she was a young widow with two small children. Joe asked for an introduction, and when he met Jimma Parnell Scott, he discovered she was teaching at the Marthal Gap School. She impressed him with her wit and independence.

They began "keeping company," and Joe quickly realized they had much in common. She had been widowed, and she also had young children to raise. Joe decided he would need to impress this lady.

He got a friend to give him a lift to Stephenville, some fourteen miles away. When they arrived, he headed for the Ford Motor Car dealership. If he had an automobile, he felt sure Jimma would see him as a worthy suitor. He had the cash in his pocket from the sale of his crops, and the price of the latest Model T Ford was $260—a lot of money. Only one obstacle stood in his way—he'd never driven a car.

The happy salesman who greeted Joe offered to teach him to drive as part of the service of the dealership's "special" that month. Joe would later realize the idea had popped into the salesman's head as soon as Joe pulled the wad of cash out of his pocket.

They got in the automobile, and Joe soon had the hang of driving a car. With that, he happily handed over his cash, and took off with his new Model T. Joe felt proud of himself. He would woo Jimma Scott, and they would live happily ever after.

If only life was that simple.

Chapter 14
Saturday, May 9, 1925

When Ruby felt excited, she noticed little shivers in her arms and legs. She tried to explain it to Aunt Margie one day. Aunt Margie thought about it, then explained that Ruby's body had thousands of nerve endings running under her skin. When she was excited or happy, these nerve endings "celebrated" and let Ruby know her nerves were happy.

Ruby thought hard about that. She was five years old now and would soon be six. She appreciated a grown-up explanation. She nodded. "I guess my skin is happy too."

Today her skin was happy. Mamma was coming home from teaching at Marthal Gap School. She could stay with Ruby and Bud for the whole summer before she had to return. They would go swimming in the creek, look for berries, maybe even have a picnic. Ruby tried to explain all this to Bud, but he was busy catching a frog and wouldn't pay attention. Ruby didn't care. Mamma was coming home. That's all that mattered.

Aunt Margie called to Ruby and Bud. Someone was coming up the road to the house, and they were in a car. Most people arrived by horse and wagon.

Ruby grabbed Bud. "Come on Bud. Mamma's coming. Put that old frog down and wipe off your hands." Ruby had been trying to teach her brother about manners and keeping clean. It didn't seem to be getting through to him.

By the time they walked around to the front of the house, the car had pulled to a stop.

Ruby saw Mamma and waved at her. But Mamma was looking at Granny and Grandpa. Mamma got out of the car, but she still wasn't looking in Ruby's direction. Instead, she turned to look at a man getting out of the other side of the shiny black car. The man walked around the front of the car. He reached out his hand, and Mamma walked to him and took his hand in hers. They approached Granny and Grandpa.

Ruby's skin wasn't as happy now. It felt confused, as did Ruby. Who was the man with Mamma, and why where they holding hands? Why hadn't Mamma looked for Bud and Ruby when she arrived? It seemed like she and Bud stood there a long, long time. Finally, Mamma turned to her and Bud. She had a big smile on her face and held out her arms for a hug.

Both Ruby and Bud ran to her and wrapped their arms around her. Mamma knelt and hugged them both.

For years to come, Ruby would remember the next few moments. Even so, she had no way of knowing then how significant it would be. Mamma released them and turned to the man. He stepped forward and smiled at the children. His smile looked nice.

Mamma said, "Children, this is Joe Parnell. We got married yesterday. He has two little girls not much older than you, and now we are all a family. He will be your 'Dad' from now on, and that's what you must call him."

Chapter 15
Sunday, May 10, 1925

Today was Mothers' Day. It was also the first day of Ruby and Bud's initiation into the Parnell family. That morning they packed up their belongings and headed for their new home in Johnsville. Ruby begged to stay with Granny and Aunt Margie.

The adults spoke among themselves. Aunt Margie took Ruby aside and promised she would come visit Ruby in her new home. Ruby reluctantly agreed to join her mother and brother.

Joe's young daughters, Veta and Rhudene, were eight, and six. They were very shy when Joe, Jimma, Ruby, and Bud arrived on that Sunday afternoon.

Over the course of the summer, the children got to know each other and played well together. Ruby relaxed and enjoyed having new playmates.

To her surprise, she and her stepsisters were also expected to perform chores around the house. Since most of her life had been spent living with her grandparents, aunts, and uncles, no one had expected her to do anything but play and stay out of the way.

Now Ruby found that after breakfast, Veta was expected to wash the dishes, while Ruby and Rhudene dried. On a farm, the workday began early to make the best use of light. For that reason, the noontime meal was called "dinner" because it was the main, heavy meal of the day. Those dishes were washed by Rhudene, and Ruby and Veta dried. The evening meal was very light and called "supper." Ruby learned how to wash the dishes for that meal, while Rhudene and Veta dried.

Ruby had her sixth birthday, and before anyone was ready for it, school started. Because Jimma had signed a contract for another year of teaching at Marthal Gap School, she and Joe decided to rent a home closer to the school. Jimma walked with the three girls every day. Ruby was excited to start school. Usually her little brother, who wasn't yet five, went along with them and played or napped in the back of the room, while his mother taught all the children.

She and Bud got to know most of Joe's relatives. Joe's grandmother, Ellen Skipper, was very old. Ruby was always called Ruby Ellen in those days, and Grandma Skipper thought Ruby had been named after her. She never understood Ruby wasn't a blood relative. And she always told Ruby she loved her.

When the Texas State Fair came along in September, Joe took his new family to Dallas to attend the festivities. Ruby and Bud were excited to see fireworks. That night the family slept in a boarding house in Dallas—another new experience. The next day they drove back home and stopped in Mineral Wells to be introduced to another one of Dad's siblings. Ruby began to feel very much a part of the family.

That Christmas as a family was a nice time for Ruby and Bud. She and Bud called Joe "Dad." Veta and Rhudene called Jimma "Mamma." It felt cozy and comfortable.

When Ruby got older, she adopted the attitude that when things are going too well, look out. But at the tender age of six, she had yet to learn that hard lesson.

Chapter 16
Early 1926

By 1926, Ruby Ellen and Bud had settled in with their new father and stepsisters. They liked having Jimma at home every night. Ruby loved having her stepsisters to play with, and she didn't even mind doing the chores so much. She also loved school and especially having her mother as the teacher. Lots of Parnell relatives and their children lived close by. She found she was happy most of the time.

Bud had his 5th birthday in February 1926. Ruby wouldn't be 7 until that August, but it didn't seem important now. The days were busy, with little time to daydream about birthdays.

It was shortly after Bud's birthday that Ruby noticed Mamma didn't seem to be as happy as she had been that day last May when she told Ruby and Bud that they had a new father. Ruby knew from long experience her Mamma had a temper. Ruby always wondered how Granny Palmer was so calm, and Mamma was quick to anger.

Ruby and her stepsisters were doing the dishes after the noon meal. It was Saturday, and the girls had planned a trip into the woods to look for a place to build a playhouse. They were laughing and talking while they washed and dried dishes and didn't at first hear Dad speak.

"Dammit, I said stop all that chatter and laughing. Pay attention to your chores."

All three girls stopped laughing and looked at each other. Veta whispered to Ruby,

"When he gets mad and yells like that, you better stop whatever you're doing."

Rhudene nodded in agreement and leaned close to Ruby's ear. "We stay out of his way when he's like this."

Ruby felt a little chill crawl up her arms. She wondered if Dad got as angry as Mamma often did. She tried to push away thoughts like that. Maybe she could simply avoid Dad when he was in a bad mood. That's what she tried to do with Mamma. But to her dismay, she had noticed Dad and Mamma arguing a lot lately.

Ruby looked at the other two girls. "Let's hurry up and finish."

She tried to push away the feeling of dread she had in that moment, but her stomach clenched up, and her eyes started to water. She finished drying the last dish and carefully hung the towel on the hook. Then she followed the other two girls as they quietly left through the backdoor.

Soon it would become a pattern in their lives.

Chapter 17
Spring 1926

By early 1926, Ruby saw her stepfather displaying her mother's type of anger.

Ruby had been spanked during her lifetime. Her mother believed it sent a message and made her children think twice before they acted up. Ruby didn't remember Granny or Grandpa Palmer ever using a spanking to discipline her or Bud. They used stern looks and explained why one or the other of the children needed to rethink their behavior. It always worked for Ruby. Not so much for Bud.

Ruby wasn't prepared for her stepfather's brand of punishment. At first it was yelling. Then the beatings started. When Ruby grew older and better understood adult behavior, she came to realize that the beatings Dad dealt out to her and to Bud were usually caused by his rage and anger at their mother.

When Jimma and Joe would start arguing, it was generally about her plans to go somewhere. Joe would become angry, tell her she couldn't go, and that made her more determined. When she left, it enraged him. Then, if either of Jimma's children did anything to annoy him, it added to his anger. He would grab something and start the beatings. Most of the time, the target was Bud, but Ruby got a good share of it herself.

Sometime in March 1926, Jimma and Joe got into a big fight. It escalated quickly, and this time Jimma packed some clothing, grabbed her two children, and headed for her parents' farm. She and the children stayed there for about six weeks, and during that time, Joe came to see her every Sunday. He would always be sweet and apologetic for the argument that caused her to leave. A few weeks into the stay at the Palmer farm, Jimma realized she was pregnant. By her calculations, the child would arrive sometime in late October or early November. The next time Joe arrived with pretty flowers he'd picked for her, she agreed to return home.

Meantime, Jimma finished her teaching contract. When that ended the last day of May, she didn't sign another one. She would take up painting again—doing landscapes and wildlife—and sell them when and where she could. It might bring in some money. Meanwhile, she awaited the birth of another baby.

Now the entire family would have to depend on what Joe could earn as a tenant farmer. Over the years, it became evident Joe was not particularly good at farming. He didn't seem to like it much, but it was all he knew. All the children would be expected to work in the fields when they weren't in school. It was grueling, dirty work—especially picking cotton. Ruby never forgot the pain produced by the sharp thorns on the cotton plants. Her hands bled from picking the cotton, and her legs bled from walking through the tight rows of stickery plants.

It might have been worth the pain and bleeding the children received if the crops had been good enough to keep the family solvent. Unfortunately, except for his unusually abundant harvest in early 1925 before he married Jimma, Joe couldn't seem to grow a decent crop.

And he never would again.

Chapter 18
Fall 1926

Things had settled down a bit in the summer. The kids did their chores and worked in the fields. The heat seemed worse than ever before. Ruby picked so much cotton that her arms, hands, and legs were covered with abrasions. With a few exceptions, the fighting between Jimma and Joe didn't seem as bad during that period.

Jimma spent a lot of time painting. One company hired her to paint greeting cards. That brought in some money, and if she could sell most of her paintings, perhaps some of the financial strain could be handled.

Joe finally realized he needed to help his wife. She found a market for a particular type of painting. To get the material for it, Joe would cut down a few elm trees about ten inches in diameter. Then he would slice the tree into slabs of about one-and-a-half inches thick. He would "cure" them for a while. Then he would give them to Jimma, who would sand the interior wood down to a smooth finish to create her paintings. They were rustic—with the dark bark of the tree still attached—giving them a "framed" look. On these slabs, Jimma painted wildlife, beautiful scenery, and moonlit cabins in the woods. She discovered people loved them and word soon got around. Her talent was a godsend that helped feed the growing family in a way Joe's farming didn't.

As summer turned into fall, the children were back in school. By this time Bud was still four months away from his sixth birthday, and he didn't have a good relationship with Joe. Jimma was often away from home. She spent time in the woods, painting pictures, which she sold in town. She often took orders for paintings. People would tell Jimma what they wanted and she would paint it.

When Jimma was working and the girls were at school, it fell to Joe to take care of Bud. Maybe Joe wasn't comfortable around little boys; maybe he resented Jimma's affection and protection of her small son. Ruby, who had her seventh birthday in August, could not understand why Joe seemed especially hostile toward the little boy.

One day, Jimma went into town for supplies. An early October cold snap had settled in. The girls came home from school and did their homework. Jimma returned just before supper. Bud was nowhere to be seen.

Ruby assumed her brother was off playing. When Jimma arrived, she remarked on how much colder it was. Then she asked the whereabouts of her son.

Bud had displeased his stepfather in some way. For punishment, Joe locked the little boy in the corn crib inside the barn. Jimma hurried out in the cold Texas wind to retrieve her son. The child was huddled on the floor, shivering. When she brought him inside, her anger erupted. The child shook from the cold and had a fever.

Joe and Jimma had a big fight that night. The girls made themselves scarce. Bud—covered up in his small bed— finally slept.

It took three weeks for Bud's recovery. Jimma suspected he had pneumonia. In those days, speculation was all they had. There certainly weren't doctors anywhere close. Even if there had been, they couldn't have afforded the cost of a visit.

Chapter 19
November 6, 1926

Things had settled down in the Parnell household. Ruby was still excited for the birth of a new sibling. Joe's girls were also excited about it. Bud had recovered from his ordeal and seemed back to normal.

On Saturday night, November 6, Joe told the four children to walk to his mother's house and spend the night. Granny Nell was a mid-wife, and Joe told his daughters to tell her it was time for Jimma to give birth. Joe's youngest sister, Estalee, was visiting Granny Nell. She had brought her new baby to show her mother. She would watch over the children during the night. It was only a short walk down the road, so they hurriedly grabbed their night clothes and walked to Granny Nell's house.

Aunt Estalee let them take turns holding her new baby—even Bud was allowed to hold it. The girls enjoyed having the chance to get used to what it would be like now at their own house. Aunt Estalee played games with them and made popcorn as a treat before bedtime.

The next afternoon Granny Nell returned and told them they had a baby sister. The children were having so much fun with Aunt Estalee, they didn't want to go home, but they were anxious to see the new baby.

So, on Sunday afternoon, all four children walked back home and met their new sister. Her name was Mary Lorena. Ruby held the little child and marveled at the perfection of her sweet face.

The baby's tiny toes and fingers fascinated Ruby and the rest of the children. None of them remembered having a baby in the house, and the girls, especially, were excited at the prospect of helping with the new baby.

Seven-year-old Ruby was selected to help with the new baby, even though both Veta and Rhudene were older. She didn't realize until much later that she had become the baby's major caregiver.

It wouldn't be long before she discovered she would fill that role for the all the babies to come.

Chapter 20
1926-1930

The next few years went by for Ruby with a sad sameness. She grew to believe it would be the pattern for the rest of her life. There would be fun occasionally and sometimes pure joy—especially when she could visit her grandparents, aunts, and uncles. But then the inevitable, angry fights would begin between Mamma and Dad.

In the late Twenties, Mamma and Joe brought home a radio. It was old, but still workable, and Ruby enjoyed hearing about the events going on in the rest of the country.

She discovered America continued to produce new technology, daring feats of adventure, amazing new civic projects, and unheard of venues of entertainment. On November 15, 1926, NBC Radio Network was formed by Westinghouse, General Electric, and RCA by opening 24 radio stations across the country.

On May 20, 1927, Charles Lindbergh in the Spirit of St. Louis set out to fly across the Atlantic Ocean, becoming the first human to do so. He arrived in Paris a mere thirty-three- and one-half hours later to find scores of people wildly cheering and waiting for him. And on October 4, 1927, work began sculpting into the stone of Mount Rushmore the likeness of the four presidents selected.

Meanwhile, Ruby's next sibling arrived on January 27, 1928. They named him Jack. By this time, Mary was walking and getting into things. Mamma spent a lot of time with her painting, so Ruby found herself busy watching the two young children unless she was in school. She realized that Dad didn't treat Jack the same as he treated Bud. Jack was his special child. As she grew older, she understood Dad resented Bud because he was another man's son. Ruby finally gave up trying to see into her stepfather's dark heart.

She loved school because it opened new worlds for her each year. Some of the children complained about school, but Ruby never felt that way. To her there was so much to learn. She read as many books as she could find and was anxious to grow up. The places described in those books made her want to explore. The amazing historic events she heard about in school and on the radio were beyond exciting. There was wonderful freedom at school, where she could express herself and learn interesting things. School was the bright spot, giving her hope for a better life someday.

It seemed like Mamma often became pregnant, but it didn't always lead to a new baby. Ruby learned years later that her mother had discovered ways to prevent a new pregnancy from continuing when she needed that outcome.

One day right after school started in 1928, the teacher told her students all about Amelia Earhart. This amazing young aviator had become the first woman passenger to fly across the Atlantic on June 17, 1928. She flew in a plane named "Friendship", with co-pilots William "Bill" Stultz and Louis "Slim" Gordon. Ruby saw pictures of Ms. Earhart and decided she wanted a haircut like that. It was cropped short, but it had soft curls.

Over the next two years, Ruby hungrily absorbed both current and historic events. The worst one she would remember was October 29, 1929, when the Stock Market Crash happened. Ruby's family was already poor. Now, she learned, many other people in the United States had become just as poor as the Parnell family.

On February 24, 1930, Ruby's half-sister Margaret was born. Shortly thereafter, Jimma sent Ruby to Fort Worth to live with Jimma's younger brother Lillard and his wife, Jewel for a brief time.

She returned to the farm a few months later, and Margaret was learning to sit up by herself. It was summer, and Mamma had been working on a new project for bringing in money for the family. She came up with the idea to create a curtain for the high school auditorium. She planned to buy the fabric and sew it together. But prior to that she would go around to businesspeople in the community and sell them ads to be painted on the curtain. When she had enough ads for the project, she went to purchase the fabric she needed. One hot day that summer, Mamma told Joe she had to go into town to pick up the money she'd been promised for a painted advertisement on the curtain.

Joe had always made his own clothes. He saved flour sacks and sewed underwear for himself. He found other fabrics to sew his pants and shirts. He must have done a fairly good job, but Ruby didn't think he enjoyed doing it. On this day, it seemed to rankle him more than usual. When Jimma announced she was going into town, Joe angrily got up from his sewing and told her she wasn't going anywhere.

Jimma never responded to a demand, or to be told she couldn't do something. The fight was inevitable.

Ruby sat on the floor, playing with baby Margaret. The fight went from bad to worse in seconds. With Joe screaming at his wife that she would not go anywhere, Jimma turned on her heel and slammed out of the house to do exactly what she had planned.

When Joe sat back down at the sewing machine, he glared at Ruby and said, "Don't you dare let Margaret cry. I don't need to hear no crying baby today, got it?"

Ruby swallowed hard, nodded her head, and prayed the baby would behave. Ruby gave Margaret trinkets she could play with, and things were going well. Just a few minutes later, baby Margaret reached for a toy just out of her grasp. In the process, the baby fell over and Ruby couldn't grab her in time. Margaret hit her head and let out a mighty scream. Before Ruby could comfort the child, Joe slammed his fist on the sewing machine and started bellowing.

"I told you not to let her cry!"

His haste getting up from the sewing machine knocked over his chair. He unbuckled his belt, ripped it off, and brought the buckle end of the belt down across Ruby's legs, repeatedly, and with force. Before he finished, blood oozed from multiple places where the leather and brass buckle had ripped open her skin. It was not the first or last time he beat her. But this one event was a defining one. She felt intense pain, shock, and anger—all at the same time.

It also fed her abiding hatred of this man who had become her "Dad."

Chapter 21
Late Summer 1930

Much to her amazement, Ruby was maturing. She grew sleek and slender, with wavy auburn hair, and sparkling green eyes. She longed for pretty clothes to wear. But in her family, that wasn't an option. Then, right after her eleventh birthday, her Aunt Margie made her a promise.

It was one of those times after Mamma and Dad started fighting more than usual. Ruby sensed so much anger in the air. She also felt overwhelmed being responsible for the care of each new baby. Fortunately, her mother realized Ruby needed to visit her grandparents before school started. Jimma hooked up the wagon and took Ruby to Granny and Grandpa's house. Aunt Margie was there prior to going back to school for the coming year.

Ruby felt sad when she arrived, but she was happy to be there with people she loved and who loved her. During the visit she told Aunt Margie about the situation at home.

Aunt Margie listened, and that alone seemed miraculous. At home there were so many chores, so much anger and frustration. Nobody wanted to hear the hopes and dreams of a pre-teenage girl. But Aunt Margie was special. She understood Ruby, and most of all, she understood the child's longing for a better future.

When Ruby finished telling Aunt Margie about the arguments between Mamma and Joe, Aunt Margie sat for a few moments. Then she took Ruby's slender hands into her own plump ones.

"Ruby Ellen," Aunt Margie said. "I'm going to make you a promise right here today. Now don't you forget it because I won't."

Ruby's heart pounded. "I promise I won't forget."

Aunt Margie nodded. "Okay, then. Here it is. I'll be graduating from nursing school just before you're ready for eighth grade. I'm going to work in a hospital as a nurse. I'll be earning a nice paycheck."

Ruby felt excitement and listened to every word.

Aunt Margie smiled. "My promise to you is this. I will buy you some nice school clothes and arrange for you to go to school someplace other than Johnsville. I'll find a way for you to live with somebody during that school year so you can concentrate on your studies. There won't be adults fighting all the time and little kids to care for. How does that sound?"

Ruby stared at her aunt. "Oh, Aunt Margie. Could you really do that?"

Aunt Margie patted Ruby's hand. "Of course, I can. I promised, didn't I?"

Ruby replayed that conversation in her head over and over. Aunt Margie would help her. It was a gift far beyond any she'd ever dreamed of having.

She never forgot Aunt Margie's promise. It was something to hold close to her heart whenever things got bad.

Chapter 22
Late 1930

When Ruby returned to school in the fall of 1930, she had a goal. She would do her best work and get good grades this year.

She vowed to avoid anything that might make Dad angry. She had learned to be aware and alert about the people surrounding her. If she paid attention, perhaps she could escape more beatings. She only needed to stay out of Dad's way, be respectful, and try not to annoy him.

Right after school started, Ruby, now 11 years old, realized her mother was pregnant again. She knew the signs, and she congratulated herself for figuring it out before it was common knowledge. Sure enough, just a few weeks later, Mamma made the announcement right after supper.

"When will it be here, Mamma?" Veta asked her stepmother.

Jimma sighed. "About the middle of May."

Joe sat quietly, finishing his cup of coffee. He didn't make any comments. Ruby wondered why.

Mary was almost four now. Jack was close to three, and Margaret was seven months. It seemed to Ruby it might be an unfortunate time to add another child. The older she got the more she understood how poor they really were. Fortunately, there were lots of Dad's relatives who lived close by. He was able to grow enough food to mostly feed the family, but not enough left to sell for a livable profit.

By this time in 1930, the Great Depression, which had started in the fall of 1929, had drastically deepened. Although it began in the United States, it quickly spread to the rest of the world.

In some parts of Texas, Oklahoma, New Mexico, and Kansas, the Dust Bowl had begun. By the time it ended, it was viewed as the greatest single human-caused environmental catastrophe in United States history.

The Depression and The Great Dust Bowl were twin tragedies in America. These events left even more people in poverty.

If Ruby thought life was difficult before, she would soon learn poor can become even "poorer."

Chapter 23
1931

Ruby's latest sibling arrived on May 20, 1931. It was another girl, but Ruby didn't worry how Dad would treat the new baby. It was around this time she figured out Dad didn't beat his own children—only Jimma's. His kids would get a spanking if they did something they shouldn't, but that didn't come close to the beatings she and Bud received.

The new baby's name was Rhonda. As expected, Ruby was tasked with the infant's care any time school wasn't in session. Unfortunately, there would be only two more weeks before summer vacation. Ruby decided to make the most of this precious time focusing on her studies.

Sometimes her grandparents would come visit in their wagon, and they often took Ruby home with them for a short stay. They had a record player in the parlor. It had a big handle on the side, and you cranked it up to play a record. The records were made of a thick, black, waxy material. The music coming out of the large cone-shaped speaker was a miracle to Ruby. She was allowed to play any of the records she wanted. Her love of music was a bright spot in her life.

Granny and Grandpa also had a radio. Ruby enjoyed listening to the music magically drifting from the fabric-covered speaker. It was fascinating to hear such a small device receive music through the air from places like New York or Los Angeles. But the news broadcasts were also a revelation. It was about this time when her awareness of the rest of the world blossomed.

One night in early May 1931, she heard about something called The Empire State Building being dedicated in New York City. She had studied geography in school and understood that New York City was a long way from where she lived in Texas. She couldn't imagine a building as tall as they described. You could take an elevator all the way up to the top. Ruby had never been on an elevator—had never even seen one. But someday, she vowed, she would ride in an elevator, all the way up to the top of that grand building in New York City.

For now, she was just an eleven-year-old schoolgirl, living on a farm in Texas, with no money, and no understanding of how she would ever pull off such a wild adventure. Someday, she reasoned, she'd grow up and be an adult. Adults could go anywhere and do anything they wanted to do.

For now, she would concentrate on her studies, and growing up to be a lady. How hard could that be?

Chapter 24
1933

Aunt Margie graduated from nursing school and announced her impending marriage to Bill McEwen. Ruby wanted to be at the wedding, but something even more exciting happened. Aunt Margie, as promised, informed Jimma she had arranged to have Ruby attend school for her eighth-grade year in La Grange, Texas. Included in that deal would be new school clothes for the growing young lady. The long-awaited promise would be fulfilled.

Ruby's birthday in August that summer of 1933 was wonderful. At fourteen, her excitement filled her with gratitude. She would live with her Aunt Ina and Uncle Benton. Their first child, daughter Margie Nell, had been born in June 1931. The little girl was now two years old, and Ruby could help with the child's care during the school year. In addition, Aunt Ina had just verified she was expecting their second child at the beginning of 1934. Ruby was more than happy to help and knew Aunt Ina wouldn't expect her to be the sole caregiver, the way Mamma did.

The birthday celebration had been held at Granny and Grandpa Palmer's farm. Granny loved baking a birthday cake for Ruby when she could. Granny also understood how much these things meant to a young girl.

When Aunt Margie arrived that day for the event, and made her announcements, Jimma expressed happiness about the marriage. But Ruby noticed Jimma's lack of enthusiasm about her being away from home for the next nine months. Even so, Ruby knew Jimma would allow her to go. Jimma had to know the way Joe treated her children was not acceptable.

Thankfully he wasn't beating the kids as often as he had been. Nobody knew why, but they didn't want to ask. There was no need to talk about things like that.

That was probably the reason Joe stayed behind in Johnsville with the younger kids while Jimma, Ruby, and Bud went to the Palmer's for the party. On the trip home, Ruby couldn't help wondering how he would react when Jimma told him about Aunt Margie's birthday surprise.

The fact that he didn't react at all made Ruby wonder what was going on in the man's head these days.

Chapter 25
1933-1934

On January 5, 1933, construction had begun on the Golden Gate Bridge in San Francisco Bay. Nobody knew it at the time, but it would become one of the many U.S. Government Works Projects providing jobs for desperate men during the Great Depression.

On March 4, 1933, fifty-one-year-old Franklin Delano Roosevelt would be inaugurated as the thirty-second President of the U.S. It was also the last time the inauguration would occur on that date, because on January 23, 1933, the Twentieth Amendment to the Constitution of the United States had been ratified. It named January 20th as the presidential inaugural day starting in January 1937.

Roosevelt became a president of many firsts—among them his inauguration on the new date, and he was the first and last president to be elected to four consecutive terms for that office.

On that cold, blustery day in March, he appeared to stand on his own at the podium, giving his stirring speech to a frightened public. The most famous line of that speech is still in the American lexicon: "The only thing we have to fear is—fear itself." The poliomyelitis which attacked him in the 1920s had confined him for life to a wheelchair, but with heavy steel braces, he managed to stand tall at this very important time in history. Many American citizens never realized he spent his life in a wheelchair.

Ruby Ellen Scott learned about all these events in her new school in La Grange, Texas. Her delight in being there, in being able to do her homework, her ability to take time to read the many books she saw in the school bookshelves, was more than she had hoped for.

Perhaps today's children in eighth grade would be surprised to learn the class schedule she had in a small-town school system in the 1930s:

Algebra I
Home Economics I
English I
American and European History
Biology
Math
Physical Education

Ruby loved it all—especially the history classes. Learning about other countries, as well as her own, gave her a better understanding of life and her looming adulthood.

One of the other joys being here was the love she saw in action all the time. Her little cousin, Margie Nell, was a sweet child. Her eagerness to learn about this exciting new world she had entered, matched the way fourteen-year-old Ruby felt about her journey through life. Aunt Ina and Uncle Benton were a loving mother and father, and Ruby's gratitude for being there, even for just this school year, would change the way she saw family dynamics. Ruby vowed she would seek the same kind of love and gentleness when she was old enough to have her own family.

Now all she must do was grow up as soon as possible and avoid her stepfather.

Chapter 26
January to June 1934

Overall, 1934 started with bright promise. The Great Depression's unemployment went down from 25.5% to a slightly better 22%. FDR set up more public works, including bridges, roads, and flood control dams all around the United States. Even the FBI had a good year. They ended the careers of several celebrity criminals, including John Dillinger, Bonnie Parker, Clyde Barrow, Pretty Boy Floyd, and Baby Face Nelson.

Ruby Ellen Scott gained a new cousin that January when Aunt Ina gave birth to James Royce Koepf on January 27, 1934. Ruby loved helping her aunt with the baby.

Spring arrived in La Grange, and the final six weeks of school began. Ruby realized her beautiful time with Aunt Ina and Uncle Benton would soon be at an end.

She felt much more confident now and had mastered all her subjects at school. She received good grades when report cards came out, and hoped she'd be able to keep up her studies next fall for ninth grade.

As each spring day dawned, anxiety crept into her thoughts. She'd always known this interlude would last only for this school year. But it didn't stop her from hoping some magic would happen that let her stay in La Grange. She would miss the little town and her aunt's family so much.

The last school day finally arrived, and Ruby dressed in one of the outfits Aunt Margie had bought for her. When classes were over, she bid her friends goodbye, and walked home to spend her last days in La Grange.

Aunt Ina, Uncle Benton, Margie Nell, and baby James would drive Ruby back to Grandma and Grandpa Palmer's house outside of Glen Rose. Jimma would come to see her sister and the new baby and take Ruby back home with her. Ruby would be glad to see Mamma, but she didn't know what to expect from Dad.

Early in the morning on June 4, 1934, they piled into Uncle Benton's car. It would take the family several hours to cover the two-hundred-plus miles from La Grange back to Glen Rose. The peaceful, gentle life in the Koepf family would be traded for the chaos in the Parnell household.

They arrived at the farm just before supper. Ruby's grandparents greeted the weary travelers. Ruby felt gratitude that her return started at her grandparents' home. It was familiar and would help her readjust to life with Mamma, Dad, and all the kids.

She slept on a daybed on the screened-in porch that night. The June weather in Texas was typically hot and humid. A slight evening breeze made the screened-in porch an excellent sleeping place on hot summer nights. That night Ruby and Margie Nell shared one of the beds, and Ruby quickly fell asleep.

She could never remember what she dreamed, but for the next few months, she often wished to be back in that time. Experiencing that night again would have been much better than the following nights.

For Ruby, it became the last sleep before the nightmares started.

Chapter 27
June 1934

The morning sun wasn't up when Granny Palmer gently awakened her. Ruby stretched, yawned, and eased out of bed. The child slept soundly.

Even before she saw the sun, heat seeped through the screened-in porch. It would be another scorcher—not unusual for Texas in June. Ruby made a quick trip to the privy, located well away from the house. On the walk back she stopped at the trough, close to the kitchen, to splash some of the cool water on her face. She longed for a bath, but with all the people in residence now she knew it wasn't possible.

At least she could put on fresh clothes. Her suitcase was under the daybed. Ruby carefully got it out and found her clothes for the day. She missed the indoor bathroom Aunt Ina and Uncle Benton had.

Ruby ran a brush through her short, thick auburn hair. Time to help Granny with breakfast preparations.

Jimma arrived right after breakfast. All the ladies there that day played with baby James. He was a sweet boy, with blond hair, blue eyes, and chubby little arms and legs.

After their main meal at noon, Ruby returned to the area where the adults had gathered. After Aunt Ina fed baby James, she asked Ruby to take him inside for his nap. Ruby took James from his mother and put him on his tummy on the bed that Aunt Ina and Uncle Benton had used the night before. He was already asleep, and she carefully put him in the center of the bed.

The men wandered off to the barn, and the women listened to Jimma tearfully recount the pain of losing her baby boy in early May. He was Joe's second son, and they named him Joe Carlton Parnell, Jr. Born on May 1, 1934, he died that same day.

Ruby felt oddly disengaged. When she left home to live with Aunt Ina and Uncle Benton for that school year, she didn't know her mother was pregnant. She tried to understand her own lack of feeling about the event. Maybe it seemed unreal to Ruby, because she had not been there through the pregnancy and birth. She felt no sadness, and she sat quietly as Mamma cried.

The atmosphere seemed heavy with grief. Ruby decided to walk to the barn and find Grandpa Palmer. Maybe he could explain why she felt so disassociated with the loss of Mamma and Joe's little boy.

Moments later, she heard a scream so full of fear it made her stop cold. She was almost at the barn and turned to run back to the house. Uncle Benton and Grandpa rushed out of the barn. Ruby's heart thudded so hard in her chest she could hardly breathe.

She reached the screened-in porch, but it was empty. Voices and crying came from the next room. She started in, but Granny saw her and shook her head. Ruby stopped, and Mamma turned around, her face wet with tears. Aunt Ina was holding baby James, limp in her arms.

The tears unshed for her Mamma's little boy, now flowed freely down Ruby's face. James Royce Koepf, the beautiful little boy she'd helped care for these past five months, was dead.

And Ruby knew, somehow, it must be her fault.

Chapter 28
June 1934

Ruby felt her stomach twisting. From experience, she knew she was about to lose the large meal she had eaten only a couple of hours ago.

She turned and ran outside. A secluded bush blessedly appeared just as she emptied her stomach's contents. She didn't know how long she'd been standing there, retching, when she felt a hand on her back. The hand reached around and held out a wet washcloth. Ruby grabbed it and mopped the sweat from her face.

Granny Palmer, her weathered face streaked with tears, held out her arms to her oldest granddaughter.

"Ruby Ellen," Granny said, "listen to me, and listen good. This isn't your fault. I know right now you think it is, but Honey, things like this happen—especially to little babies."

"But, Granny," Ruby straightened up to look at the older woman, "I put him on the bed for his nap. I was so careful to put him in the middle of the bed. What happened?"

Granny shook her head. "Somehow, he managed to roll over by himself. He probably woke up and tried turning over. Ina said he had just learned to do that in the last few days."

"How could he die by just rolling over? I don't understand." Ruby brushed away new tears.

Granny sighed. "Sweetheart," she said, "babies are so unpredictable. Baby James is a husky little boy. If he just started rolling over, he would keep doing it every chance he got. He fell between the bed and the wall, and he smothered."

A fresh supply of tears rolled down Ruby's cheeks. "Aunt Ina must hate me. She's been so kind to me all my life, and now, because of me, her baby died."

Granny grabbed her granddaughter's shoulders and shook her softly. "Ruby Ellen, you listen to me. Self-pity is unbecoming in anyone, and right now, it's bad for you—and even worst for your aunt."

Ruby took a ragged breath and wiped her face and nose. "I'm sorry, Granny. I don't know what to do. How can I help?"

Granny said, "Now, you're getting there. Stop thinking about yourself and think about Aunt Ina and Uncle Benton. They don't need to be dealing with your grief. They have to make arrangements for a funeral and final resting place for their baby."

Ruby nodded. "Just tell me what I can do now."

Granny put her arm around Ruby's shoulders. "Let's go back

inside. You must try to be a grown-up today. Everyone is upset. They don't need to be worrying about you, or me, or Pa, or anybody. We all have our grief, and we'll just have to hold it inside while we get through the next few days."

Ruby hugged her grandmother. "I love you so much. Thank you for understanding."

They walked back to the house together, with Ruby's hand in Granny's. Somehow, Ruby had to get through this without upsetting her aunt and uncle.

It would be the most difficult thing she'd faced in her short life.

Chapter 29
Fall 1934 to Spring 1935

Ruby's sorrow over the death of baby James Royce hung over her like a thick, heavy blanket. When she and Jimma returned from Johnsville, all the kids were eager and happy to see her.

She wondered how to explain the pervasive sadness and guilt she felt from the moment she woke up each morning since that awful day. She worked hard to do what Granny had said. Ruby's grief was nothing close to what Aunt Ina and Uncle Benton were feeling. She knew that—deep inside—but it didn't sooth her own feelings of loss and regret.

Veta would have her 18th birthday in July, and Rhudene would be 16 in November. A wave of remorse hit Ruby at breakfast the first morning after she and Mamma returned from Glen Rose. At that moment, she thought about how unremarkable her childish pride in schoolwork would be to her older stepsisters. That's when she understood what Granny Palmer had been trying to tell her that horrible afternoon. One's own problems weren't any more important than those of others.

When school started in September in the Johnsville School District, Ruby—now 15—felt happy being back in classes. She knew and understood what happened in her life, good or bad, still gave her the choice of how to make things better or worse. Sometimes simply accepting what you were dealt made life easier. Other times, finding a new, better way to move through situations gave you opportunities to improve.

One day, Joe came home from the post office. He had a summons for jury duty. Joe's frustration at having to miss working the fields at that time of the year made him build up a steam of fury. When Jimma made some comment, it made Joe even angrier.

He turned to Jimma, summons in his hand, and shook it in her face. "Your father is to blame for this. He knows I'm behind in the planting this year. He wants me to fail."

She screamed at him. "My father had nothing to do with your stupid jury summons. How dare you blame him."

"He's the damned Deputy Sheriff," Joe yelled back. "Of course, he's the one who did it. I'm getting my rifle and I'm going over there and kill that old bastard."

Joe headed out to the barn for his rifle, and Jimma took off after him. It was then that Veta, the oldest sister, gathered up the other kids.

She, Rhudene, and Ruby, each grabbed one of the little ones, and headed out the door in the opposite direction. Bud followed along behind the others, holding little Jack's hand. They had a special place at the top of a big hill. It was far enough away from the farm that they could no longer hear the yelling. The older kids kept the young ones entertained. After a period of peaceful quiet, they came down from the hill and went home. By the time they arrived back at the farmhouse, it was as though nothing had happened.

Grandpa Palmer would never know how close he came to being shot that day.

Chapter 30
Late 1934 to Early 1936

Ever since Ruby had returned from La Grange in the summer of 1934, she sensed a slightly different attitude in her stepfather. It happened right before her 15th birthday in August, about the same time her routine each day had changed.

Mamma had assigned Ruby the task of making breakfast each morning. Since she was almost 15, it was only right she learned more cooking skills—at least that's how Mamma thought. So, each morning her stepfather came into the bedroom she shared with her half-sister, Mary, and awakened Ruby for her job as breakfast chef. He would tap her on the shoulder and tell her it was time to get going on breakfast.

Ruby understood why her mother wanted her to do it. In the first place, Jimma was frequently pregnant (although she never gave birth to another baby after the one who died in 1934.)

Besides, Jimma didn't like cooking, and even more, she hated getting up early. So, Ruby became used to doing this chore. It was certainly a lot easier than caring for the parade of babies all those years.

In August 1935, Ruby had her 16th birthday. Once again, she spent the day with her grandparents, and Granny Palmer made her a birthday cake. For Ruby, having her birthday with her grandparents was a treat she'd enjoyed for years, but especially this year. In the fall, Ruby would be in 10th grade—a sophomore at Duffau High School. She sensed, deep down, that these annual birthday celebrations with her grandparents would come to an end much sooner than she wished.

By the time the New Year arrived in 1936, Ruby Ellen Scott had taken another small leap into adulthood. When she looked in a mirror, she saw how much taller she was this year than last year. It made her smile. By now she was five feet, nine inches tall. Her young body had lost its childish frame and had been replaced with a curvy, more mature adult one.

About a month into the New Year, Joe's behavior toward Ruby took an unexpected turn—at least in Ruby's mind.

Each morning, when he came into the bedroom where she and Mary slept, he awakened her with a kiss—at first on the forehead— then a few weeks later, he kissed her on the cheek. This was the man who, when she was only ten years old, beat her with a belt buckle. Now he kissed her awake. It felt more than a little creepy. A deep-down warning rang a little bell in her sleepy head.

In late March 1936, Duffau High School burned to the ground, a devastating turn of events. The education she so desperately sought had been taken away—her only ticket out of here. Without the ability to attend school, mornings became even stranger. That first morning after the school burned down, her stepfather came in to awaken her. But this time, he placed the unwanted kiss on her lips.

If alarms went off inside Ruby's brain earlier, they now became a loud, wailing siren.

Chapter 31
April 1936

On Saturday afternoon, April 4, 1936, Ruby walked to the General Store about a mile up the road from home.

Saturdays in the country also brought old men to the General Store. It was their chance to socialize with their farming neighbors, catch up on the gossip, and exchange ideas about the latest news. On this day, the men were wound up tighter than a fifty-cent watch. The latest big news to discuss was the execution, on the previous day, of the notorious Lindberg Baby kidnapper, Bruno Richard Hauptmann.

"I think he got off easy," one gray-bearded, tobacco-chewing, old-timer said, as he aimed brown juice into the spittoon in the center of their circle of chairs. "Should ah hung the bastard."

The others nodded agreement, adding their own ideas of appropriate indignities. Ruby waved to the men and went to the counter to talk with Mr. Belcher.

"Hello, young lady. What can I do for you today?"

Ruby pointed to a box on the shelf behind the counter. "I need one of those Easter egg kits."

Mr. Belcher handed Ruby a Paas Easter Egg dye-kit.

"Ruby Ellen, don't you think you're too old for colored Easter eggs?" He grinned as he took the dime she handed him.

"It's for my little sisters and brothers, Mr. Belcher. I can't let them down this year. We couldn't do eggs last Easter."

Mr. Belcher nodded. "Yeah, I remember. I ran out of the egg dye last year, but I did give them some chocolate Easter eggs, didn't I?"

Ruby smiled. Mr. Belcher had always been kind to her. She said, "Yes, you did, and the kids were thrilled. I don't think they ever saw a chocolate Easter egg before."

"Well, I'm just glad you made it in here today. By next Saturday I will be all out of dye kits again."

Ruby nodded. "That's why I made the effort to get here today."

Turning to leave, she heard one of the gossiping men speak the name Joe Parnell. Ruby stopped in her tracks. The group around the spittoon wasn't looking her way. She turned and approached a shelf of canned goods. With any kind of luck, they wouldn't realize she could hear them. She picked up a can of beans and absently studied the label.

"I swear I heard him say it. Wouldn't ah believed it otherwise."

Another man let out a low whistle. "He better be careful. Man could get hisself messed up real bad doin' that kinda thing."

A slightly deeper voice said, "Are you sure you heard right? Why would he say that right out to folks?"

The first speaker grunted. "Probably had a few slugs of that rot gut whiskey old man Thompson sells out of his barn. Why else would Joe tell me he's thinking about 'doin' his stepdaughter. Man would have to be drunk or crazy to go around town saying stuff like that."

One of the other men shushed the speaker. In a low voice, he said, "Keep your voice down. She'll hear ya."

Ruby took another can from the shelf and pretended deep interest in comparing the two labels. Her heart beat so fast she thought she might faint.

The original speaker said, "Might be a blessin' if she did hear it. Hate to see something like that goin' on 'round here. Folks gotta stop that nonsense."

"Anything else you need today, little lady?"

Mr. Belcher had walked up behind her, and Ruby almost dropped one of the cans. "Oh, no, sir. I just wanted to see the recipe on this one can. But I don't really need it today."

Ruby mentally willed her shaking hands to steady as she put the cans back on the shelf. She retrieved her package of egg dye and turned to leave. The gossiping men had abandoned the spittoon.

She left the store and saw them standing in a clump a few yards up the road. They weren't going in her direction, and they didn't see her. She turned away and started walking but couldn't hold back the angry tears.

It took longer than usual to get home. Her mind whirred and churned. What should she do? No, the better question was what *could* she do? Time to talk to Mamma.

And the sooner, the better.

Chapter 32
May 1936

It had been more than a month since Ruby heard the men talking that Saturday at Belcher's Store. She'd been anxious to talk to Mamma about it that same day but didn't have the opportunity. In the end, she decided it was better to have a plan before she did. The very next day, the idea formed, and that's when she went to Mamma.

Sundays were different from other days. First was the scramble getting all the kids ready for church. Then, on return from church, there was dinner to prepare. The sameness of Sundays helped Ruby steady her mind and build up her courage.

After dinner, a familiar ritual played out. The two youngest girls would go with their sister Mary to visit Parnell relatives. Jack and Bud went hiking in the woods. Veta and Rhudene visited friends. Joe always arranged to go down to the creek for a swim in the nude, then took a nap under a tree. He'd be gone two hours.

Mamma would get out her paints and work on a project. Ruby liked to watch, especially today.

When she told Mamma what she heard the men say, Jimma didn't reply at first. She finished adding a couple of strokes of green paint on a leaf, put her brush in the jar of turpentine, and turned to her oldest child.

"Has he ever touched you in a way he shouldn't?"

Ruby blew out a breath. She told Mamma about the morning kisses, the escalation from tapping on the shoulder, to kissing her forehead, to a kiss on the cheek, and finally to kisses applied to her lips.

Ruby had turned away from Mamma as she talked. When she finished and turned around, she saw tears on her mother's cheeks.

Jimma shook her head. "I didn't expect this, but I should have known. I don't know what to say."

Ruby felt strangely calm. Once Mamma knew, Ruby believed things would work out. She needed help coming up with a plan.

Jimma said, "Let me think about this. Meanwhile, I'll tell him I want Rhudene to make breakfast for a few days so you can get some rest. I'll say you may be coming down with something—maybe chicken pox or measles. That ought to keep him at a distance."

"I want to go to Fort Worth. I could get a job—I know I could. I just don't know how I'll get there."

Jimma nodded. "That's what I'll be working on—the way to get you there. Maybe you could take the bus, but I don't know how much that would cost. Let me think on it a bit. We'll come up with something. Meanwhile, keep to yourself as much as you can."

And Ruby had done exactly that. Now Mamma had a plan, and everything would depend on their closest neighbor down the road. Today was Saturday, May 9, the day after Mamma and Joe's tenth wedding anniversary. Things like that were ignored in the Parnell family. On Saturdays, Joe went to visit his sister and her family. On this Saturday, Mamma would walk up the road to the neighbors' house. Maybe the plan would come together for tomorrow.

All Ruby could do was maintain hope.

Chapter 33
Sunday, May 10, 1936

When Ruby woke up, the irony of the date struck her immediately. On this day exactly eleven years ago, Mamma and her new husband Joe Parnell, took Ruby and Bud away from Granny and Grandpa's house to start their new lives. It was Mother's Day then, and it was today.

Now, eleven years later, she would get away from her stepfather. The plan was easy. She still felt nervous.

Yesterday, Mamma went down the road to their neighbors. The Turners said their daughter Marie, and son-in-law Burt, would arrive with their new baby early Sunday morning to meet his grandmother and grandfather. They would have Mother's Day dinner and afterwards, Burt and Marie would drive back to Fort Worth. Ruby's plan hinged on accompanying Burt and Marie on their return trip.

Jimma warned Ruby not to mention to the Turners anything about this being a get-away plan. If they knew the sordid details, they might not want to be involved. Ruby agreed. She carefully gathered the clothes she would take with her. Mamma had given her an old suitcase which usually kept painting supplies.

Ruby stashed the empty suitcase under her bed, and after church, she took it out and packed.

At dinner, she barely touched her food. Joe frowned. "Are you still feeling sick?"

Jimma stepped in smoothly. "It's nothing, Joe. Just another stomachache. She'll be fine by tonight."

He seemed satisfied and went back to his meal. Ruby relaxed. They talked about Mary, Margaret, and Rhonda's planned visit to see their cousins that day. The children were excited because their aunt promised homemade ice cream and Mother's Day cake. The girls would leave the house as soon as the dishes were done.

The meal ended, dishes were washed, and everyone went their separate ways. Joe left for his weekly swim. Ruby was all packed when Jimma came in.

"Are you ready?" Jimma absently smoothed Ruby's already well-made bed. She touched her hair with both hands, and they shook, ever so slightly.

"Don't forget this photo of your grandparents." Jimma took the photo and handed it to Ruby.

"Thanks." Ruby opened her suitcase and put the photo in. "I didn't think you'd want me to take it."

Jimma shrugged. "You should have it. They love you so much, and you'll miss them most, I think."

Ruby felt a little twinge around her heart. "Oh, Mamma, I'll miss you too."

Jimma sighed. "You have to get going."

They walked back to the kitchen, and for the first time, Ruby noticed her mother seemed tired. She'd had her 40th birthday last month—just four days after Ruby heard the men talking about Joe. Ruby couldn't imagine herself ever being 40. It must feel awful being that old.

Jimma reached in the cupboard, pushed aside some jars of canned tomatoes, and pulled out an envelope. She extracted a wad of dollar bills.

"Here," she said, and handed Ruby ten one-dollar bills. "I wish it could be more."

Ruby felt tears sting her eyes. She took the bills and stuffed them in her small purse. "I'll pay you back as soon as I can."

"No, you'll need to hang on to your money. You'll be needing food and a place to stay. I hope it's enough to hold you until you find a job."

Ruby brushed at her eyes. "Thank you, Mamma."

Jimma tilted her head. "Call your Aunt Ina. She'll want to know you're there. Tell her what happened."

"Once I get settled, I'll let her know." But Ruby had no intention of telling her aunt about Joe.

"Now don't forget to write me. Mail the letter to Belcher's Store. I'll check with him once a week. You gotta get goin.' We don't want him to see you leaving. There'll be hell to pay—for everybody."

"Okay." She quickly headed out the front door.

She headed to the neighbor's house and gently knocked on the door. She heard laughter and knocked again, harder this time. Finally, Mae Turner came to the door.

"They'll be ready in five minutes, Ruby. Do you want to come inside?"

Ruby shook her head. "No thank you, ma'am. I'll just wait here on the porch."

Mrs. Turner went back inside. Ruby looked down the road and prayed her stepfather stayed extra-long at the creek today.

Time seemed to stop. Ruby mentally begged Burt and Marie to hurry. The heat felt intense today, but Ruby noticed her hands were cold.

Ten minutes later the young couple came to the door. Ruby jumped up and grabbed her suitcase. The family spent a few more minutes saying goodbye before the young couple finally joined Ruby. Burt offered to take her suitcase.

She said, "Thanks, I'll just hold on to it."

He shrugged, opened the back door of the car, and Ruby slid in. Burt got in the driver's seat, but Marie hung back, talking to her mother. Ruby's nerves were almost at the breaking point as Marie inched toward the passenger side and got in. Burt started the car.

"Did you get everything you needed?"

Marie nodded. "I just had to thank Mother for the lovely dinner. I felt bad I didn't help her more."

Ruby's brain felt like screaming. *"For crying out loud, let's get on with it."* But she said nothing. Instead, she turned and looked out the rear window. Her stomach lurched. Her stepfather stood in the road in front of the Parnell's house, looking toward the car.

Ruby made a little noise in her throat and Marie looked over her shoulder. "Did you say something?"

"I was just saying how much I appreciate the ride."

"Glad to help. Have you ever been to Fort Worth?"

When Ruby looked out the rear window again, Joe was running up the road. She leaned forward, almost touching the front passenger seat. "Yes, I have relatives there."

The car took off, and Ruby willed herself not to look back until they were further up the road. When she finally did, she saw something she would never forget.

Joe Parnell stood in the middle of the road, halfway to the Turner farm, furiously shaking his fist at the retreating car.

Part Two

May 1936 to June 2, 1939

Chapter 34

Wednesday, May 13, 1936

The day had been humid from the moment Ruby awoke in her room at Mrs. Murphy's Boarding House.

The Magnolia Street Commercial Laundry hired young women to work on washing, drying, and pressing the loads of sheets, pillowcases, tablecloths, napkins, and towels. Hotels, restaurants, and boarding houses sent their linens to The Magnolia. Ruby feared she might ruin their good reputation.

The sweat slid down her face, falling on her arms, and dripping onto the sheets she had been given to put through the mangle. The name itself made Ruby shudder. She felt only marginally better when the supervisor told her it was for ironing sheets and wouldn't really mangle the operator—unless said operator became careless.

She reached up and wiped away the moisture on her face. The heat drifting from this monster only made the May heat and humidity ten times worse. She felt queasy and weak. Life seemed to get worse at every turn.

"Hey, girl," the supervisor glared over at Ruby. "You're falling behind. I thought you said you knew how to do laundry."

"I'm sorry. I'll do better." The noise in this hellhole was so loud, she doubted he heard her limp apology.

The man sighed, and walked over to Ruby. He put his hand on her shoulder. "Look, kid, you aren't fooling anybody. You've never worked in a laundry, have you?"

Ruby slumped. She fought back tears "No, Sir. This is the first time I've ever done the washing this way."

The supervisor pressed his lips together. Then he shook his head. "I can put you back in the washing floor. I'll get one of the regulars to take over the mangling."

Fear crawled up Ruby's back. She couldn't afford to lose this job. So many people were out of work. It had been hard enough convincing the lady doing the hiring to give her this chance.

"Please, Sir. I need this job. I'm almost out of money, and my rent is due at the end of the week." She stopped herself. It would make her sound pathetic—the last thing she wanted.

Then the most unbelievable thing happened.

Her supervisor reached over her shoulder, turned off the mangle, and pulled her up. At first, she kept her head down, reluctant to meet his gaze.

He extended a forefinger and lifted her chin. To Ruby's amazement, he was smiling.

"What did you say your name was?"

She frowned. "Ruby. Ruby Ellen Scott."

The supervisor nodded. "Okay, Miss Ruby Ellen Scott. I want you to walk a couple of blocks over from here and talk to the manager of the Brite Spot Café. He's looking for a young woman to work the afternoon shift."

He gestured for Ruby to follow. He led her to his tiny, cluttered office, and rummaged through a few papers on the desk. He found one of his business cards and extended it to Ruby.

"Here," he said. "Take this to the Brite Spot and ask for Mr. Frasier. When you give him this card, tell him Wally from The Magnolia sent you to fill the waitress job. He's a buddy of mine. Tell him to give me a call if he needs a reference."

Questions fired around inside Ruby's brain. Why would he be helping her? She had done a lousy job for the past three days, trying to learn the simple job of washing and pressing linens. Now he seemed willing to give her a reference. What was in it for him?

Wally tilted his head at Ruby. "Is something wrong? Wouldn't you rather have a more pleasant job in a restaurant than here in this hot box?"

Ruby sucked in a quick breath "Oh, yes Sir, of course. And I'm beholden to you for overlooking my lack of skills. I just can't for the life of me think why you should be so kind to a country girl who can't even do the work in a laundry."

Wally's kind face shifted to sadness. He took a deep breath—the kind of thing she'd seen her grandfather do when he was worrying over something. He looked over her head, and she knew he wasn't really looking at the here and now.

After a few seconds, a tiny little smiled seemed to sweep away the last of the sadness. The smile reached up to his eyes when he focused again on Ruby's face.

"You remind me of my baby sister. Her name was Pearl, and she was about your age the last time I saw her. They drafted me into the Army during the Great War. I went home after boot camp before they shipped me overseas. That was the spring of 1918, and Pearl wanted to go to Houston to work that summer.

"We only had two days, but we talked a lot. She told me all about her plans for her future—about becoming a teacher. She looked so excited as she talked, and I was very proud of her. She was bright, beautiful, and looking forward to her future."

The smile on his face slid down a bit, leaving his eyes with a sadness so acute, Ruby could feel it in her own chest.

He swallowed before continuing. "Two weeks later, my mail caught up with me in France. There was one letter from Pearl, but I opened the one from my mother first. It explained how Pearl had suddenly come down with some strange flu-like illness. It happened so fast; they didn't even have time to get her to the doctor in the little town closest to our farm."

Ruby felt a lump in her throat the size of a small frog. She felt tears welling in her eyes. Somehow, she knew what was coming.

Wally swallowed one more time, wiped an invisible tear from his left eye, and smiled down at Ruby. "Pearl was the first person in our little county to die of what became known as the Spanish Flu. I never understood why they called it that, but I hated it. It took my beautiful little sister away from us, with all her hopeful plans and dreams."

He shook himself, plastered a smile on his face, and said, "Anyway, you remind me of her, and I want you to have something in your life better than this. Maybe what I can do for you will make up, in some small way, for what I couldn't do for Pearl."

Chapter 35

Wednesday, May 13, 1936

Ruby tugged at her skirt. It almost didn't fit anymore, like most of her clothes. What else could she do? Would Mr. Frasier find her clothes inappropriate for the waitress job?

The sign on the door indicated the restaurant hadn't yet opened for the early dinner crowd. She marveled at the kindness of Wally at The Magnolia, then she took a deep breath and tapped lightly on the glass door. The young woman who unlocked it flashed Ruby a big smile.

"You must be Ruby Ellen Scott," she said. She opened the door all the way and gestured Ruby inside. "Wally called and told us you are a very nice, willing worker."

Ruby felt an unexpected warm glow settle around her. The day seemed to improve with each hour since her talk with Wally that morning. The young woman opening the door stuck out her hand.

"Name's Ruth. Ruth Nance. Welcome to our home-away-from-home."

"Thanks," Ruby said. All her worries about fitting in at this new, different job, melted away.

Ruth turned to her boss. "Whadda ya say, George? Think she'll fit in?"

George Frasier's weathered face broke into a big grin. "Shucks, she looks like she belongs here. Welcome, Miss Ruby. Are you ready to start today?"

She hadn't expected she'd be hired immediately. It surprised her when she heard herself reply.

"Absolutely! Should I go home and change clothes?"

Ruth chuckled. "No need for that, Sweetie. Come with me." She put her arm around Ruby's shoulder. "We have uniforms in the ladies room. We'll find you one that fits."

Relief surged through Ruby's entire body. She realized she'd been fearful and hopeful at the same time. Less than a week had passed since she left her home outside Johnsville, and already she had a nice room at Mrs. Murphy's. And now she had a better job than when she started at the laundry on Monday.

But by far the most important change had to be the wonderful, kind people she'd met these past three days—especially Ruth Nance.

Chapter 36

May 1936

The moment they were introduced at the Brite Spot Café, Ruby felt like she'd known Ruth Nance from somewhere, in another time, and another place. In later years, after she'd heard of such things, she would believe they were probably connected in another lifetime.

That first day, Ruby's new boss asked her how she wanted her name tag to read. She hadn't thought about it until that moment, but she knew her answer instantly. "Well, most people call me Ruby Ellen. That's what I'd like on my nametag."

"Okay then," he said. " I'll have it ready for you in a few minutes."

"Thank you, sir." Ruby took a big breath and turned back to folding the napkins she'd been given.

Ruth said, "I think Ruby Ellen is a beautiful name. It sounds very distinguished—exotic even."

Ruby's eyes opened wider. "Oh, no, it's nothing like that. Really. It's just that Ellen is my middle name, and well, when I was little . . ."

Ruth put her hand on Ruby's arm to quell the nervous gestures. "No, no. I meant that as a compliment. I think Ruby Ellen is a beautiful name." She returned to her napkin folding.

"Take Ruth, for example. I find most women with that name are usually old and uninteresting—plus it sounds so Biblical. But Ruby Ellen. Now there's a woman who will go on to do big things in this world.

Ruby felt tears stinging her eyes. She hated when she did that and coughed to cover her actions.

She said, "My mother has a bad habit of calling me 'Rube.' I really hate that. It sounds so harsh."

Ruth frowned. "Rube? You mean like Rube Goldberg the cartoonist? That's an awful thing to do to your name."

"I know." Ruby stood, smoothed her apron, and straightened it. "But as for me doing big things, well . . ." She shook her head. "I don't know about that, but I'm determined to get my high school diploma this fall. That's going to be a landmark moment for me."

"You're smart," Ruth said. "I wish I'd done that at your age instead of what I actually did."

Ruby opened her mouth to ask what she meant. But at that moment, Mr. Frasier interrupted their conversation.

"Here's your name tag, young lady. Are you ready to start your shift?"

Ruby's face melted into a happy grin. "Oh, yes sir. I'm very ready."

George Frasier shook his head. "Never saw anybody so anxious to wait on tables." He turned to Ruth. "Ok, Ruthie. Show her the ropes and get her started. I'm ready to open the doors for that hungry early-dinner crowd."

Chapter 37

Memorial Day, May 31, 1936

Even though Ruth was several years older, Ruby found they had similar tastes and enjoyed many of the same things. They became fast friends and made a pact that if one of them had a problem, the other wanted to know about it. Having a friend with whom to discuss life's inevitable problems helped each woman.

Ruth's husband, Dub, was an interesting fellow. He obviously loved Ruth, and he welcomed Ruby into their home. He was Ruth's second husband, which surprised Ruby. After she met him, she realized what a wonderful relationship they had.

George Frasier decided to close the Brite Spot Café for the morning and lunch crowds on Memorial Day so his employees could have at least part of the holiday to enjoy time away from work. They would open again for the dinner crowd. Since Dub had to work that day, Ruby and Ruth decided on a picnic together to celebrate their time off. The women made sandwiches for themselves and packed a lunch. They took the bus to Forest Park and found a great spot under a grove of trees. That's the day Ruby heard all about Ruth's past.

Ruth eloped at sixteen in July 1927. Homer, her new husband, moved her from one little town to another. Soon Ruth realized Homer was an alcoholic and had a bad temper. This resulted in beatings for Ruth. The only good thing about the marriage was their baby, Rex Dennis, born in October 1928. Ruth adored the sweet little boy. But Homer's alcoholism and raging temper made him a lousy father and husband. The beatings escalated, and in 1930, she finally got up her courage to leave. She packed for herself and the toddler, and headed for her parents' home in Dennison, Texas.

She received a rude shock.

A stern, distant sort of woman, Ruth's mother said, "You made your bed, now go back and lie in it." Ruth's father said nothing, looked at the floor the entire time, then turned his back on his daughter.

Fear and sadness gripped her in that moment. But it seemed as though a bright light suddenly illuminated her. She was 21 now—not the sixteen-year-old child who ran away from home. Her parents' rejection of her now made her realize how cold and uncaring they had always been. She realized that was why she'd run away at sixteen and married Homer.

Ruth headed to Fort Worth, determined to find work to support herself and her child. She filed for divorce and tried to put the ugliness behind her.

The depression in 1930 made jobs scarce. Men stood in bread lines. When rumors of someone hiring surfaced, dozens rushed to the source—hoping to get a job.

As a very young, divorced woman with a small child, Ruth quickly realized she had zero chance of finding a job paying enough to support herself and her son. She realized she shouldn't have been surprised. Still, she didn't expect Homer to file for custody of Rex Dennis—not because he wanted the boy—it was just the easiest way to hurt Ruth. Even though the man was an alcoholic and a wife beater, societal beliefs during those years allowed him to win custody of the child. The courts considered Ruth a "bad mother" since she couldn't find a way to support herself and her son.

Ruth shook with emotion as she told the story. Ruby felt her own anger rising.

"That's horrible. Didn't they understand his violent behavior?" Once triggered, Ruby's thoughts immediately went to the beatings she'd survived from her stepfather.

Violence seemed to be something they shared.

Ruth took a deep breath. "That's enough for now. Tell me about your life BFW."

Ruby's anger drained. " BFW?"

"Before Fort Worth. We have that in common. Coming to Fort Worth, from wherever we lived an unhappy life, gave us both a chance to start over."

"I hadn't thought of it that way," Ruby said. "I did not attach Fort Worth to the good fortune I've had since arriving here on Mothers' Day."

"Understandable, and I'm not saying Fort Worth is actually the magic charm. All I'm saying is that leaving a 'place' where bad things happen, and going to a new 'place' with no bad memories . . . well, don't you see? It can be like getting a second chance—an opportunity to take whatever baggage you brought with you and change it into the life you always wanted to live."

Ruby grinned. "Lady, you are something else. Two months ago, I wouldn't have understood, but now I do"

She looked at Ruth. "I'm so glad we had this talk. I've been feeling sorry for myself for a long time, but I'm finally realizing how being in a new place gives me a chance to be what I want to become."

Ruth grinned and glanced at her watch. "This has been lovely, but we need to be at work in the next hour."

They grabbed their purses and empty lunch sacks. Walking back to the bus stop, Ruby said, "Thanks for sharing your story. I know it must have been difficult."

"I used to be ashamed of my youthful mistakes, but now, I simply count my blessings for the life I've made since then. I'm nine years older than you, yet somehow, I don't think of our age difference. I know we're going to be good friends for a long time."

They sat on the bus stop bench, and Ruby said, "I know we will. Our meeting was meant to be. I think we were destined to be friends. You have so much to teach me—stuff I wouldn't have learned before. And I know you're someone I can trust. I've never really had anyone to talk to about things like this. You are a gift."

Ruth said, "Please never forget you're also a gift. Remember that as you walk along life's highway."

They grinned at each other as the bus edged up to the stop. Ruth stood. "Let's get a move on. There are hungry people out there depending on us."

Chapter 38

Early June 1936

Of the many things Ruby treasured about her friendship with Ruth Nance, her friend's wise guidance topped the list. Ruth's focus on speedy and efficient service helped Ruby conquer her worst fears—being fired on the first day.

She realized the job was not much different from what she had done at home—just more fun. Best of all, she received tips in addition to her salary. She was eager to do a good job. It made her a favorite of their regulars.

Thanks to Ruby's newly gained efficiency, Mr. Frasier allowed her half an hour off each day for running quick errands. Today she needed to tell Mrs. Murphy she was moving to a new place. The room there seemed much larger than her current one. Best of all, it was closer to Ruth and Dub's apartment.

Ruby felt embarrassed about leaving her sweet landlady because the woman had been so kind to her.

But Mrs. Murphy gave her young tenant a big smile when Ruby explained about finding the new room,

"Sweet child," Mrs. Murphy looked into Ruby's eyes, "God has a habit of organizing things to happen in certain ways when you need them to."

Relief flooded through Ruby. "I'm so grateful to you for the hospitality you've shown me. I feel bad about leaving you with an empty room."

"No need for that." The older woman patted Ruby's cheek. She pulled out a small photograph from her pocket and showed it to Ruby.

"My son, Ben. He'll be home from college at the end of the week. I didn't know where to put him, so I said a prayer. Now Ben can have his old room back."

Ruby shook her head. "I didn't know prayers worked so quickly. They haven't worked much for me."

Mrs. Murphy took both of Ruby's hands in her own. "Believe you're worthy and promise me something."

Ruby felt her heart beating. "I'll try my best."

"Promise me from now on you will stand up straight and tall. You're a beautiful girl, and your height is one of your best features. First thing in the morning, stand up straight, look in the mirror, and say, 'I'm worthy of good things in my life and the love of good people.'"

Ruby felt a strange warmth and excitement flowing through her. Mrs. Murphy released Ruby's hands.

Ruby said, "I'll pick up my things tonight."

"I'll get them ready for you."

"How can I thank you for all your kindness to me?"

"You already have. Now don't be a stranger. Just because you're moving doesn't mean you can't come to visit me sometime. In fact, why don't you come over for Sunday dinner this weekend. Will you be off?"

"Oh, that's so kind of you. I'll let you know. But I don't want to put you out. Your son will be here by then, and I'm sure you'll have lots to talk to him about."

Mrs. Murphy's eyes twinkled. "Don't worry I know he'd be happier talking to you. Haven't you noticed most of my boarders at the dinner table are over 50?"

And with that, Ruby hurried back to the Brite Spot for her afternoon shift.

Chapter 39

June 1936

Ruby's move from Mrs. Murphy's boarding house to her newer, more spacious room on Lipscomb Street had unexpected perks. First, there were several young people in residence, even though they were at least six years older. Still, seeing their bright shiny faces whenever Ruby had the opportunity to join them at dinner made her happy.

The most important thing was her proximity to Ruth and Dub's house. They often walked to work together. This morning, Ruby's shift started an hour before Ruth's, so she had served the early birds before Ruth arrived.

Ruth's abrupt wave when she arrived alerted Ruby. Rather than going to change into her uniform, she headed for Mr. Frasier's post behind the cash register. The two chatted quietly while Ruby took care of her last customer. Her curiosity went into overdrive.

Ruth finished her talk with Mr. Frasier and joined Ruby. She sat on one of the stools.

"Sorry to keep you in suspense."

Ruby's pulse quickened. "What's going on?"

Ruth sighed. "I wish I had more time. It all happened so fast. . . .

"Just tell me what's going on."

Ruth looked at her friend, and her shoulders drooped. "I'm going to work at Dub's old job."

Ruby said, "I'm confused."

"I know, and I'm sorry. I didn't know anything about this yesterday. Dub found a better job. He got it in his head to offer my services when he gave his notice."

"Wait a minute," Ruby said. "So you're leaving here to work at Fort Worth Poultry and Egg?"

Ruth nodded. "It wouldn't be my first choice, but they need to replace Dub. It pays twice as much as I make here. We're trying to save for our own house. This could make the difference."

Ruby had to be supportive.

"I'll miss you, but I'm happy for you. Can we still be friends?"

Ruth's face seemed almost comical. Ruby couldn't help herself. She giggled and said, "I'm sorry for laughing. You look startled."

"Well, I am. You surely can't believe our friendship is that fragile. It won't matter where I work. We will always be friends."

"I know," Ruby said. "It just took me by surprise. I apologize for doubting you."

Ruth reached over and patted Ruby on the hand. "Apology accepted. Now, I must go change into my uniform. I told George I'd finish out the week. Fort Worth Poultry and Egg Company will simply have to wait until Monday for this girl."

Ruby watched her friend as she walked away to change. She shook her head. Things certainly would be different around here. Perhaps she should look for a better salary too. She'd need it when she started school in the fall.

Once the idea lodged in her brain, it rattled around and started growing.

Chapter 40

June 1936

When Monday morning rolled around, Ruby remembered she would be working at The Brite Spot today without her best friend. For Ruth, having a new job—even one she didn't particularly like—was a blessing because she would earn more money. But for Ruby, it meant less time spent with her friend.

As she dressed for the day, it occurred to her that life was very different now than the one she'd led as a schoolgirl, with a stepfather who made her life miserable. She realized the difference could be not living in fear all the time. Living in a city, having a job doing something she enjoyed, and meeting nice people, gave her satisfaction. She saw herself in a new way.

She finished dressing and realized she could happily go to work today—even though Ruth wouldn't be there. Many of their customers came in every day, and she knew them by name. It made her happy to know they looked forward to seeing and talking to her.

Then she remembered Mrs. Murphy and went to the full-length mirror. Standing up tall, she adjusted her shoulders and straightened her back.

The girl she saw in the mirror no longer looked like a schoolgirl. She saw a young woman, who had a job, lived on her own, and planned a great future. Ruby grinned at her image and winked.

And just for an instant, she thought her image winked back.

Chapter 41

July 1936

The window in Ruby's room faced south. The house next door sat back from the street, so Ruby's view was unobstructed. A row of beautiful old oak trees stood between the two houses. She watched the songbirds gathered there each morning, and especially loved the Cardinals. She knew the male Cardinal helped the female feed and tend their young. She hadn't realized the male's bright red color changed to a duller shade of brown while helping with the baby birds.

Gratitude filled her heart as she watched the beautiful creatures. She loved her expansion of possibilities, and the joy of steering her own ship.

Ruby learned that to enroll at Paschal High School, a test would be given, placing her as a junior or senior. She'd probably qualify as a senior, based on courses she'd taken the past few years.

Soon after, Ruby learned the Brite Spot would close in the evenings after July 15. Ruby's dream of going to school evaporated like dew in the morning sun. The Brite Spot Café location attracted ordinary blue-collar laborers for breakfast and lunch. It appealed to their appetites and pocketbooks. Mr. Frazier believed those same people would continue to eat there for breakfast and lunch. But he knew dinner was out of the question.

Ruby could either continue working days at the Brite Spot or find another waitress position at a dinner establishment. She discussed it with Ruth, who encouraged her to stay at the Brite Spot, save her money, and set her sights for school next year. But Ruby longed to go to school now. She would think about it. For now, she would stay at the Brite Spot.

Though she wasn't thrilled at this setback, she still felt the joy of making her own decisions.

Ruby stepped outside and noticed a stranger walking toward the Boarding House. The woman seemed stooped and old. When she lifted her head, Ruby drew in a sharp breath of air.

"Hi, Rube. I hope you don't mind me showing up, but I need a place to stay."

Jimma had stopped at the bottom of the steps. The first thing Ruby said seemed unfriendly.

"What happened, Mamma?"

Jimma looked so tired it made Ruby embarrassed. Jimma shook her head and sat down on the top step.

"I can't take it anymore. I left him."

Jimma had lost weight since Mother's Day. Now she needed help. Ruby sat on the step beside her.

"I'll take you to my room."

Jimma pulled herself up.

Ruby settled Jimma in bed and went looking for her landlady. Ruby explained the situation, and Mrs. Evans set out her requirements.

"I'll need an extra $1.00 a week for the room, and an extra $3.00 if she wants to eat her meals here."

"Can I give you the money when I get paid?"

"Sure, kid. Just don't forget."

Ruby stood there a few seconds, searching her brain for a solution. The only thing she could do was look for another job. If Mamma stayed with her very long, her current salary wouldn't sustain them both.

Chapter 42

July 1936

Ruth Nance tilted her head when Ruby finished her story. The look on her face was unreadable, and Ruby, wondered if Ruth disapproved.

"Sweetie, what else can you do? Maybe she's embarrassed to go to her sister's house." Ruth shook her head. "If she has no money, and no other place to go, it looks like you're it."

Ruby didn't try to suppress her disappointment. "I know you're right. I just hoped I could find another solution. I don't think she has a dime in her purse, and I told my landlady I'd give her some money today."

They had been sitting in Ruth and Dub's cheery kitchen since Ruby got off work at the Brite Spot that afternoon. It was Saturday, and Dub worked on Saturday's. Ruth only worked every other Saturday.

Ruby looked at the kitchen clock. "Oh, no. I didn't realize the time. I need to get back. Mamma will be wondering where I am."

She almost knocked over the wooden chair when she stood. Ruth smiled at her friend.

"I can loan you a few dollars until next payday if you need it. My new job is paying well."

Ruby shook her head. "No, I can't take money from you. I got my pay today. I'll be fine until next week. I'll figure out something." She felt her heart beating faster than usual. Truth was she had no idea how she'd pay for her mother's food and lodging at the boarding house.

Ruth walked into the living room. She opened her purse without a word, took out her billfold, and extracted two five-dollar bills.

"Give me your hand," Ruth said.

Ruby frowned as Ruth reached for her hand and pressed the folded money into it.

"No, I told you. I can't take money from you."

Ruth shook her head. "Of course, you can. Don't be a goose. What are friends for?"

Ruby felt the tears forming. With her other hand, she tried to wipe them away, but it was no use. The dam collapsed, and the tears flowed freely. The past two months had been such a blessing, but she also felt afraid a lot of the time. All her life she'd lived with a big family, either with her grandparents, or with Mamma, Bud, Dad, and all the other kids. Being truly alone, with no one to guide her or admonish her for being stupid and foolish, was both exhilarating and terrifying. Ruth had become her rock—a person she trusted and who she felt shared a strong bond with her.

Ruth put her arm around Ruby's shoulders and led her back into the kitchen. The older woman dampened a washcloth and held it out to the tear-streaked Ruby.

Ruby took the offered washcloth and dabbed the tears from her face. Then she reached into her pocket and pulled out the handkerchief she always carried. She blew her nose and let out the breath she'd been holding.

"What would I do without your friendship? You always make me feel better, and I don't know how you do it."

Ruth grinned. "Practice my dear friend, lots and lots of practice."

Chapter 43

Mid July 1936

Fort Worth, Texas, back in 1935, found itself in an unusual situation. The residents of "Cow Town" were proud of their city and for years had struggled in the shadow of Dallas, thirty miles east. But Fort Worth had a wealthy benefactor on their side—Amon G. Carter, the wealthiest man in town, owner of the *Fort Worth Star-Telegram*, and radio station WBAP.

The Texas Centennial would occur in 1936. Dallas was the lucky winner of the state-wide contest for the "official" Centennial celebration. To the residents of Fort Worth, it was just another humiliation to be endured. So, while Dallas proceeded to make big plans for their celebration, the movers and shakers of Fort Worth decided they would host their own event and garner some well-deserved attention for their beloved city. Fort Worth would put on an extravaganza like nobody had ever seen in Texas.

In October 1935, the Fort Worth City Council adopted a resolution to declare an emergency existing for the construction of the Fort Worth Centennial Stock Show buildings. The City Council felt it was in the best interests of their city to begin construction immediately. The funds for this larger-than-life entertainment were set at $1,862,727.00, with funding coming from a variety of grants, bond elections, and federal centennial funds. (If this had been 2021 money, it would have been about $35,082,000.00).

Texas Congressman Fritz Lanham from Fort Worth received this message from Amon Carter:

"It is our purpose to build the finest exposition grounds to be found anywhere in the United States . . ." The Fort Worth Frontier Centennial would attract visitors from all over the U.S. and other countries.

Fast forward to July 1936, when this fantastic and expensive centennial celebration would be kicking off in Fort Worth with a show put together by Billy Rose, the famous New York City producer. In addition to multiple venues of entertainment, there would be several dining places. Opening day would be July 18, 1936.

Ruby knew nothing of all this whoop-tee-do.

A few days after Jimma showed up, Ruth invited both Ruby and Jimma to dinner. Jimma begged off.

"Rube, I really don't feel like meeting your friends tonight. I just want to crawl in bed and get rid of this god-awful headache. I've had it all day."

Ruby knew better than to argue the point.

At Ruth and Dub's house, Ruby tried to dismiss her money concerns.

Dub said, "Sweetheart, tell her about what we heard today."

Ruth turned to Ruby. "Do you know anything about what's going on at the Fort Worth Centennial?"

"What's that?"

By the time she'd heard the details of this fantastically huge celebration, things started looking much better. Maybe tomorrow would bring her the job she needed to solve all her problems.

Maybe it was the answer to her recent prayers.

Chapter 44

The Casa Mañana Summer of 1936

Ruby looked out the window of the bus, and noticed how the dense, muggy air revealed the waves of heat. The temperature felt intense today. She watched the people walking along the sidewalks, sticking to whatever available shade could be had at noon in downtown Fort Worth in the middle of a hot, humid July. They went about their daily business. Ruby wondered if any of them felt as disappointed as she did.

Her hopes had been high for getting a job at Casa Mañana when it opened. The people who interviewed her were very nice, but she couldn't work there because she was too young. Two nice things about the situation happened: they suggested she reapply when she was 18, then they referred her to a lovely restaurant much closer for her. Since that place didn't serve alcohol, Ruby's age wouldn't be a factor for them.

It hadn't occurred to Ruby that her age mattered. Even as a child, she was taller than her peers. She had attained a height of 5 feet, 6 inches by the time she had her 14th birthday. Not only that, but her young, slim, body began taking on even more curves when she was 15. At her 16th birthday, Granny Palmer measured her at 5 feet, 9 inches. Most people just assumed she was a "grownup" after that.

When she looked in her mirror, she saw a grown woman. Everybody treated her like one without asking her age. People assumed she was what she looked like: young, but legal age.

In one way, she felt grateful for the unintended lesson. From now on, she'd monitor herself and try to correct any childish behavior.

Ruby saw her bus stop coming up next, so she reached for the cord above the window and pulled it, alerting the driver she wanted off. When she stood, she purposefully stretched up as tall as possible and relaxed her shoulders. She held her head high—but not in a snooty way—and walked smoothly down the aisle. When she stepped off the bus, she maintained her posture all the way to the boarding house.

The young woman who walked back into her rented room that day felt officially prepared to pass as a grownup. And when she looked at her reflection in the mirror on her closet door, she knew in her bones it was true.

Chapter 45

End of July 1936

Ruby had good things to celebrate. She had landed a new job, and Jimma had a lead on one herself. The two of them decided to rent a small, one-room apartment not far from Ruth and Dub's home. They hoped to move in right after Ruby's 17th birthday.

Of course, not everything was great. Nobody in 1936 could expect that, but Ruby felt truly grateful for the things which had come her way recently—especially the new job. Ruby had resigned from the Brite Spot. Mr. Frasier was such a sweetheart about everything. He completely understood Ruby's need for work in the evenings. He knew how much she wanted to attend high school in the fall. He wished her well and told her if she ever wanted to return to the Brite Spot, he would welcome her back. When she left on her last day, she thought she saw him swipe a tear away as she turned to go.

She needed to get home and check on Mamma. Jimma's new job at the tanning factory was hard on her. She had a lot of stooping and bending with her work. Ruby noticed that after work Jimma needed to soak in the small bathtub down the hall from their room each night. But she did seem somewhat better than she had been that first day.

Mamma finally told Ruby all about the ruckus with Joe. Apparently, his anger at Ruby running away had not cooled down during the month and a half she'd been gone. He accused Jimma of helping her leave, but Jimma steadfastly reminded him of the way he had treated his oldest stepchild. Joe didn't want to hear it. He kept reminding his wife that he'd taken in not only Ruby, but her brother Bud. Bud was now 15, and he'd taken off too. There would be no strong young man to help Joe in the fields. How would he pick the cotton? Who would help him harvest the measly crop of vegetables he'd planted that spring? His own daughters, ages 20 and 18, were left to deal with it, and he needed them to cook meals, take care of the little ones, and take care of the house. The younger children were still too young to be of much help.

He went on like this day, after day, and each time he grew angrier and meaner.

As her mother poured out the story, Ruby found herself feeling a little bit sorry for Joe. Poor man had built such a castle of anger and frustration that he never could see what had caused most of the misfortune he now endured.

When Mamma finally finished her story, Ruby asked what would happen to her half-brother and her three half-sisters. To Ruby's amazement, Joe had said he would "allow" Jimma to leave, but the children must stay with him.

Jimma's new job was demanding, but she kept telling Ruby she could handle it. The job started early in the mornings, and her exhaustion seemed to increase each day. Ruby hoped the poor woman could continue working at the tanning factory.

If she couldn't, Ruby had no idea how they would manage.

Chapter 47

August 12, 1936

The morning of her 17th birthday, Ruby Ellen Scott happily realized she was one year closer to being an adult. Now she would focus on finishing high school.

During the last two weeks, Mamma had managed to find a job at a laundry. It was hot working in the heat of summer, doing all the washing and pressing of laundry, but at least she was out of the tanning factory. Jimma's new job, had allowed them to move to the furnished apartment at 1600 South Lake Street two days before Ruby's birthday.

Ruby had worked the evening shift for ten days. The new restaurant was a step up from the Brite Spot. The pay was better, and the tips were usually more generous. With Mamma working a new job, Ruby felt she could stash away money to buy clothes for school.

Today she planned to meet with the school principal to see if she qualified to become a senior. They would have until Tuesday, September 8 to receive her records from Erath County.

When she walked out of R. L. Paschal High School at 1:30 p.m. that day, Ruby sternly reminded herself crying right now was not an option. Paschal couldn't verify Ruby's last year at school. Mr. Roberts would need to contact the school board to see if they had her records. It wouldn't be possible to have that information before the 1936 Paschal School year began.

Ruby left the apartment for work that afternoon and when she opened the door, she saw a strange man approaching. A woman with him seemed unable to walk on her own, and Ruby realized it was Jimma.

Jimma lifted her head.

"Mamma, what happened? Are you okay?

The man seemed annoyed. "Help me get her inside. She fainted at work today. She could barely stand up."

Ruby and the man put Jimma on the bed. The man started to leave. Ruby frowned. "Wait a minute. Who are you? What's wrong with my mother?"

Ruby noticed the irritation on the man's face.

"Look, lady. She needs a doctor. This is the second time she's passed out. The boss told her last week he didn't need no sick people workin' there."

The man reached into his pocket. He pulled out a ten-dollar bill and extended it to Ruby.

"Here," he said. "The boss told me to leave it with Ms. Parnell. It's what's owed her for the week. She's bein' let go. Ever' bodies got to pull their weight."

With that the man turned and walked out the door. Ruby looked at the bill in her hand and sighed. Better than nothing, but not much. Paying for this apartment was going to require Ruby to make more money. Now what?

She walked over to the bed. "Mamma? I need to get to work. My shift is ready to start. Will you be okay while I'm gone?"

Jimma smiled, but it was weak. "I just need some rest, Rube. You go on. I'll be fine till you get back."

Ruby put her hand on her mother's forehead. It was warm, but it could just be the heat of a hot August afternoon. There was nothing else she could do for now. She'd come up with something soon.

Chapter 48

August 1936

Obviously, something was wrong with Mamma, but so far Ruby couldn't convince her to see a doctor. Nowadays, Ruby felt like the parent, and Jimma seemed like the difficult child. Then Ruby got her big idea.

Margie Palmer McEwen was a nurse. She was also Jimma's youngest sister, and Ruby's favorite aunt. Margie and Bill McEwen had married shortly before Ruby's school year in La Grange for her eighth-grade year. Aunt Margie also arranged to pay Aunt Ina and Uncle Benton room and board for Ruby's stay.

Unfortunately, whenever Ruby thought about that wonderful year, she was reminded of the death of Aunt Ina's baby boy. She hadn't contacted Aunt Ina, even though she had arrived in Fort Worth three months ago.

Ruby weighed the wisdom of going behind Mamma's back and calling Aunt Ina. At least Aunt Ina was in Fort Worth. Aunt Margie and Uncle Bill lived in Houston. Ruby had no idea how to contact her. Aunt Ina would know, and Ruby needed someone to convince Mamma to seek medical help.

Ruth came to the rescue. Ruby stopped by her house on Saturday afternoon and outlined the problem.

"Do you have a phone number for your Aunt Ina?"

Ruby nodded. "Mamma gave it to me before I left. She wanted me to let Aunt Ina know I was in Fort Worth, but I couldn't do it. I can't face her."

Ruth said, "Okay. Is this problem about you or is it about getting your mother into medical treatment?"

Ruby said, "Oh, Ruth. You're right, of course."

Ruth laughed. "Sweet girl. You remind me of me a few years ago. We all learn eventually."

Ruby shook her head. "I've learned more from you about being an adult than I ever learned from my mother. I suppose I always felt like I needed to protect myself because no one else would."

Ruth grinned. "As I recall, you have a loving set of grandparents, and several amazing aunts and uncles. I gather they've cared a lot about you, don't you think?"

The truth of what Ruth said made Ruby feel ashamed.

"Okay." She opened her purse and pulled out an old address book Mamma had given her. It was filled with addresses of most of her relatives, and the phone numbers of any of those lucky enough to have a telephone.

Ruby reached for Ruth's telephone and dialed the number next to Aunt Ina's name. It rang three times before it was picked up.

"Hello?" The sound of Aunt Ina's cheery voice made Ruby's heart swell. She was afraid it might burst.

"Aunt Ina? It's Ruby Ellen."

"Oh, Ruby Ellen, my precious little niece. It's so good to hear from you. What's going on sweetheart?"

That familiar warm laugh and sweet Texas drawl made Aunt Ina's voice sound welcoming and full of love. Ruby's fear instantly melted away. She felt tears rolling down her cheeks and brushed them aside. There was nothing to cry about here. This was her aunt who loved her and had taken her in for an entire school year.

She sincerely hoped the rest of her maturing wouldn't be as rocky as this one small step had been.

Chapter 49

August 15 to 16, 1936

When she left Ruth's house that afternoon, Ruby's whole body felt lighter than a gentle breeze. After all the worry and hesitation about phoning her Aunt Ina, the outcome had been the best of all possible solutions.

Aunt Ina listened as Ruby explained about Mamma. Aunt Ina wasn't even aware that Jimma had left Joe. She was more than happy to give Ruby the telephone number for Aunt Margie. When Ruby spoke to Aunt Margie about an hour later, the news was even better. Aunt Margie said she and Uncle Bill would drive up from Houston the next day. Both Margie and Bill were off on Sundays, and they would pick up Jimma in Fort Worth around noon and be back in Houston by time for supper. Aunt Margie listened carefully to what Ruby told her about Jimma's frequent fainting. When the phone call concluded, Ruby felt a huge wave of relief.

She tried to pay Ruth for the cost of the long-distance call, but Dub stepped in at that moment and told her to not worry about it.

"Listen here, young lady," Dub said, a tiny smile around his mouth. "You are almost a part of this family. You've never made a long-distance call in your life. Let us be the ones who pay for your very first one."

Now all Ruby had to do was confess to her mother that she had intervened on her behalf with Aunt Margie.

Surprisingly, Jimma didn't seem upset at all. In fact, she appeared glad someone had stepped up and acted for her. That evening, Ruby helped her mother pack the few clothes she'd brought with her.

The following morning, Jimma was already up and dressed when Ruby woke up.

"Gracious, Mamma. They won't be here until noon. You could have spent a few more hours sleeping."

Jimma's face looked less sad and swollen. "Rube, I'm just so grateful to you for doing what I was afraid to do. I don't guess I've given you very many compliments during your lifetime, but what you did for me yesterday was the most loving, kind, and brave thing anybody ever did for me."

Ruby felt her throat tighten, and fresh tears spring into her eyes. She swallowed and turned away. "Thank you, Mamma. I was afraid you'd be mad at me for calling Aunt Margie."

"I know," Jimma said. "If you'd suggested it before doing it, I'd probably have told you not to. But once you did, and when you told me about it, I felt the biggest load lift from my heart. I guess I just didn't have the courage to ask for help from my little sister."

"Come on," Ruby patted her mother's arm. "Let's have some breakfast. I bought a few groceries yesterday, and I knew you'd love to have some crispy bacon this morning."

Jimma grinned, and it was the first such expression Ruby had seen on her mother's face in a long time.

"You sure know the way to my heart, little girl. I'll have two slices."

Chapter 50

Late August 1936

As a little girl, Ruby Ellen Scott often sat quietly just outside the perimeter of the group of adults in her family. Most times, especially in the long, daylight hours of summer, the time after supper was the spot in the day when the grown-ups had time to sit and discuss events, or news they'd heard from a neighbor or friend.

It occurred to her now that she missed those educational episodes with the adults in her life. Without her even being aware, a lot of the things they discussed helped her understand the world around her. It also taught her how important kindness was to any interaction you might have with others. From her own experience with her stepfather, she learned firsthand that anger and violence caused a person's brain to register fear. It also created animosity against the person who caused the violence.

Then there was Granny Palmer. Her gentleness, patience, and unceasing love filled Ruby's heart and mind with warmth and happiness. A simple compliment or some sort of praise for a job well done could carry a person through an otherwise difficult time.

Without even being aware of it at the time, Ruby now understood why she was drawn to the people she so admired. Her friend, Ruth, for example, was always kind—even when someone treated her with unkindness. She had often responded to Ruby's questions with one of her own. "What do you think?" Or sometimes, "What can you do to change the situation?"

Ruby had subtly learned from her association with Ruth that it was more important to gauge the other person's need from a question, than to impose your own feelings and possible prejudices.

Since she had arrived in Fort Worth on that hot, sweltry Mother's Day in May, almost everyone she'd met or had association with had been unfailingly kind to her. She found herself responding to them in the same way. It had now become a habit for her, and it surprised her when she made the connection.

Today she felt that kindness flowing from George Frasier at the Brite Spot. She had decided to check in with him and see if she could get some additional work by taking the early shift there. She knew it was harder to fill that shift than the one for lunch. It started at 6:30 a.m., and workers just beginning their day needed hot coffee, a solid breakfast, and a kind person to serve it. Ruby felt deep gratitude when

Mr. Frasier offered it to her. He apologized and said he was sorry he didn't have a place for her at the lunch hour, but Ruby assured him she was happy to help where she was needed.

When she walked out of the Brite Spot that afternoon, she felt honored that he considered her the right person for that slot. She must always remember "kindness begets kindness."

Chapter 51

September 1936

Ruby came to a difficult decision. It occurred to her that being on her own had its downside. As a child, the adults around her ordered her life.

Almost four months had gone by since she left the farm outside Johnsville. It seemed more like four years. She found herself unable to remember how everything looked. Maybe she didn't really want to.

These past four months, she had held onto the dream of going back to school for her diploma. She had even gotten the okay from the principal at Paschal High School. But just because you wanted something didn't mean you could, or should, get it. As an adult, you had to measure the pros and cons. If you were in charge of your own life, it was important to gage what was really needed at that time.

And that's why Ruby decided her dream of finishing school couldn't happen right now. If nothing else, these past four months had shown her she needed to keep her priorities straight. A teen-age girl, who had left her home, needed a job to maintain herself. Dreams and wants kept people focused on a goal. But the reality of being on your own sometimes meant dreams had to be put aside so you could eat, have a place to live, and put clothes on your back.

So, Ruby visited Paschal High School, one more time, and spoke to Mr. Roberts. When she finished explaining, she waited to hear what he would say.

Mr. Roberts smiled at her. "Miss Scott, I really admire your decision. I can tell you're mature for your age, and you impress me quite a lot. You should know you will still be able to start your senior year at this time next year—provided, of course, you still want to and are in a position, financially, to do so."

Ruby's heart almost pounded out of her chest. "Oh, Mr. Roberts, that's so kind of you. It never occurred to me I'd be able to try again next year. How can I ever thank you?"

"Don't thank me, young lady. This is something you did all on your own. You are the sort of student teachers dream of. I can promise you we'll still be here, and I really hope to see you next year."

When Ruby walked out of the principal's office, she felt dazed but excited. The dread she'd had going into this meeting completely disappeared, and in its place was a massive determination to make sure she did her part to report back to Paschal High School in the fall of next year.

Now she needed to keep on target and not let anything upset her plan. She would work to make sure she could go to school next year. But this moment in time gave her faith in her own ability to care for herself and her future.

And since she wasn't a fortune teller, she couldn't possibly know what would be most important to her this time next year.

Chapter 52

Fall-Winter 1936

Once Ruby understood her options for completing an education, her entire mindset changed. Looking back through the prism of time seemed like watching a movie of someone else's life. She now felt completely comfortable in her new hometown. Best of all, her mother's life had improved dramatically.

When Aunt Margie and Uncle Bill arrived that day in August to take Jimma back with them to Houston, Ruby worried that she might never see her mother again. During all the years growing up, she never saw her mother sick or unable to work—other than when she was close to giving birth, or right afterwards.

Ruby felt immense relief when she learned Mamma's illness boiled down to having a major issue with her teeth.

Jimma had been the only child in her family to inherit a mouthful of buck teeth, along with all the problems they caused. J.R. Palmer had never known his own father or any of his relatives on that side of the family. He and Ellen decided Jimma must have been saddled with her problem teeth through one of those unknown forebearers. Whoever or whatever had caused it, this woman at age 40 had some major mouth problems. Most photographs of Jimma up until 1937 portrayed her with a closed mouth and a grim look. With the overlapping teeth, food particles stayed stuck and caused tooth decay. Because of bacteria, many of her teeth had been damaged to the root.

In the long run, they decided to remove all her own teeth and supply her with dentures. They believed the infected teeth caused the sickness and fainting. Ruby wasn't clear on all the details, but she didn't press for answers. Blessedly, Aunt Margie had paid for the entire procedure. Jimma assured her youngest sister she would repay every penny, no matter how long it took.

Within a short time, Mamma returned to live with Ruby. Jimma smiled more often, and the new dentures enhanced her appearance. Her entire demeanor changed noticeably. Thanks to her renewed health she managed to get better jobs (which paid more,) and when she had enough money, she moved into her own apartment. Ruby felt relieved her mother had gotten rid of her terrible teeth.

Ruby's relationship with her Mamma had moved into a mostly comfortable place now. Understanding the physical and emotional pain her mother had endured so long opened a new window of understanding about being an "adult."

Christmas turned into a quiet time because Mamma went back to Johnsville to visit the little kids, while Ruby stayed in Fort Worth. When Ruby returned from work one day, she was stunned to find a gift from her mother. Since that first time she'd been allowed to listen to her grandparents' small radio, Ruby had yearned for one of her own. She never expected to have one until she was much older, but Mamma apparently thought her oldest child needed something to repay her kindness. It brought tears to Ruby's eyes to find a lovely radio sitting on her bedside table, along with a note from Mamma. The note simply said, "Merry Christmas to my dear daughter."

As soon as Ruby turned on the radio, she searched for station WBAP in Fort Worth. With any kind of luck, she'd be able to hear the Light Crust Doughboys. Not only that, but she discovered a selection of other stations bringing her the music she loved and the news and entertainment she needed.

New Year's Eve, December 31, 1936, arrived on Thursday, and Ruby spent the evening with Ruth and Dub. Upon arrival, she saw a young man she didn't know. He seemed unattached and had arrived ahead of her. Dub introduced his co-worker.

Frank seemed like a nice enough human being, but he was at least two inches shorter than Ruby, and had little to say. After dinner, Ruby excused herself and went to help Ruth in the kitchen. She found her best friend cutting a pie and waiting for the coffee to perk.

Ruby reached into the cupboard for the dessert plates. "You have to be kidding me, right?" She spoke softly, but with annoyance in her voice.

Ruth rolled her eyes toward the ceiling. "I told Dub it was a dumb idea. I never met the guy, but I think Dub feels sorry for him. He does seem a little bit out of his element."

"Out of his element?" Ruby whispered louder than she had intended. "I don't think he's even a citizen of this world."

"No one is expecting you to marry the guy."

"Don't even mention the word 'marriage' to me."

Ruth grinned and shook her head. "Oh, sweet girl. Never say 'never.' You must know I didn't plan to ever marry again after I got away from Homer. But, as you can see, I found a wonderful man, and marrying him was the smartest thing I ever did. Be patient. When the right one comes along, you'll feel it."

Ruby switched subjects. "I expected to see Rex Dennis tonight. You said Homer was bringing him to spend the weekend. I thought he'd be my date."

"Well, as usual, Homer changed his mind. No big surprise there." Then Ruth turned to her friend and tilted her head. "Anyway, what's this about a date? Can't you find a better boyfriend than my eight-year-old son?"

Ruby leaned in close to Ruth's ear so she could whisper. "I'd rather date eight-year-old Rex Dennis than poor old Frank."

They both started giggling, but quickly stopped when they heard Dub calling them from the living room. "What's going on in there, ladies? We're still waiting for our coffee and pecan pie."

They straightened up, composed themselves, and returned with the requested refreshments.

But each time they looked at each other, right up until they heard the Guy Lombardo version of Auld Lang Syne on the radio, their laughter threatened to bubble up again. Frank never seemed to notice. A couple of times that evening Dub looked at the two women and shook his head, while allowing himself a small grin.

Ruby would remember that evening as her first, real adult party event—even though, thankfully, she never saw poor old Frank again.

Chapter 53

A Brand-New Year – 1937

Ruby decided to treat herself to a movie on New Year's Day. Its cost was a quarter, so she decided a small bag of popcorn at five cents wouldn't be extravagant. She and Ruth had gone together several times before, but this was the first time Ruby attended all by herself. She considered it another milestone. A real adult woman could go alone to a movie, and not be embarrassed she wasn't with someone.

Today's movie line up offered, in addition to the main feature, two short subjects, a cartoon, and the most recent newsreel. The newsreels shown in movie houses fascinated Ruby. They offered more access to the history unfolding around her. She enjoyed listening to her new radio. The voices delivering the news kept her much more informed than she had been prior to moving to Fort Worth, but the newsreels put faces to many of the voices on the radio. She was shocked the first time she saw a newsreel showing Adolph Hitler. He seemed like a horrible caricature of a human being—short, an ugly piercing voice, and a maniacal look as he shouted at the hordes of people. She wondered how he had managed to become the leader of a country.

Also in the newsreel, for only the second time in her life, she saw the current president of the United States—Franklin D. Roosevelt, and his wife Eleanor. They seemed surrounded by happy people congratulating him on his soon-to-be-inauguration for a second term as the nation's leader. The newscaster in the reel reminded the audience that this big event would take place for the first time on a new date—Wednesday, January 20, 1937.

The sun sat low in the west when she left the theater, and walking to the bus stop, a brisk wind ruffled her hair. She couldn't stop thinking about all the things she'd seen that day in the newsreel. For the first time in her life, she felt part of the larger world around her. This year she would become eighteen. Three years after that, she would be able to vote. It occurred to her she would need to learn how all that worked, and what had to be considered before casting a ballot.

Becoming a real adult might turn out to be more terrifying than her childhood.

Chapter 54

The Next Few Months, 1937

Before Ruby knew it, January was gone, and February had replaced it. She always felt better in February, perhaps because January usually had the worst weather. Maybe it was because January seemed such a letdown after all the holiday cheer in December.

Mr. Frasier had asked her to come back and work for him a few weeks on the breakfast shift. Ruby was delighted to have another income—especially at the Brite Spot.

One cloudy February morning, she looked over her shoulder and saw a familiar face, Larry Johnson, a friendly young man she had waited on many times at the Brite Spot. "Hi, Larry. Good to see you again. What'll it be?"

Larry glanced up at her, and Ruby saw a big smile spread across his features.

"Well, if it isn't Miss Ruby Ellen. I thought you'd left us forever. Are you back for good?"

Ruby blushed. "I'm filling in for Irene."

"Hey, George," Larry motioned to Mr. Frazier to join them. "Why didn't you tell me you brought this beauty back? I'd a been here every day."

Ruby felt her cheeks burning.

"Well, Larry, sometimes beauty just shows up at your door and begs to be let in. I'm the sort of fellow who's happy to oblige."

Both men chuckled, and Ruby shook her head. "Mr. Frazier's pulling your leg. He's helping me out."

Larry nodded approval. "Glad to hear things are going well for you."

Ruby took his order, and then a flurry of activity kept her busy for several minutes. She had been too busy to notice that Larry and Mr. Frazier were in deep conversation.

She approached with Larry's order, and Mr. Frazier said, "Well, Larry, here she is. I guess you'll have to ask her yourself."

And with that, Mr. Frazier moved on to seat a newly arrived man and woman.

Ruby set the hot platter in front of Larry, then reached for the coffee pot to help another customer. Larry reached out and grabbed her free arm.

"Can you please come back and talk to me for a minute when you've delivered that coffee?"

Ruby was caught off guard. "Ah . . . sure . . . just give me a minute."

She poured the coffee for her new customer and handed him a menu. "I'll be right back."

She returned to Larry. "Is something wrong? Did I make a mistake on your order?"

He took a sip of the coffee, then looked squarely at her. "Would you ever consider going out with me sometime?"

Ruby blinked. Larry waited. Everyone in the café seemed to vanish. At that exact moment the sun popped out from behind an early-morning cloud. Bright sunlight poured into the Brite Spot Café.

"Yes," she said. "I would."

And the world started turning again.

Chapter 55

Spring 1937

It was April before Ruby realized it. Next month would mark one year living in Fort Worth. She felt right at home now. It occurred to her she'd made a lot of friends since that hot Mothers' Day in May when she arrived in the city. She'd even been dating.

It started last year when Ruby accepted a dinner invitation from Mrs. Murphy. Ruby never forgot how kind Mrs. Murphy had been, and she often stopped by to see the woman. They would sit in Mrs. Murphy's homey kitchen, having a cup of coffee and sampling some of her wonderful recipes. It was during one of those visits she finally met Mrs. Murphy's son, Ben.

Ben was a sweet young man. He was tall, a little bit overweight, and had the biggest blue eyes. He blushed when he talked to Ruby, and she tried to put him at ease. Then one afternoon he asked her for a date. He suggested they take in a movie at the Majestic Theater that evening. Before she had a chance to respond, she saw the happy glow on Mrs. Murphy's face.

"That's awfully sweet of you Ben. I'd love to go to the movie with you."

The instant the words left her mouth, she wondered why she'd accepted his invitation. She really didn't have time for dating.

But the pure joy she saw on Mrs. Murphy's face caused Ruby to answer in the affirmative.

After that, they went out a few more times, but they couldn't get together very often. Eventually Ben met a girl who worked close to where he worked.

One day when Ruby had stopped by to have coffee with Mrs. Murphy, she seemed a little sad.

"I guess you heard Ben has a girlfriend," Mrs. Murphy said. She stirred sugar into her cup. "She's nice, but I sure had hopes the two of you would hit it off."

Ruby thought quickly. "You know, Mrs. Murphy. I enjoy Ben's company, but did you know I'll be going to high school this fall? I don't think it would be proper for Ben to date a high school girl, do you?"

Mrs. Murphy's eyes widened. "Oh." She frowned. "I assumed you were older than that."

"Why thank you." Ruby grinned and sipped her coffee. "It's important that people think I'm older than I am. But just so you know, I'll be 18 years old on August 12 this year."

Mrs. Murphy shook her head. "Don't mind me, dear. I'm just a typical mother who wants to make sure her son meets the right girl. To me, you fill the bill."

Ruby put her hand on Mrs. Murphy's. "I consider that quite a compliment."

They chatted a little longer and finished their coffee. Ruby stood up to leave, and Mrs. Murphy took the cups to the sink and rinsed them out. She turned back to walk Ruby to the door.

Mrs. Murphy's face now displayed a conspiratorial grin. "Well," she said, "if you don't have any better prospects after your birthday, let me know. I have another son who graduates from college next year."

Chapter 56

May 1937

Ruby Ellen Scott regarded her image in the full-length mirror on the door of her closet. She had already purchased several outfits she thought would be suitable to wear to Paschal High School this fall. The one she had on today was her favorite.

Ruby knew how to sew, but without a sewing machine she had little ability to make her own clothes.

Her mother's sewing machine had been in their home for as long as she could remember. Mamma used to tell her about Lester buying the machine just before Ruby was born. She had taken it with her every time she moved. Sometimes, it had to stay at Granny Palmer's house. Granny Palmer always cared for it until Jimma found a place to live. Ruby wondered if the machine was now with Granny Palmer again, or if Mamma had left it with Joe. She really hoped it was in Granny Palmer's possession.

Ruby's interest in clothes had skyrocketed once she became a working girl. Even though she usually wore uniforms, she wanted to look nice on her own. Since arriving in Fort Worth, she was more interested in clothes than she ever had been. She now noticed what other women wore and discovered the styles she liked and those she didn't.

She and Ruth had gone to a movie recently where the Movie Tone News showed footage of the May 12, 1937, Coronation of King George VI and his wife, Queen Elizabeth. All the beautiful gowns on display for that occasion were so splendid, and the grandeur of Westminster Abby made Ruby long to visit it in person someday.

But in that same newsreel, they saw the May 6, 1937, disaster of the Hindenburg as it attempted mooring at The Naval Air Station in Lakehurst, New Jersey, in a sudden lightning storm. A crowd of people turned out that evening to witness this landing. Even a newsreel crew waited to welcome and film the huge, rigid-framed hydrogen airship. That crew caught, in horrifying detail, the swift burning of the aircraft's skin, and some of the victims falling through the flames. A radio announcer from New York started out announcing the impressive size of the airship, and almost immediately switched to describing the horror of what he witnessed each moment. He ended up, tears in his voice, stunned as all the rest of the spectators that terrible evening.

Those two events—the coronation of a monarch and the swift death of so many people—caused Ruby to think about more than her own private world. For all her perceived problems with money and learning how to manage on her own, it was a huge initiation into world events. Becoming more aware of the vast number of people sharing the planet with her, was a giant leap from childhood to grown-up status.

It also showed her how life could be very good in one place and could suddenly turn horribly bad in another.

Chapter 57

August 1937

In March 1937, Billy Rose announced he would return to Fort Worth to stage a new version of Casa Mañana and the Frontier Centennial. The boarded-up grounds of the 1936 celebration would open and once again provide entertainment, food, and drink for the eager crowds. Ruby was ecstatic when she heard that confirmation.

On June 26, 1937, Casa Mañana and The Frontier Centennial officially opened for its second season. Ruby and Ruth made sure they visited the extravaganza very soon after that. Ruby wanted to know where to go to be hired at one of the restaurants. When she found it, she filled out an application, and handed it in.

On Thursday morning, August 12, 1937, Miss Ruby Ellen Scott presented herself at the Pioneer Palace. At last, she was old enough to work in this amazing venue and support herself while she went to school. By this time, she had purchased a small, inexpensive Kodak camera. She loved taking photos of her friends, relatives, and the sights in Fort Worth. One day she took her camera to work with her and took a picture of her two male bosses at Pioneer Palace. When all the film had been shot and processed, she happily made notes on the back of many of them and placed them in a photo album she'd received for her birthday from Ruth and Dub.

Ruby's life in a mere fifteen months had changed so radically she almost forgot what it had been like before. But the best thing by far was her belief she could have a future unlike any she'd ever imagined. She loved working in places where she could meet lots of new people. They seemed to value her service, and they apparently liked the way she performed her job. Because she was young and strong, waiting tables each day, carrying multiple plates, and swiftly serving her customers, people were impressed. Her employers valued her "can do" attitude, and her customers loved being pampered by such a lovely and friendly young woman. Never in a million years would Ruby have imagined herself doing the work she now performed. Her shyness had lessened, and her youthful exuberance impressed all those around her. Life was good.

She had supplied the name of her Duffau High School teachers from the 1935-36 school year to the principal at Paschal. Those grades had now been received, and Ruby was set to enroll in September. Now she focused on working more hours.

By the time classes started at Paschal, Ruby had the clothes she needed for a young woman attending her senior year. She would still have her job at Pioneer Palace until it closed for the season in October, and she'd already found another one she would step into for the winter. Yes, things were looking good for Ruby Ellen Scott.

She had yet to learn that God, apparently, has a sense of humor.

Chapter 58

Fall, 1937

On that first day of school in September, Ruby awakened an hour earlier than the alarm on the small Bulova bedside clock. She realized she might have a good chance of getting into the bathroom down the hall before the rest of the building stirred.

Her one-room apartment had a kitchenette in the corner of the room and a toilet and basin installed in a sort of closet. But getting a bath or shower in the large bathroom down the hall depended on how many other residents had the same idea.

The luxury of a quick shower made her happy on this most important day. She managed the entire process in a little less than ten minutes, and happily noted none of the other people on her floor were waiting in line when she exited the shower room. Now she would have plenty of time to dress, fix her hair and makeup, and make some oatmeal and coffee.

Ruby's nervousness drained away when she walked into the halls of R.L. Paschal High School that morning. This was nothing at all like the schools she'd attended previously. Thankfully, she had been supplied with a map of the building so she could quickly find the proper classroom for each period. English would be the first period, followed by Geometry, Chemistry, Typing and Shorthand, Public Speaking, and Home Economics. By the end of the day, Ruby's mind reeled from all the different classes.

In her old schools, one or two teachers taught all the subjects. Not so here at Paschal. She'd made notes during each class, starting with the name of the instructor for that subject. But rather than making her feel overwhelmed, she realized her year away from school had somehow actually prepared her for what she now faced. The homework might present a bit of a problem, she realized. Classes were over at 3:30 p.m. each day. Her job at Pioneer Palace required her to be there by 5:00 p.m. It would take some major shuffling of schedules to allow her to go to school, work, and get her homework done each day. Of course, the homework would only be for English, Geometry, and Chemistry. If she could manage her time properly, it should all fall into place.

It dawned on her she could probably only see her friends on the weekends. Not a big problem. The point was doing what she set out to do. Dating and socializing would have to take a backseat for now.

How difficult could that be?

Chapter 59

October 30, 1937

By the 25th of October 1937, Ruby Ellen Scott had completed six weeks of school. Already she realized how different things were in the city, as opposed to the one-room schools she had attended thus far. Of course, it also made a difference having to work for a living, while attending a full day of school, plus finding time to do her homework. She simply hadn't fully realized how limited time would be because of her situation.

Her first report card was a good one. But the cost to her sleeping schedule left her tired and a bit panicky. If this would be her life for the rest of the school year, she honestly didn't know if she would make it. For the first time in her young memory, she didn't trust her strength and enthusiasm for school to get her through the entire year.

She struggled through the next four school days, hoping to improve her time management, and find a way to enhance her sleep schedule. On Saturday morning she stopped by Ruth and Dub's home to see if Ruth had any suggestions.

Ruth had her usual pot of coffee on the stove, ready for drinking, and Ruby gratefully sipped a cup of the hot, steamy brew.

"The way I see it," Ruth said, "you have to make a decision pretty quick."

Ruby frowned as she set the empty cup back in its saucer. "I'd love to if only I actually knew what that decision should be."

Ruth grinned. She didn't speak until she had refilled Ruby's empty cup. "Have you eaten anything today?"

"That depends on what you mean by 'anything'."

"Anything more than a piece of toast?"

"Not really. I plan to go to the grocery store when I leave here."

Ruth shook her head. "You are really stubborn, aren't you? How about a scrambled egg, a couple of warmed up slices of bacon, and some fresh orange juice?"

Ruby's eyes lit up. "That sounds fantastic! How do you always know exactly what I need?"

"I suppose because I was your age once. I know what it's like, and I know eventually things will be better, but this fall has been terrible for all working people. Just when we thought the Depression might be fading, it's crashed down on us again."

Ruby nodded. "It certainly didn't help my plans when the Casa

Mañana Frontier Fiesta was shut down on September 25. It was supposed to stay open until late October. I heard there was some sort of "lawsuit" that forced them to close sooner than planned. I had to take the first evening job I could get just to stay in school.

Ruth dished up the scrambled eggs and bacon. "Didn't you go back to that restaurant where you worked before you were old enough to be hired at Pioneer Palace?"

"Yes, but the girl who replaced me this summer was able to work longer hours. I knew I couldn't be there in the mornings and afternoons. So now, they're putting me on just a two-hour shift in the evening. That won't make me enough to survive." She took a bite of toast.

"It sounds like you've already made your decision."

Ruby shook her head. She sipped her orange juice and felt the tears starting. The anger she felt for resorting to tears was becoming more familiar every day.

Ruth poured herself another cup of coffee. "Sweetie don't berate yourself. I think a good cry is what you need."

Ruby swiped at the offending tears and shook her head. "No. Crying never got me anything but a stuffy nose and bloodshot eyes. I need to come up with a plan."

"Such as?"

"On Monday morning, I'm going to the principal's office and tell them I need to drop out until I can find a better job in the evenings."

Ruth sipped her coffee. "Someday, you'll figure out how precious an education is. There's no sense in wringing your hands about things you can't fix—especially right now. But if I ever have a daughter, I'm going to insist that she not only finish high school, but that she goes on to college. The world is changing. A woman can't afford to be left behind, with no education, and dependent on a man to take care of her."

Ruby felt a chill down her back. "Oh, Ruth, I almost forgot what you went through when you were my age. You're right, and I believe someday I'll be able to do all that."

"My sweet friend, I'm really talking about myself here, so pay no mind. You do what you need to do for your own situation. You need to survive the best way you can. Maybe you can finish school later."

Ruby sighed and finished her last few bites of bacon. "Sure. But who knows? Maybe my Prince Charming will come along and sweep me off my feet. He'll be handsome and smart, and he'll take me away on his white charger."

Ruth grinned. "That's the spirit. Think positive."

Ruby nodded, but in the back of her mind, she didn't think that was a plan to depend on.

She stood. "I guess we'll see, won't we?"

Ruth said, "Don't forget. Tomorrow night's the Halloween party. You promised you'd go with me. Dub says he's not up for it."

Ruby nodded. "I'll be here by 6 p.m., okay?"

"Yes, and wear comfortable shoes. Josie said we're going on a scavenger hunt."

"I've ever been on a scavenger hunt. How does that work?"

Ruth grinned. "It's easy, really. We split up into teams. They give each team a list of weird things we're supposed to bring back—like a burned-out light bulb, or a book of matches. Stuff like that. Then the team who brings back the most items on their list wins the prize. You know, maybe boxes of Cracker Jacks or some other silly thing."

"Well," Ruby said, "I'll try to not set my expectations too high. It doesn't sound like an earth-shattering evening."

Ruth shrugged. "True, but it's more fun than staying home alone on Halloween. And who knows? You may have a wonderful time?"

Ruby hugged her friend as she prepared to leave. "From your lips to God's ears."

Chapter 60

Halloween 1937

When Ruby woke up Sunday morning, the first thing she saw were the gray clouds outside her window. If it rained today, what would happen to the planned scavenger hunt this evening? At first, she thought that might be a great idea. But then she remembered how much Ruth was looking forward to the party.

She turned on her radio, hoping for a weather report for the day and evening. Instead, she found herself in the middle of a sermon from Fort Worth's most famous Baptist preacher: J. Frank Norris. Even though Ruby had grown up 65 miles south of Fort Worth, everyone with a radio had heard of the man. He had a reputation for filling the First Baptist Church in Fort Worth with huge crowds every Sunday. But on a darker note, he had murdered a man back in 1926. Even so, Norris had been acquitted of the murder, and his outlandish style and forceful personality seemed to draw people in. Ruby had no interest in anything someone like that had to say. She quickly dialed her radio to another station.

There she found the weather report. While there might be light showers in the early part of the day, forecasters predicted the sun would shine by early afternoon, and the evening promised to be dry and pleasant for the city's trick or treaters and party goers.

Ruby took care of her weekly chores of laundry, grocery shopping, and general cleaning of her small apartment. She occupied her mind during her chores by planning her speech for tomorrow's meeting with the Paschal school principal. The man had been so kind and helpful to her, and now, in addition to letting herself down, she felt in some way she was letting him down, too. She dreaded the meeting, so she decided to think about something else instead.

By 5:00 p.m., Ruby had finished all her chores, dressed for the party, and was on her way to pick up Ruth. Ruby loved that she could walk to most of the places she needed to go. Sometimes she caught one of the many buses that ran late into the evening, but when it was still light, she preferred walking.

When Ruby rang the doorbell at Ruth and Dub's little rented house, she heard Dub's heavy footsteps approaching. He opened the door and grinned at her.

She said, "Trick or Treat."

Chapter 61

Halloween Night, 1937

Ruby had already met many of the girls at this evening's party. Some of them worked at the Fort Worth Poultry and Egg Company with Ruth, and some of them worked at various restaurants in this area of town.

A week ago, Ruth and Ruby had gone grocery shopping together. When they returned to Ruth's house, Ruth explained the rules of a scavenger hunt.

"You don't have to do it all by yourself. We split up into teams."

Ruby frowned. "How many teams will there be?"

"Depends on how many people show up. We need to have the same number on each team."

"I don't get it. What difference does it make?"

Ruth shook her head. "Look, I didn't make the stupid rules. I don't know why they made them like they did. Just trust me when I tell you. It works better when the teams are evenly divided."

"You really do know the rules, don't' you?"

Ruth squinted at Ruby. "You've been putting me on, haven't you? I thought you'd never been on a scavenger hunt."

"I haven't. I've just enjoyed watching you explain the rules. You're the best explainer I've ever met."

So tonight, Ruby felt fully prepared.

The party had an array of women who differed in both age and physical ability. It hadn't occurred to Ruby that some of the women might not be able to participate in a scavenger hunt. When the teams were formed, three women opted not to participate because of all the walking. That left three teams of five, plus one. Ruth immediately offered to stay back at the party to help the hostess. Ruby understood but felt disappointed.

The teams were given a list of items to bring back and each team started off in a different direction. Ruby's team headed into an area she knew well.

The first three items on the list took only ten minutes to acquire. The next item seemed appropriate for Ruby. It was a menu from a particular restaurant close by.

The group arrived in front of the Paris Coffee Shop at 614 West Magnolia just a few minutes before 6:00 p.m. They huddled briefly then shoved the reluctant Ruby inside. Her job was to ask for a menu from that restaurant. Once inside, Ruby's nerve almost failed her. What if they didn't want to give away one of their menus? Those things, after all, did cost money.

She noticed there were quite a few people sitting at tables and several more at the marble counter. Obviously, the dinner hour was in full swing. Everyone looked busy, and it seemed rude to bother the workers about a silly scavenger hunt. She came close to simply leaving, but then she saw a young man walking directly toward her.

He was a bit taller than her, dark-haired, and handsome. A devilish smile lit his face, and he had a hint of sassy-smartness about him. Ruby felt strangely mesmerized. Then she heard his voice.

"Hi, Beautiful. My name's Jimmy Valentine. What can I do for you?"

Chapter 62

Halloween Night, 1937

When Ruby exited the Paris Coffee Shop, her team teased her about the young man. They didn't believe she'd never met him before. When they returned to the party, the first topic was Ruby's "handsome friend."

She had a moment alone with Ruth and tried to explain. "I swear I never laid eyes on that guy. I've only been there one time. I never saw him before."

Ruth grinned. "I believe you, Sweetie. They're just having fun at your expense."

On the way back to Ruth's house, Ruby still insisted she'd never met Mr. Valentine.

Ruth said, "You are so wound-up nobody would take you seriously. Even I, who knows absolutely you've never met him, can tell something's up with you."

Back at Ruth's house she said, "The girls teased you. You made it easy for them. Do you get that?"

Ruby sat down on one of the kitchen chairs. "I don't know what's gotten into me. I'm nervous and agitated. It's not like me. I'm usually calm."

Ruth smiled. "How many young men have you dated since your move here?"

Ruby shrugged. "Maybe six or seven. Why?"

"Have you ever reacted to any of them the way you did this young man?"

Ruby started to speak, but Ruth said, "Just think about it. Is there something different about him?"

"I don't . . . I mean it seems to me . . ." Ruby frowned. "He's different from anybody I've met . . ."

She shook her head. "I don't know, but there was something about him. It felt like we were the only people there. I heard his voice—asking my name."

Ruth sighed. "I assume you told him your name."

Ruby blushed. "I think so. I don't remember."

"Well, if I were in your place, I'd see what I could find out about this dreamboat of yours."

"Whoa," Ruby frowned. "I said he was nice looking. I never called him a dreamboat."

"I gather you agree it applies to Mr. Valentine."

"Okay, I suppose that's true. But who ever heard of anybody named 'Valentine?' That must be phony, don't you think?"

"I'd suggest you ask Mr. Valentine, himself. He's likely the only one who knows."

That remark from Ruth started Ruby thinking.

If I go back to the Paris Coffee Shop, maybe I can find out if he was lying to me.

"I think I have a better idea."

"Oh?" Ruth frowned. "What mischief do you have up your sleeve?"

"Not much," Ruby shrugged. "It occurred to me the best plan would be to speak to the owner of the place. I'm guessing he'd be a better source of information."

Ruth grinned and shook her head. "That, my dear, is a sterling idea. Go straight to the boss."

Ruby's smile hid the little tinge of excitement she felt about going back to the Paris Coffee Shop tomorrow morning.

And why, she wondered, did that suddenly make her heartbeat faster?

Chapter 63

November 1, 1937

Ruby woke up early Monday morning. She would stop by the Paris Coffee Shop first, and then go to Paschal before the school day started.

She intended to put to rest the question of Mr. Jimmy Valentine. She would speak to the Paris Coffee Shop owner. If she remembered correctly, his name was something like 'Jones' or 'Smith.' It was sort of weird though, because the man spoke with a heavy accent and looked to be Italian or something.

When she arrived at the coffee shop at 7:00 a.m., she was surprised to see how many customers were already there. Two men got up from the counter and headed to the cash register. A young woman took their money, thanked them, and turned to Ruby.

"Where would you like to sit? Counter or a table?"

"The counter. I just want coffee. Do you know when the owner will be in?"

"He's in the kitchen. Did you need to speak to him?"

"Yes, if he has time."

Ruby sat at the counter and took a menu from the stack. Maybe she should order more than coffee.

"Could I order buttered toast with that coffee?"

The cashier/waitress leaned in with a grin, and said, "Why don't you try the biscuits? They're the same price as the toast and taste better."

It didn't take Ruby long to agree, and she nodded.

Ruby sipped coffee. A huge clock on the back wall showed 7:06 a.m. She had time to talk to the owner.

Two beautiful steaming biscuits, with a delicious aroma arrived on a small plate. She hadn't realized how hungry she was. She bit into one and closed her eyes.

"So, you like-ah my biscuits?"

Ruby's eyes popped open. A nice-looking, balding man, whose ample girth made her think of Santa Claus smiled at her. His deep brown eyes twinkled. It made him look more like an impish detective than Santa.

He smiled at Ruby. "You enjoy da biscuits, so I answer your questions?"

She couldn't place the accent, but it wasn't Italian. "You must be the owner."

"Gregory K. Smith. I own this place for last seven years. You been here before?"

"Only once," then she said, "Well, I was also here last night. I want to ask you about a young man who helped me. He said his name was Jimmy Valentine. I wondered if he was a manager here?"

Mr. Smith shook his head. "He is night supervisor for kitchen staff. He use crazy name 'Valentine' when he want to impress pretty girl."

"Oh." Ruby sighed. *Great. Just another guy full of himself and showing off.*

Mr. Smith turned to go back to work. "But he's one smart fellow. His real name Jimmy Smith." He pushed open the swinging door separating the kitchen from the eating area, and then turned back to Ruby one more time. He winked at her.

"He's my oldest son. He'll be here for night shift at 6:00 p.m. Maybe you should get to know him better?"

Chapter 64

Still November 1, 1937

After her delicious breakfast at the Paris Coffee Shop, Ruby walked to Paschal High and explained her financial situation to Mr. Roberts. He was sympathetic to her plight, understood her concerns, and encouraged her to try again next semester.

She went around to each of her classes, had her teachers sign off on her request to leave, and returned the course textbook. She was able to say, "Good-bye" to some of her classmates, and assured them she would be back when she could.

With that chore out of the way, Ruby suddenly felt adrift. As tough as it had been trying to juggle school, homework, job, and everyday life, her sadness surprised her. Somehow, she felt like a failure. She had worked so hard to construct her life so she could finish school. Now there was an empty place in her heart. Once again, the thing she'd worked to achieve had been ripped away. But she knew, without a doubt, she'd done the right thing. It was obvious she needed a full-time job now. She also realized she wasn't the only one in bad financial shape these days.

She'd gotten in the habit of turning on her radio each night to hear the news of the day. Frequently it didn't seem encouraging. Just last night, she heard that people in Europe were suffering even more than most Americans. Not only were they struggling with the financial depression, but more and more countries were gearing up to protect their citizens from the Nazi threat.

When Ruby was a child, her mother and other relatives often talked about the Great War of 1914 to 1918. Now, it seemed if things went on the way they were headed, there could be another Great War. She heard conflicting opinions on the radio. Some people said the United States would be dragged into this on-going problem. Others said it was a problem strictly for the Europeans. Then just recently, she'd heard that Japan was invading China, and was likely to take over that huge country.

She decided to push all of that out of her mind for now. This afternoon would be the perfect opportunity to start the job search again. Restaurants needed energetic and willing employees.

All that remained was finding the best place for her.

Chapter 65

Life Can Turn on a Dime

Ruby Ellen Scott was not superstitious. At least she didn't think so. Sometimes, she marveled at the unexpected events which caused her life to change. But even that day in the early autumn of 1937, she wouldn't understand the beginning of the very big detour about to happen.

Ruby's landlady took both the morning and evening editions of the *Fort Worth Star-Telegram*.

This generous lady offered her renters both editions to read at their leisure. The only rule was the newspapers needed to remain in the parlor. That way, everyone had access to them.

Early on, Ruby had noticed that yesterday's editions of both papers were removed to the screened-in porch at the back of the big house. There, they awaited disposal on trash day. Neither the landlady nor anyone else had an interest in "yesterday's news". But Ruby knew most job postings ran more than one day. For her, yesterday's postings could still be interesting and helpful.

Within minutes after helping herself to yesterday's editions, Ruby was back in her tiny apartment going through the help wanted ads. She found several interesting possibilities and cut those ads out to take with her on her search.

It was close to 10:00 a.m. when she was ready to hit the street. By Noon, she was tired and discouraged. Even though the ads ran more than one or two days, an early-bird applicant for those ads had a better chance of getting the job. Today, that's what Ruby had faced.

She walked out of the latest restaurant which had advertised a job. Just like the other three places she'd visited today, that job was already filled. She felt tired, hungry, and discouraged. The lunch hour would be the worst time to continue the job search. So, she looked around to get her bearings, and realized she was back on Magnolia Street.

She hadn't paid much attention. Now, it seemed like a little omen. Thinking about those wonderful breakfast biscuits made her wonder how lunch would be. She turned around and headed back to the Paris Coffee Shop. Perhaps some of their great food would give her strength to keep slugging along.

The restaurant was even busier than it had been at breakfast. She looked around for a place at the counter and saw one all the way at the end of the room, close to the serving window from the kitchen. Ruby gratefully settled in and picked up the lunch menu.

The choices were reasonably priced and sounded delicious. She decided on the meatloaf special with mashed potatoes, gravy, and green beans. She closed the menu and looked around for the waitress who should have been behind the counter. To her amazement, she saw Mr. Smith come out of the kitchen with two plates of fried chicken. For a heavy-set older man, he moved fast. Ruby saw him deliver the plates a few seats down from where she sat. When he hurried back toward the kitchen, he turned his head and seemed to recognize Ruby. He grinned and stopped in front of her.

"I don't suppose you could possibly be a waitress, could you?" His frown looked almost comical.

The question startled Ruby, but her answer was completely automatic. "Absolutely," she said, adding, "I'm actually a very good waitress."

Mr. Smith's eyes widened. Words Ruby didn't understand poured out of his mouth. He stopped when he realized he wasn't speaking English. "I'm sorry, I forget sometimes. I fall back into speaking Greek. Are you really a waitress?"

Ruby caught her breath. He wasn't kidding. "Yes, sir, I am a waitress looking for a new job."

Mr. Smith reached for her hand. She extended it to him, and he covered her hand with both of his larger ones. "If you can help us get through this lunch hour, I will hire you."

Ruby's heart almost stopped beating. Could this really be happening? Did life bring such surprises? She quickly nodded.

Mr. Smith said, "Come with me. I show you dressing room and find you a uniform, okay?"

"Okay, sure." She swallowed hard. The excitement of the moment, the fast pace, and this incredible happenstance—just when she needed it most—gave her a charge of energy she didn't know she had in her.

She followed him to the back, took the uniform he handed her, and he grabbed one of the busy waitresses working the back tables.

He turned to Ruby. "I forget to ask your name."

"It's Ruby . . . Ruby Ellen Scott."

"Okay, Ruby Ellen Scott. You go with Lizzie. She show you ropes." And he was gone before she could respond.

Lizzie grinned at Ruby. "Come on, girl. You're a gift sent from Heaven. We've been struggling all day."

Ruby said, "I was here early this morning, and it was busy then. But everything seemed under control. What happened?"

126

"It's a long story, but one of our waitresses was in an accident this morning. She's in the hospital. We were already down two waitresses when that happened."

Ruby quickly changed into the uniform as they talked. She was ready to go in under five minutes. Lizzie grinned at her.

"Girl, if you can serve as fast as you get dressed, you'll do great here."

Ruby couldn't believe her luck. "Do you really think he would hire me? He doesn't know anything about me."

Lizzie said, "Don't you worry. You'll soon realize Mr. Smith knows the score. He sizes up people fast. He must have seen something in you he liked."

And with that, Ruby followed her newest friend and emerged into the noisy lunch crowd.

Someday she'd look back and realize this was the day her life changed again.

Chapter 66

Afternoon, November 1, 1937

Even though she was exhausted, Ruby experienced a thrill of accomplishment. When Mr. Smith locked the front door after the last lunch customer left at 2:00 p.m., the entire group enthusiastically thanked her for all she had done.

"What we really need," Lizzie said, "is for Ruby Ellen to come work with us here. We couldn't have done it without her."

Mr. Smith nodded. "You want job here, Miss Ruby? We can use good help like you. If you come back for evening shift, I'll give you a full-time position."

Ruby couldn't believe it. "That's exactly what I've been looking for. What time do you want me?"

Lizzie spoke up. "We open for dinner at 5:30. Can you be here by 4:45?"

"Oh, yes," Ruby said. She hurried to the dressing room to change into her street clothes. She and Lizzie walked out of the dressing room together.

"There's just one thing I need to do right away," Ruby said. "But I'll definitely be here by 4:45."

"Great. We'll see you then," Lizzie said. They walked out the door together. Lizzie turned the corner.

Ruby crossed the street, just as her bus arrived.

The job she had secured after Casa Mañana was a small, older restaurant. She had to take a bus to get there and returning late at night was spooky. The people she worked with seemed okay, but the patrons were a disappointment. None of the other workers, or even the management, seemed to mind the course language, and inappropriate comments many of the male customers made. The other girls took it in stride. Ruby decided a long time ago she wouldn't.

She wasn't scheduled to work until Friday night. Today she would turn in her notice and agree to work her shift this Friday. Maybe such a gesture would make her sudden departure less disturbing. She opened the front door and approached her boss.

Mrs. Jenkins was an older woman who looked as though she'd seen hard times and blamed the world for it. Ruby walked in, and Mrs. Jenkins informed Ruby they didn't need her any longer. Mrs. Jenkins handed her a check with the amount she had coming for last week's wages.

Ruby was stunned but started to thank her boss for giving her the job in the first place. Mrs. Jenkins shook her head.

"Never mind. I've been told you have one of those 'high-and-mighty' attitudes about yourself. Seems some of my customers don't talk to you the way you'd like. Well, Missy, I can't have that kind of girl working here. Times are tough. Men need to blow off steam after a hard day's work and have some fun. If you can't take it, you need to find another job."

Unexpected anger flooded Ruby's body, but she forced herself to smile. "Thank you, Mrs. Jenkins. You've made this so much easier for me. I hope you have a beautiful rest of the day."

With that, Ruby Ellen Scott held her head high, turned on her heel, and walked out of that sorry place for the last time.

Chapter 67

Late Afternoon, November 1, 1937

Ruby stopped by her apartment, stashed the severance check from Mrs. Jenkins in her lingerie drawer, and hurried to get a quick shower before returning to the Paris Coffee Shop. She donned a clean dress, touched up her makeup and hair, and grabbed her work shoes. Then she walked back to 614 West Magnolia.

The break for employees between the lunch crowd and the more subdued dinner crowd gave the staff time to clean up and restock the kitchen. The breakfast and lunch cooks came in early to get things started before opening at 6:00 a.m. The evening cooks took over after the lunch crowd departed. The dinner preparations needed more time, and the pace was somewhat slower. The dinner guests usually wanted to relax with a delicious meal. The tables with fresh white tablecloths, matching napkins, and candles gave an air of elegance.

By this time, Ruby had been working in various restaurants for eighteen months. She understood the rhythm of the different shifts and enjoyed the changing routines. After her brief encounter with Mrs. Jenkins, she felt absolute excitement at the prospect of being able to work the evening shift in this fine establishment.

She arrived at 4:30 that afternoon and was pleased Mr. Smith and Lizzie were already there. There were two other waitresses scheduled for the shift: Katie and Estelle. Katie would be there by 5:00; the unfortunate Estelle was the lady currently hospitalized, and Ruby would be standing in for her shift. With all the fast-paced action during the lunch shift, then the bizarre encounter with her previous employer, Ruby had temporarily forgotten about one of her plans for that day.

She had changed into her uniform and was conferring with Lizzie when they heard loud noises from the kitchen. A man seemed to be arguing with someone. Ruby looked at Lizzie, and her puzzled face set Lizzie laughing. Lizzie shook her head.

"Don't mind him. He's more bark than bite. Anyway, I don't think he'll give you any trouble."

Just as Ruby opened her mouth to respond, she saw a tall man coming from the kitchen area. The stern look he wore seemed out of place for such a boyish face. It took less than three seconds for Ruby to realize who he was.

He had a piece of paper in his hands, and he appeared to be reading it as he walked toward Mr. Smith. He reached the boss, and the two men spoke quietly for a few seconds. The young man straightened up, turned, and finally noticed Ruby.

The look on his face transitioned from mild irritation to wide-eyed surprise.

Lizzie grinned as she and Ruby walked up to the front. She leaned in and whispered to Ruby. "That's the boss's son, Jimmy."

Ruby swallowed hard and felt a grin slipping across her face. "Yes, I met him last night," she whispered back.

Lizzie whispered again, "Be careful. He thinks he's God's gift to women."

Ruby didn't reply, but her next thought stunned her.

He probably is.

Chapter 68

November 22, 1937

Ruby couldn't remember another period in her life when time had passed so quickly. It had been three weeks since that day on November 1, when she returned to the Paris Coffee Shop to: a) inquire about a job; and b) discover the true name of Jimmy Valentine.

She felt deep gratitude for her amazing good luck at being in the absolute right place at the perfect time on that first day. A full-time job, during the depression, was the answer to prayer.

Her second discovery surprised her. Jimmy Smith had far more depth to him than she had seen in those few seconds of their first meeting. There was no question the man was handsome.

The first time she saw Ruth after that, she gingerly mentioned to her friend that this young man was far too handsome to be interested in her.

"Ruby Ellen," she said, "I'm sure he's a nice-looking man. I'll withhold my judgement until I meet him. But you are definitely a beautiful young woman."

Even as Ruth spoke, Ruby was shaking her head in disagreement. "Get serious, Ruth, whatever I am, beautiful isn't the word anyone has ever attributed to me. My stepfather constantly berated me for being too tall, too skinny, and too lazy. He told me more than once I was downright ugly, and no man would ever marry me."

Ruth shook her head. "It infuriates me to hear you say that. You must know by now your stepfather was just another angry man, who didn't have much going for him anyway."

"Well, Mamma thinks he's handsome, but with the anger and meanness I've seen in him most of my life, I don't see much in the way of handsome."

"Has it ever occurred to you that he said things like that so he could control you? Why do you think he started kissing you awake each morning? It certainly wasn't because you were homely, or unattractive in any way."

One thing had changed since that day with Ruth. Before the end of the first week when Ruby went to work at the Coffee Shop (as she now called it), she no longer felt unattractive. Jimmy Smith seemed unable to stay away from her. He started coming to work earlier in the evening. He would help with the tablecloths, napkins, and candles. Even his father noticed the change.

One afternoon right after Ruby changed into her uniform and came out of the dressing room, Mr. Smith walked over to her and smiled. "I think you are good influence on my oldest son. He comes to work earlier than before. He never seemed happy to do tablecloths and things like that. Now he seems more interested in helping you than doing his own job."

Ruby drew in her breath. *Oh, great. I'm gonna get fired before the week is out.*

Mr. Smith laughed heartily. "I don't mind. I feel glad first son is in better moods these days. I think it is good you are with us for many reasons."

Ruby felt herself blushing, but her heart fluttered happily.

Chapter 69

Thanksgiving 1937

All through the month of November, Ruby saw the ads in the *Fort Worth Star-Telegram*. Among the For Sale and Want Ads was a well-placed, four-line ad:

Turkey Dinner With All Trimmings
Paris Coffee Shop
"We do not keep good food—we sell it"
614 West Magnolia Ave.

Ruby swelled with pride when she saw it. She was proud to be part of the staff and liked the employees she worked with, and the customers she had come to know. It was like a great big, happy family. Even the fact that she had to work on Thanksgiving didn't bother her.

Ruby looked forward to seeing all the customers today for the big dinner. She enjoyed being with her fellow workers and—Jimmy.

Jimmy. His full name was Thomas James Smith. The first couple of days, they had a cup of coffee together before opening the restaurant for the dinner crowd. After that, they started taking their meal breaks together. Lizzie and the other girls teased her, but Ruby just grinned and shook her head.

The Thanksgiving crowd would start arriving at 11:00 a.m. Ruby changed her clothes and got busy helping with the preparations. They took a break about 9:30, congratulating each other for a job well done.

The delicious smells from the kitchen had all the employees hungry before they sat down to their meal. They loaded up their plates and kept an eye on the clock. Ruby chose a place toward the end of the counter, and Jimmy quickly joined her. The others pretended not to notice that these two seemed more interested in each other than the food in front of them.

As they were finishing their meal, Jimmy mentioned that his mother and four younger brothers would dine here today. "Mom will think you're great," he said. "My grandmother is also supposed to be here."

When they finished eating, they gathered up their dishes and took them back to the kitchen. Ruby said, "I guess your dad will be glad to have his wife and other children with him at Thanksgiving."

Jimmy said, "Well, I don't know about that." He hesitated a moment. "I guess there's no way you could have known, but my parents have been divorced for several years now."

"Oh," was all Ruby could think to say. She tried again. "I'm sorry. I didn't mean to pry."

"Nah," he said, shaking his head. "No big deal. It's better than hearing them arguing."

Ruby sighed. "My mother and stepfather argued all the time. I understand."

Jimmy grinned at her. "See? There's something else we have in common."

She smiled at him, but she felt sure his family couldn't be as crazy as hers.

Chapter 70

December 1937

For the most part, December flew by for Ruby. Having a job, with enough hours to work, gave her a sense of confidence. A couple of days a week, she worked both the breakfast shift and lunch crowd. The other days, she worked either breakfast or lunch, and then worked the dinner shift. Those hours resulted in a dependable amount in her check every week. On top of that were the tips she received. Another large perk came in the form of meals for employees. Whatever shift they were assigned, they were allowed a free meal during those hours.

After Thanksgiving, Jimmy often asked her for a date. Usually, they took in a movie, but one night, he invited her to a "dance party." She begged Ruth's help to come to her apartment and pick out an outfit which could be "gussied up." Fortunately, she had a couple of nice dresses she was able to afford while working at Casa Mañana. They selected the best one for dancing, and Ruby thanked her friend profusely.

"I haven't had many occasions to dance."

Ruth said, "The way people dance these days you can do pretty much whatever you want. Follow his lead, and don't step on his toes. You don't have to dance like Ginger Rogers. He's probably no Fred Astaire."

Ruby grinned. "I just hope he doesn't wear his cowboy boots."

"You didn't tell me this paragon of male perfection wears cowboy boots. Does he ride horses too?"

"As a matter of fact, he does. His uncle Ed taught him how to ride horses. They go riding often, and Jimmy wears his cowboy boots just in case. He says it's better to be ready, because his uncle is a detective on the police force, and he never knows when he's going to get a few hours to relax, riding his horse."

A few minutes later, Ruth said, "This is serious, isn't it?"

Ruby said, "I'm not sure what you mean by that."

"Oh, I think you do. I've never seen you so flushed with excitement about some guy. This is different. He seems different. Where is this going?"

"I've never felt this way about any guy—well, maybe a little bit with one or two I could name—but this is something else. When I think about him it makes my heart beat faster. When I see him, I feel all quivery and like I need to sit down."

"In other words," Ruth said, "you are in love with love."

Ruby frowned and shook her head. "What in the world does that mean?"

"It means, my sweet, vulnerable, lovely friend, you've been bitten. The 'love bug' has gotten into your brain, and it's making your pulse quicken and your stomach quiver. You are on the brink of a decision."

Ruby blew out a breath. "Okay. What do you think this is?"

Ruth chuckled and stood up to leave. She picked up her purse and walked to the door. She turned and looked at Ruby.

"When he asks you to marry him, think ten seconds before you say, 'yes', okay?"

Chapter 71

January 1, 1938

Ruby gingerly opened her eyes. Her head hurt, and her eyes felt scratchy. It took a few seconds, but she finally remembered last night— New Year's Eve, 1937 style.

Today was an unintended departure from her usual Saturday mornings. She looked at her bedside clock and moaned when she realized it was after 9:00 a.m. Then she remembered it was New Year's Day, and the Coffee Shop would be closed.

Her first order of business would be finding and taking a couple of aspirins. Then she made a quick bathroom trip, found her robe, and made herself a cup of coffee. She took the cup and saucer back to her nightstand, and just a minute before 9:30 a.m., turned on the radio to station KRLD.

She waited to hear the opening theme song of "Let's Pretend." Ruth had introduced Ruby to the show one Saturday morning when Rex Dennis was staying with his mother. Today, she wanted to feel like a child one more time.

By the time "Let's Pretend" had ended, the aspirin had done its trick. She felt much better and was eager to get going with her free day. Ruth and Dub had invited her for an early dinner, and she needed to complete all her chores before that.

Ruby prided herself on her ability to deal with whatever chore she was doing, yet still think through problems, or issues. Having her brain engaged in deep thought made the chores go faster. Today's brain work was more like a mammoth decision, and she decided to seek help from her best friends.

From the day she met Ruth at the Brite Spot, they seemed more like long-lost sisters than friends. And Dub was the big brother Ruby had always wished for. They were both so leveled headed and far more experienced in life's ups and downs. Ruby knew the advice they gave her would be the best she could find.

When Ruby arrived at their house for early dinner that afternoon, she realized how hungry she was. She'd had several cups of coffee that morning but ate only a piece of toast. The wonderful smells of Parker House rolls, roast beef, and a host of savory vegetables made her hunger more ravenous.

After they finished dinner, they elected to wait half an hour before indulging in the dessert Ruth had whipped up. They sat back and sipped coffee as they talked.

"So, what is this decision which has you so puzzled?" Ruth set another full cup of coffee in front of Ruby then returned to her own cup.

Ruby took a sip before answering. "It has to do with Jimmy's mother. I was nervous about meeting her, but I hadn't given much thought to how that would pan out."

"How much time did you spend with her?" Ruth leaned back in her chair. "I would think with all the hustle and bustle of Thanksgiving Dinner at the Coffee Shop, there wouldn't be a whole lot of opportunity for her to get to know you."

"That's true," Ruby said, "and I didn't really get to talk to her all that much. But the sad fact is I don't think she likes me."

Dub sat back, crossed his arms, and frowned. "Now, what gave you that impression? I suspect she didn't have any more time to evaluate you than you did to get the low down on her."

Ruby nodded. "That's true. The only real thing she had to evaluate was me running around, delivering dishes, bringing more rolls, and filling coffee cups. I didn't have a lot of time to notice her while I was busy. It was when Jimmy called me over to introduce me to her, and the rest of his family."

Ruth leaned in. "What did she say to you that made you think she didn't like you?"

"That's just it. She said all the right things, but there was just the hint of—I don't know what to call it—I guess 'snobbery' would come closest."

Ruth said, "What did she say to give you that impression?"

Ruby tried to remember that day. "There was this tiny 'smirk' I saw on her face— it was just a brief second or two. Jimmy stood beside her when he introduced me, and she reached over, took his left hand in both of hers, and looked up at him as though he were some Greek god. Then she turned her head back to look at me and said, "He's my first born, you know. Mothers always cherish their first born.""

Dub spoke up. "That doesn't sound too bad. She's probably just proud of him."

Ruth took a deep breath before speaking. "Dub, your mother was always nice to me. You had both brothers and sisters. But I've noticed that some women, who have only male children, become rather possessive of them. And I'm guessing that after giving birth to five sons, and then having your husband divorce you, she might be feeling a bit vulnerable. There are lots of women out there who behave rather 'bitchily' if another woman appears on the scene as a rival."

Ruth saw the look on Dub's face and couldn't suppress a giggle. "You look so stunned. Didn't you know some women jealously guard their male offspring?"

Dub blinked, and Ruby smiled at him. "She's right, my friend. Even I've noticed that. I just didn't expect Jimmy's mother to be one of those women."

"Well," Ruth said. She stood up and began gathering the dinner plates. "I think it's time for a piece of that pecan pie I made. Once we have some of that under our belts, perhaps we can solve Ruby's problem."

Ruby stood up to help her friend. "Don't worry about me. I don't plan on giving Jimmy's mother any reason for worry about me stealing her precious son from her."

Ruth shrugged. "From what I've heard from you these last two months, I suspect she has plenty to worry about."

Ruby followed Ruth into the kitchen and put the dishes on the counter. She wanted to say something—anything—to deny it. But the truth was right there in front of her.

She might really be the problem Jimmy's mother dreaded.

Chapter 72
February 1938

Each year Jimma used to remind Ruby that her daddy's birthday was in February. As a child Ruby had the impression she should feel sadness in February due to that connection.

Last year when February rolled around, she and Mamma were still living together, and the subject came up several times—especially on his birthday. Ruby finally aired her feelings about it.

"Mamma, birthdays are supposed to be happy memories. Just because Daddy died shortly before his birthday doesn't mean we have to be sad about it the rest of our lives."

Jimma clammed up after that. But Ruby felt freed. Today, she went to the window, looked out at the sunlit trees, and smiled. "Daddy," she said, "if you can hear me, I'm wishing you a Happy Birthday this entire month."

When February arrived in 1938, Ruby felt happy. Valentine's Day occurred on Monday, and Jimmy arranged to take her to a nice restaurant in downtown Fort Worth. Since they both had to work that night, they celebrated the day with a lovely lunch, surrounded by complete strangers. When the waiter had taken their luncheon order, Jimmy grinned and handed her the first Valentine she'd received as a grown-up woman. It was fancy, beautiful, and signed with love. She felt herself blushing as she read it.

She said, "I'm glad we could be here today for Valentine's Day. At the Coffee Shop, it seems like everybody's watching us."

Jimmy grinned. "I know. But we have to keep our relationship sort of quiet. I don't want to get grief from Dad—or my mother."

Ruby said, "I don't think they'd like it if they knew how we feel about each other."

"I don't care. You know how I feel about you."

She almost couldn't catch her breath. "I hope you know how I feel."

The waiter brought their food, and Jimmy looked around at the other diners. He let go of Ruby's hand and, in a quick maneuver, was on one knee looking up at her. He took her hand again and said, "Ruby Ellen Scott, would you marry me?"

Ruby's heart felt like it would burst. "Yes, Jimmy Valentine. I would be ever so happy to marry you."

He broke into the grin Ruby loved. He returned to his seat beside her and said, "Let's figure out a good day to go buy a ring. I want you to help pick it out."

"Okay," she said.

Days later, when she told Ruth about it, her friend asked what she'd ordered for that special Valentine's Day lunch.

In response, Ruby shook her head. "I have absolutely no memory of even eating lunch—much less what was on the plate."

Ruth grinned. "That's the way it should be."

Chapter 73

March 1938

The month of March 1938 seemed unusually damp to Ruby. It had rained several days in a row, and that made winter more challenging. Her current landlady had given her an old umbrella left behind by a long-ago tenant. It kept her dry, but it was bright red—not a color she particularly liked. She thought it called attention to her when she used it, and that made her uncomfortable.

Today was Monday, and maybe the sun would shine. She decided to carry the umbrella anyway. She was headed downtown to meet Jimmy, and she decided to take the bus. They planned to meet at Haltom's Jewelers and pick out her wedding ring. When Ruby arrived, she saw Jimmy, and he was already talking to the salesman behind the counter.

"What do you think of this one? I think it's beautiful, and it's one I can afford." He handed her a ring box.

Ruby hadn't expected an engagement ring too. She made up her mind quickly. "I think it's lovely."

Jimmy seemed happy with her response. "You're worth a lot more. Someday I'll buy you a better one."

Ruby smiled at him. Sometimes he seemed so vulnerable—almost like a little boy. When they first started dating back in late 1937, she had asked him how old he was. He grinned and said, "How old do you think I am?"

"Well," she said, "I was eighteen in August this year. I assume we are about the same age. When is your birthday?"

"August 28. That's when I became eighteen."

Today, watching him sign the contract to pay one dollar a week until the ring was paid off, Ruby suddenly realized she was two weeks and two days older.

When they left the jewelry store Jimmy said, "I don't think you should wear the engagement ring just yet."

"Why? It's not like we're a couple of kids. We're both eighteen years old now."

"I know," he said, "it's just that I don't want to have to deal with my dad yet. Besides, I have an idea."

Ruby felt a small chill. "What?"

"Let's go to Weatherford to get married this Friday."

"Friday? Weatherford? You've got to be kidding.

"Come on," he said. "I already asked to have Friday night off, and Dad said okay." He grinned at her with that look that always left her heart pounding. "Besides, you already have the day off. I saw it on the schedule."

He looked so pleadingly at her, as though everything were dependent on her answer.

She opened her mouth and heard herself saying, "Okay, but we don't have our marriage license, we don't have witnesses to go with us, and I don't know what to wear."

"I asked the Mahanays to stand up with us. We'll work out the rest this week."

Ruby sensed they might be missing something about this plan. They had been walking during the entire conversation, and Ruby suddenly felt raindrops on her cheek. She opened the red umbrella, and Jimmy joined her under it.

With another big grin on his face, he said, "How did you know that red is my absolute favorite color?"

Chapter 74

March 28, 1938

Ruby and Jimmy went their separate ways after their walk in the rain. She had the dinner shift, as did Jimmy But she needed to talk to Ruth— sooner rather than later.

At Ruby's knock, Ruth opened the door. She frowned. "What are you doing here at this hour? I thought you had to work this afternoon." She opened the screen door and Ruby entered.

"I have to be there by 4:30, but I needed to talk to you first."

"Ok, what's up? You look a little bit like the cat who swallowed the canary and upchucked it all over the kitchen floor."

Ruby laughed. "Where do you come up with stuff like that?"

"Don't try to change the subject. I thought you were out wedding ring shopping today."

Ruby sat in her favorite chair. "I was, and we did. He bought me an engagement ring, which I never expected."

"So why aren't you wearing it?"

"I can't be wearing an engagement ring now. Jimmy could be in big trouble if anybody knew about us."

Ruth was quiet for several moments. "Okay, here's an idea. Rather than me trying to drag all this out of you, why don't we skip the newsreel, and get right to the main feature?"

Ruby shrugged. "Jimmy wants to elope this coming Friday. We both have the day off, and he wants us to go to Weatherford and get married at the courthouse. He's asked two of our friends at the Coffee Shop to be our witnesses."

Ruth arched her eyebrows. "Have you told your mother?"

Ruby looked at her friend and sighed. "I haven't talked to Mamma in months. She's thinking about moving back to Johnsville to be with Dad and the kids?"

"Doesn't answer my question."

"Not until I absolutely have to. She'll give me grief."

"What about Jimmy's mother?"

"He hopes to keep this from both of them."

"You'd better brace yourself for the explosion once they learn he ran off and got married and didn't tell them.

"I just hope I don't get fired."

Ruth said, "Okay, back to my original question. When's the last time you really talked to your mother?"

Ruby frowned. "I haven't even seen her since Christmas. That's when she said she 'might' get back together with Dad, and I didn't encourage her."

"I understand why you wouldn't want her to reconcile with your stepfather, but I imagine she misses the other kids. Besides, she's probably lonely—especially since she doesn't have you to talk to these days."

"You're probably right. But we seem to clash more often since she followed me here. When she first got here, I thought we'd be okay living together. But I've grown up more than she realizes. She still treats me like a little kid. I'm glad she got her own apartment."

Ruth nodded and smiled. "Now we're getting somewhere. You've grown up, and she's feeling left behind."

"I never thought of it that way. It does make sense, but there are other issues too. She and I don't do things the same way. When she first arrived, she said I was too 'fussy' about cleaning the apartment. She also said I was too vain about the way I dress. But then Mamma has always been more interested in her art than cleaning house or caring how she looks."

Ruth nodded. "And when you got away from the family in Johnsville, you decided you wanted to live by your own standards. Just so you know, that's not at all unusual."

"That's good to hear."

"One more thing," Ruth said. "Do you think if she knows you're getting married, she'll try to stop you?"

Ruby didn't reply immediately. "No . . . at least I don't think so. But I don't want anybody trying to talk me out of it either."

Ruth said, "I admire your courage. If you really love this man, and if you think the two of you would be good for each other, I encourage you to be firm in your own mind before you do anything. Then, after you've thought through all the possibilities, and you still believe this is what you want for your future, I say 'go for it.'"

Ruby blew out her breath. "I love him like crazy, Ruth. I've never felt this way before. But I do appreciate your wisdom."

"That's great," Ruth said. "Please remember it's nice to be married to the man you love, but don't forget you're still two separate people. Sometimes you won't agree with each other, and that must be okay—with both of you. You give the marriage all you've got to make it work, but you shouldn't lose yourself in the process."

"Gee, that sounds pretty difficult to manage."

"That it is, my sweet friend, so keep this in mind. Your marriage will work if you both care enough to make it work."

Ruby looked at the clock on Ruth's bookcase. "I've gotta get going, or I'll be late for my shift. Thanks for the advice. I appreciate it more than you know."

Ruby hugged her friend and left. The overhead clouds made her decide to take the bus to work. There weren't many passengers on board, and Ruby found a nice, empty, window seat to watch the scenery. But soon her attention shifted to replaying the conversation with Ruth. Then, just as the bus approached her stop, a brilliant ray of illumination took hold of her brain.

This might be the most important decision I'll ever make.

Chapter 75

April 1, 1938

The weather looked breezy and seemed to have a bit of spring chill in the air. Ruby had gotten up early—mostly because she woke up at five in the morning and couldn't go back to sleep. She gazed at her dress draped over the back of a chair. It was an impulsive purchase when she went shopping yesterday. But she liked the dress more than any she currently owned. It was pink, and pink was her favorite color. She took her best shoes out of the box and arranged her underthings.

Last night she wound small sections of her hair into pin curls. Now she removed the bobby pins and brushed out her hair. Good so far. All she had to do was arrange it the way she'd learned from one of the girls at the Coffee Shop. It was a chic, glamorous look—at least that was Ruby's opinion. It seemed perfect for today's occasion.

She put on her new lingerie—another small splurge for her—and stepped into the new dress. As she looked in the mirror on the closet door, she realized her heartbeat faster as the minutes clicked by. Little surges of something which felt like a small electrical charge coursed through her entire body. While she watched herself in the mirror, she tried to catalogue this feeling. It reminded her of waiting to blow out the candles on the birthday cake Granny Palmer made for her fifth birthday. This was much more than that, so she tried to remember the most magic, most exciting event she'd ever experienced. That had to be the roller coaster ride at the Texas State Fair when Dad took them there so very long ago.

But her elation during that long past adventure was mundane when compared to today's feelings. Today she felt on the verge of bursting with excitement—especially when she pictured herself and Jimmy standing together, pledging their vows of love and commitment.

Her attention still focused on her reflection in the mirror when she heard Jimmy knock on her door. It caused her breathing to stop for a few seconds, and she had the odd feeling she was frozen in time. When he knocked the second time, her senses returned, her blood once again flowed through her veins, and her breathing—although rapid—seemed mostly normal now.

She glanced at the clock. Where had the time gone? It was 10:00 a.m. on Friday, April 1, 1938, and her soon-to-be-husband was on the other side of that door. She reached for the knob to open it.

Jimmy stood on the other side, displaying a huge grin which spread across his entire face. His eyes widened when he took in the vision of his bride-to-be.

"You are so beautiful. You take my breath away." The big grin crept back onto his face. She could tell he was waiting to hear her first words to him on this, their wedding day.

Ruby opened her mouth to speak, but what came out stunned her.

"It's April Fool's Day."

Chapter 76

The Rest of the Day

The deed was done. There were even photographs to prove it. A photographer, who hung around the courthouse for just such occasions, had offered them his services. Of course, they still had to be developed, but at least they would have something to look back on over the years. In one photo, the newlyweds stood on the steps of the courthouse with their friends. The men stood in back, and the ladies stood one step down and in front of their husbands. The next photo featured the new couple alone. Later, they would have one of the larger prints tinted to show the color of Ruby's pink dress. A north Texas wind flattened the skirt of her wedding frock, pinning it against her legs. She wore a lightweight gray coat for warmth. Jimmy was dressed in a dove gray suit and matching Fedora hat. That big, silly grin still creased his face.

During the return trip to Fort Worth, Ruby sat beside Jimmy in the front seat, while the Mahanays chatted in the back seat. They talked about how honored they were to have been involved in the wedding, and how beautiful Ruby looked in her new dress.

The drive to and from Weatherford (in Parker County) was not all that far from Fort Worth (in Tarrant County). But in Ruby's mind it seemed farther than the 20 miles or so each way. Why had she thought the ceremony would take longer? In the books she read as a young girl, there were always elegantly dressed crowds of people in the church pews. Those guests would then enjoy a beautiful reception with extravagant foods served on china plates, using real sterling silverware, and drinking fine wine from crystal goblets.

Jimmy and Ruby Smith's after-wedding- celebration would be hot dogs and Dr. Peppers with the Mahanays at the Pig Stand Drive-up in Fort Worth.

But Ruby truly didn't mind. She needed time to think about her new status as a wife. More than that, where would they be living?

She had already decided for now she would simply notify her landlady that she had a new roommate. Well, on second thought, she ought to tell Mrs. Thunderberg that she'd gotten married this morning.

It wouldn't do to have the poor soul think Ruby was a fallen woman.

Chapter 77

April 3, 1938

The secret marriage didn't stay a secret very long. In fact, it was pretty much out of the bag by Monday.

The newlyweds had gone to Ruth and Dub Nance's house for dinner on Sunday afternoon so they could meet Jimmy. Ruby explained they planned to keep the marriage a secret for a time, and Ruth looked at the shiny new rings, pointing out they were a dead giveaway. Then Dub suggested Pauline might wonder why her son stopped sleeping at her house. Might that not be one of the first questions asked when he arrived at his mother's home today?

The newlyweds realized they needed a revised plan.

Ruby felt panicky about standing in front of Jimmy's mother. She suggested Jimmy should go visit his mother, grandmother, and four brothers Sunday evening without her. He could just explain they were married. Maybe Ruby wouldn't have to face them.

"I don't think my mother will even believe me if I don't bring you along."

Ruby could barely breathe even thinking about Pauline. "She'll think you made a huge mistake. She'll think I tricked you into getting married."

Jimmy shook his head. "No, she won't. She knows me well enough to understand I have a mind of my own. We're ready to become our own family. You come from a broken home and so do I. We're the oldest children in each of our families. We've both been working and earning a living for two years now. We had to grow up fast, and we needed to become independent. We've done that, and we're ready to be together."

He stopped talking, and Ruby saw the distress in his eyes. The fierceness of his explanation made her heart melt. She couldn't bear to make him unhappy.

She nodded. "Okay. I guess you're right. We'll have to tell them sometime. It might as well be now."

Immediately Jimmy's face relaxed into a big smile. "That's my girl. Anyway," he said as he took her hand in his, "my grandmother will certainly understand. She'll be the voice of reason if Mom gets her nose out of joint."

The next day Ruby reported to Ruth that the reveal had gone better than she expected. Jimmy was right about his grandmother stepping in and approving the union. It turned out "Grammaw Honea" heartily approved. Ruby could tell her mother-in-law wasn't quite as pleased. The difference seemed subtle.

Ruby asked Jimmy's mother how she wanted Ruby to address her and, the woman said, "Call me Pauline. I'm not quite ready to be called 'Mom'."

Ruby decided to ignore the tone.

To Ruby's surprise, Pauline was amenable to giving Jimmy the automobile they both shared. She said she could use the bus or call a taxi if she needed that sort of transportation. Then Pauline pointed out her sister had a car and often took her shopping. Ruby felt confident that, with any kind of luck, perhaps they wouldn't have to be in contact with his mother all that much.

But of course, that's rarely the way things happen in real life.

Chapter 78

Still April 1938

Ruby would remember the spring and summer of 1938. If for no other reason, the world-wide scourge of war seemed to creep closer each day. The world was dividing up sides, preparing for another bloody conflict.

Some parts of the world focused on the still lingering depression, and other parts girded themselves to attack or be attacked. U.S. citizens scanned their newspapers and listened to the radio commentators—like Gabriel Heatter, Walter Winchell, and Edward R. Murrow—to keep abreast of events happening across the world. Ruby and Jimmy were aware of these events, but they focused on their new marriage.

The fallout started almost immediately. When they returned to work at the Coffee Shop on Monday, it hadn't occurred to them that "Smitty" already knew. Ruby guessed her new mother-in-law probably spilled the beans to her former husband.

Ruby felt grateful for being allowed to continue her job, and Jimmy took the "dressing down" from Smitty. His father said they were too young for marriage, and he resented not being told. Smitty expected obedience from his offspring. Ruby realized Smitty wasn't truly angry they were married, but that they failed to let him in on it. She walked a tight rope that day, not wanting to "poke the bear". Fortunately, his sunny smile had returned by the next day, and he welcomed Ruby into the family.

Ruby eventually found time to let her own mother know about the elopement. Jimma assumed Ruby would be happier. Jimma still teetered back and forth over returning to her husband and children.

Pauline told Jimmy she wanted them to have Sunday dinners at her house. Ruby decided it would be a good opportunity getting to know his entire family.

The first Sunday dinner they attended was April 10. Upon arrival, Ruby offered to help set the table, but it had already been done. She had about twenty minutes to spend with her new "brothers-in-law."

The boys seemed eager to be friends with her, and she set them at ease after the first few awkward minutes.

When they all sat down to eat, Ruby noticed both the lovely table setting and the amazing dishes of food. Her experience back home with Mamma and Dad wasn't anything at all like the elegance Pauline displayed. Pauline asked Ruby about her family.

"Tell us their names, and what they're like," Pauline said.

Ruby did the best she could to put them in a good light, but she knew her heart wasn't in it. She didn't feel like giving her stepfather any credit.

Grammaw Honea nodded sagely and said, "Some men just ain't worth the powder it ud take to blow 'em up."

Ruby almost choked on her bite of food. She quickly swallowed and smiled at the old woman. "I never thought about it that way, Grammaw, but you're right."

Ruby felt drawn to this crusty old woman who dipped snuff, drank whiskey, and fiercely loved her family.

The time would come when Ruby depended on her.

Chapter 79

The Rest of April 1938

Two weeks after their first "Sunday" dinner, the family celebrated Easter. Without little children in the house to hunt Easter Eggs, it was about family being together. None of Jimmy's four younger brothers wanted to be "a little kid."

The one closest in age to Jimmy was Paul. He was an energetic fifteen-year-old, eagerly awaiting his 16th birthday in November 1938. He had light brown hair and fairer skin than Jimmy. Already he was spending some of his off-school hours at the Coffee Shop. He started out in the kitchen as a dishwasher and moved on to learning how to cook. Ruby often encountered him on days when she worked the evening shift. He was an industrious kid and worked hard.

Next in line was brother Bill. He was a bit shy and wore thick glasses. He had dark hair and the same fair skin as his mother. His 14th birthday would be in May 1938. Bill was interested in cars, and he was a sweet kid at an awkward age. He tried harder than the others to get Ruby's attention. Bob also wanted to be older. He had already celebrated his 12th birthday in February. He had blond hair, blue eyes and, when he reached his full height, would doubtless be taller than his older brothers. The last of the sons of Pauline and Gregory was David.

David, who had his birthday in January, was named Thomas David. Ruby found that surprising. Technically, Jimmy's name was Thomas James Smith, though no one ever addressed him as "Thomas." Ruby wondered—but would never know why—two of the sons received the same first name. David, now ten years old, was a sweet, happy little boy. David had light brown hair and hazel eyes. Ruby felt especially drawn to him.

That Easter, the day was warm and sunny. Everyone gathered on the front porch. Sitting on the porch with the family reminded Ruby of happy days at her grandparents' farm. She had never lived in a city before moving to Fort Worth and surprised her that lots of the "city people" liked walking in their neighborhoods on Sunday afternoons. The neighborhood where Jimmy's mother, grandmother, and brothers lived was no exception. By the end of the afternoon, Ruby felt sure she'd met all of Pauline's neighbors. They obviously had heard about the quick, secret marriage of Pauline's oldest son, and they were anxious to meet his new bride. At dusk they abandoned the front porch and moved inside. Jimmy and Ruby thanked Pauline and Grammaw

Honea for the lovely dinner and the opportunity to meet so many neighbors.

Driving back to their apartment, Ruby said, "I'll bet they think we had to get married."

Jimmy frowned. "Why would you say that?"

"Because" Ruby said, "when people rush out to get married, without telling other people about it, those other people think there must be some reason to get married so quickly."

Jimmy shook his head. "Let them think whatever they want. It won't make a difference for us."

Chapter 80

Monday, May 2, 1938

Jimmy slept soundly. He and his kitchen crew worked until midnight on Sunday, doing a major cleanup job. It was a chore he did every two months. He wasn't alone, of course. Smitty started the team off by telling them what things needed cleaning, which annoyed Jimmy because he'd done it a dozen times on his own.

Ruby grabbed some coffee and went downstairs to get the morning newspaper Mrs. Thunderberg provided for her renters. She found this morning's *Fort Worth Star-Telegram* and settled in with her coffee. On page four, she found what she sought:

Couple Married At Weatherford

Mrs. J. Parnell of Stephenville has announced the marriage of her daughter, Miss Rubye Ellen Scott, to Mr. Thomas James, son of Mrs. Pauline E. Smith, 1216 East Maddox Avenue, on April 1 in Weatherford.

Rev. Charles T. Whaley read the ceremony. The couple were attended by Mr. and Mrs. W. A. Mahoney of Fort Worth. They are at home at 1600 South Lake Street.

Ruby felt sure she was missing something—like where was Jimmy's last name? And why wasn't Smitty mentioned as being the groom's father? Maybe Pauline wanted people to think she was widowed. That would be easier than explaining why Smitty didn't also live at 1216 East Maddox. Maybe there was a limit on how many words were allowed when announcing an elopement.

Funny how putting an article in the newspaper made it seem more real.

Chapter 81

Summer 1938

Probably all newlyweds go through several months of learning how to live with each other. There's often a problem about getting along with each other's parents or friends. Another issue is learning what each partner expects. The wife for example, may want kudos and praise for cooking and cleaning. The husband might expect being pampered—especially if his mother did.

With both people employed outside the home, compromises are needed. It usually takes the young a bit longer to pick up on that. Both Ruby and Jimmy had their ideas of what married life should be like, and it took a few months before everything settled in.

A large problem was how their money would be spent. Ruby had experienced more frugalness in her young life than Jimmy could imagine. Buying groceries seemed to be Ruby's "job" in the marriage. Her salary was already paying for the apartment they shared because he had simply moved in with her. It became more difficult to buy enough food and incidentals with an extra person sharing these things. Somehow it hadn't occurred to Jimmy he might need to help by contributing part of his salary. Ruby felt hesitant to mention these obvious problems. If she had known then what she would learn months later, she might have been more inclined to express her needs. For now, she tried using gentle hints.

One day in July, the humidity was off the charts, and she finished her shift at the Coffee Shop. She went back to the dressing room to change into her street clothes. She felt tired, sweaty, and discouraged. Tears flowed down her cheeks. That's when Lizzie came in to change her clothes.

"Miss Ruby, are you crying?"

Ruby took a handkerchief from her pocket and dabbed at her eyes. "No, of course not."

"Well, it sure looks to me like those are big ol' salty tears. What's got you all riled up?"

"I'm just tired, that's all, and I still have to go get groceries before I can go home and put my feet up."

Lizzie patted Ruby on the back. "Sweetie, I know what you mean. What I wouldn't give right for a swim at Forest Park pool. Today's been a scorcher. I'm glad the boss put in air conditioning. It's a blessing."

Lizzie sat beside Ruby. She took off her work shoes as she talked. "Here's an idea. Why don't we grab a bite to eat before we leave? Might as well rest a bit and let someone else wait on us."

"Okay," Ruby said. "I guess that wouldn't hurt."

Lizzie finished changing shoes. She grinned at Ruby. "I'll go get us a table. You dry your face and 'git' yourself ready. You'll feel better in no time."

"Sure thing," Ruby said.

Maybe Lizzie, who had been married for ten years, could give her some helpful advice about the care and feeding of husbands.

Ruby joined Lizzie at a table by the window. The cool breeze from the new air conditioner in the restaurant felt like heaven on her face. She sighed and picked up a menu. This felt like a treat tonight—just what she needed.

Chapter 82

August 1938

Texas in August can be extremely hot and humid. This information isn't news to Texans, but it's good information to have if you're new to the area or just passing through.

Back in 1938, cars didn't have air conditioning, and most houses didn't either. Some businesses were able to afford it, and movie theaters were some of the first. Restaurants, too, jumped on board when they could justify the expense. Cool customers were happy customers.

Unfortunately, boarding houses and most homes 'made do' with electric fans, or water-cooled units which were set into an open window. Ruby and Jimmy's boarding house didn't have those things, so the newlyweds saved up for a couple of electric fans. Both of their birthdays were coming up, and they talked about perhaps finding another place to live that did have some air conditioning. But money was always tight, so they decided to wait. Maybe in the fall something good would happen.

Older people weren't that optimistic. They listened to their radios every night and read the papers each day. Germany continued to build up their military, and they worked even harder to find new ways to disrupt the lives of their Jewish citizens. On August 10, 1938, Nuremberg's synagogue was destroyed by the Nazis. On August 12, 1938, Hitler called up 750,000 German troops for an unprecedented series of military exercises.

In Fort Worth, Texas, on Friday, August 12, it was Ruby Ellen Scott Smith's 19th birthday. When she went in to work that day, the girls presented her a birthday cake with 19 candles on top. She blushed at the friendly gesture and blew out the candles. Later that day, she and Jimmy were supposed to have dinner with Ruth and Dub Nance. Ruth wanted to have a celebration for her friend, and Ruby looked forward to the evening. She hoped Jimmy could get off work for the occasion.

Around 1:30 p.m. that day the lunch crowd had thinned out significantly. Only three customers lingered over their dessert and coffee. Ruby and Lizzie sat down at the counter for a quick lunch, and at that moment, Jimmy walked in the door with a bouquet of red roses. The grin on his face made Ruby melt.

"Happy Birthday, Sweetheart." Jimmy handed her the flowers, and she hugged him. It was such a sweet gesture, and the remaining few customers applauded. Ruby felt heat racing up her neck.

"You shouldn't have been so extravagant," she chided.

He shook his head. "I couldn't think of anything else."

At that moment, Smitty came from the kitchen. He saw his daughter-in-law holding the bouquet of roses, and his son grinning like a little kid. He said to Jimmy, "I'm going to need you here tonight. I hope you didn't have plans."

Chapter 83

Sunday, August 28, 1938

Sunday dinner on August 28 would be special, because it was Jimmy's birthday. Ruby and Jimmy arrived at his mother's house, and the boys crowded around their older brother, eager to give him the cards and the present they had picked out.

Ruby drifted into the Grammaw Honea's bedroom. Grammaw was propped up on top of the bedspread, and she gestured Ruby to sit in the rocking chair.

Ruby enjoyed these chats. The old woman was amazingly direct and had distinct opinions about most things. Today, the subject was birthdays.

"When's your birthday, Grammaw?"

"April 1, same as your anniversary."

"Jimmy didn't tell me that," Ruby said.

Grammaw snorted. "He's still a kid."

"Well," Ruby said, " he's 19 years old now. He's not a kid. Let's hope he'll remember your next birthday."

Grammaw picked up the small metal coffee can on the floor, spat out a wad of the snuff she'd been holding in her mouth, and set the can back down on the floor.

"My dear, today is Jimmy's 18th birthday."

Ruby frowned. "On no, Grammaw, he's 19. I just had my 19th birthday. He's two weeks and two days younger than me. You're mistaken about his age."

Grammaw bowed her head for a moment, and at first Ruby thought she might be saying a silent prayer. But when Grammaw raised her head, there was just the trace of a grin on her face.

"Ruby Ellen, I guess I know how old my first grandchild is. I was there when he was born in 1920. I know this because I had been living with my daughter Jessie that year. When the census people came in April, I had just moved in, so they counted me as a member of Jessie and Ed's household.

"Pauline and Gregory had a house over on Baltimore Avenue. Pauline was pregnant at that time, and one day she felt pretty sick. So, Jessie drove me over to take care of her. The census taker came to Pauline's door, and I answered. It was the same one who'd recorded the census at Jessie's house just a few days earlier. She had already put me

162

down as living with Jessie and Ed, and here I was opening the door like I lived at Pauline's too. We had a good laugh about it at the time."

Ruby felt anger bubbling up. Grammaw had to be right. It made sense.

"I can't believe I married a 17-year-old boy. You must have thought I'd taken advantage of him."

For the first time ever, Ruby heard a chuckle from Grammaw. The old woman shook her head. "Ruby, I can guarantee you none of us thought that. We know our Jimmy. I'm just sorry he tricked you."

At that moment her boyish husband walked into the room. "Hi Grammaw. Did you and Ruby have a good talk?"

Ruby said, "We certainly did. She told me all about the year you were born."

"Oh," Jimmy said, a grin spreading across his face. The grin froze and slid away.

When he spoke again, Ruby barely heard him.

"Oh."

Chapter 84

Fall 1938

In north Texas, the promise of cooler days ahead often presented itself at the beginning of September.

Ruby and Jimmy planned to have a picnic at Forest Park, but at the last minute, Ruby had to fill in for one of the waitresses. There went their fun Labor Day plans.

The rest of September seemed determined to place obstacles in the path of the newlyweds. Jimmy started taking on more responsibility at the Coffee Shop. Sometimes he went in to work for the late morning shift rather than his original starting time of 5:00 p.m. Ruby spent her off time looking for a new rooming house. She loved where they were, but she realized it now seemed overcrowded with Jimmy's belonging. Ruby would keep her eye on the "Rooms for Rent" ads.

She found one, though it wasn't what she'd hoped. But it was larger and had more storage.

Jimmy now offered to pay the rent most of the time, which helped Ruby breathe better about buying groceries. She realized she'd never thought about how husbands and wives managed their money. Mamma and Joe fought about money all the time.

She realized there were lots of things she didn't know—especially when it came to being married. Thanks to Ruth Nance, Ruby figured out what a "normal" marriage was like.

The Great Depression was still an issue for most citizens. It seemed to Ruby things had always been this way, and there was never enough money to go around. The new wrinkle in people's day-to-day worries was the possibility of another war.

Ruby and Jimmy both followed the news closely. The pundits on the radio talked about the possibility of another war. Some folks thought it wouldn't involve America, but Ruby heard concern that it would.

In just one week in September 1938, Adolf Hitler once again demanded self-determination for Sudenten Germans in Czechoslovakia. Prime Minister Neville Chamberlain of Britain made a trip to Berchtesgaden to try negotiating the situation. But Chamberlain never had the least chance when it came to Adolph Hitler.

Chamberlain left from Munich two days later. Within a week, British politician Winston Churchill condemned the annexation of

Czechoslovakia by Hitler, and four days later, Chamberlain once again arrived in Munich to confer with Hitler.

As always, Adolph Hitler would have his way. On September 30, 1938, the Treaty of Munich was signed by Hitler, Benito Mussolini of Italy, Édouard Daladier of France, and Neville Chamberlain of Britain. That treaty forced Czechoslovakia to give up the Sudenten territory to Germany.

When Chamberlain returned to London, he declared that by signing the Munich agreement there would be "peace in our time."

The war-weary world would hold its breath and hope for the best.

Chapter 85

October 1938

Ruby loved October. The changing of the seasons was more interesting with Jimmy by her side. To her delight, the comfortable weather index Fort Worth was enjoying became a welcome relief from the summer.

After being here for the past two years, she found living in the city gave her a completely different feeling about autumn. The city was a vibrant place, and for the first time in recent memory, Ruby felt truly happy.

One afternoon Ruby had a few extra hours before her shift, and she decided to drop in on Ruth Nance. She hadn't recently spent time with her friend.

Ruth opened the door, and her face instantly crinkled into a big grin.

"Oh, my stars," she said, as she threw her arms around Ruby. "You are definitely a sight for sore eyes."

Ruby returned the hug. "I'm so sorry I haven't seen you lately. Time seems to pass so quickly now."

They settled in with cups of coffee and chatted non-stop for half an hour. Ruth got up to get the coffee pot. When she returned, the smile on her face gave her a Madonna-like glow.

"Okay," Ruby said. "What's up? You look like the proverbial cat having snagged a canary."

Ruth poured them each another cup, and looked up.

"I'm pregnant," she said softly.

"Oh, Ruth," was all Ruby could manage. She grabbed Ruth's hand and squeezed it. "I know how much this means to you. When did you find out?"

"I went to the doctor last week. He did a 'rabbit test' and called me yesterday to say it was positive."

"I've heard the Rabbit Test is really pricey."

Ruth shrugged. "It is, but Dub wanted me to stop working. If I turned out not to be pregnant, I would keep working. But now, I can quit. He wants me to be careful. We're both very excited."

"That makes sense," Ruby said. She grinned. "I'm so happy for you. When is it due?"

"The doctor said somewhere around the first week or two of May."

Ruby said, "Can you tell me what made you think you *might* be pregnant? I know if you stop having your period that would be a clue. Is there anything else?"

Ruth grinned. "Why sweet Ruby. I think you're just as anxious as I am to have a baby."

Ruby blushed. "Oh, no. Heavens, we can't afford to have a baby. We're barely making ends meet as it is."

Ruth picked up the empty coffee cups and took them to the sink. "When it does happen for you, I hope you'll be in a better position, and you won't worry."

"Me, too."

Chapter 86

End of October 1938

Life moved on as it usually does. What happened on the other side of the world was hard to associate with life for Ruby Ellen and Jimmy Smith. But the newscasters on the radio, and even the newsreels at the movies always had the latest information about how the world moved closer, day by day, to a reckoning with all those terrible things nobody wanted to face at home.

While Germany required all Jewish passports be stamped with the letter "J", the United States passed a law forbidding child labor in factories. Japanese troops occupied Canton, China, and in the United States the DuPont Company announced its new synthetic polyamide fiber. It would be called "Nylon."

The cosmic duality of the "Yin" and "Yang" of the world continued on its path of ultimate history.

Meanwhile, Ruby and Jimmy had recently moved twice. With a short supply of money, it wasn't easy for young people to find good living accommodations. Ruby wondered if the Great Depression would ever be gone. They both worked hard and did all they could to save a little money. That turned out to be a running joke between them. When something happened requiring extra money, one or the other of them would say, "Oh, don't worry. We'll just take it out of savings."

Ruby started using her days off to work other waitressing jobs. She now knew several restaurant owners in town who needed extra help on some days. She was grateful when they called upon her. Even Jimmy was attempting some extra overtime. He tried to keep that from his dad. The Old Man wouldn't be happy if he knew Jimmy was moonlighting.

It was right at the end of October when Ruby realized something she'd been too busy to notice. In retrospect, she decided it was probably inevitable, but when it hit her that day, she felt completely unprepared.

Not only had she just realized that Halloween night would occur on Monday this week, but that it would also be the one-year anniversary of their meeting. And there was one other big event which somehow managed to slip her mind

She had not had a period in more than six weeks.

Chapter 87

November 1938

In Ruby's mind it wasn't procrastination. After all, the cost of a visit to the doctor needed to be considered. Just because she hadn't had a period recently didn't necessarily mean she was pregnant. There could be all sorts of reasons to explain that

But, since she couldn't think of any logical ones or even an illogical one, she eventually decided it was time to consult a doctor. She had been to only one doctor her entire time in Fort Worth. For that matter, he was the first doctor she'd ever seen. It was when she started working at Pioneer Palace during Casa Mañana that she had been sent to Dr. Crawford to make sure she wasn't a disease carrier. All the waitresses had to get their health certificates, and they had to be signed by a licensed medical doctor. Ruby liked Dr. Crawford, so that's where she would go.

It never occurred to her she would need an appointment. So, when she appeared at his office on Monday morning two weeks later, she ended up explaining she didn't have access to a phone where she lived. She'd quickly improvised and said she came in person to set up the appointment. It all sounded very reasonable to her, and she felt sure the nurse at the desk hadn't thought anything of it. Ruby was in luck. The doctor had an opening that very afternoon.

When she left the appointment, she felt a mixture of emotions. When she was little and playing with her dolls, she'd fantasized about being a grownup and having a baby of her own. Now that she was grown up, her fear centered on how she and Jimmy could take care of a baby.

She felt excited about having one; she simply didn't know how they could pull it off.

Dr. Crawford pronounced she was in good health, and he recommended several supplements to make sure the baby received enough nourishment. He said Ruby could expect the birth to be in early June 1939.

Who to tell first? Jimmy? Probably not yet. She hadn't even mentioned the possibility to him. Mamma? Definitely not because she already knew what Mamma would say. Pauline? Ummm, soon, but maybe not the first one. Grammaw Honea would be best, but that didn't seem feasible without telling everyone else at the same time. She finally settled on Ruth. Ruth could give her information. She could help Ruby understand what lay ahead.

Maybe Ruth could even give her strength to tell the rest of the family.

Chapter 88

What a Coincidence

Ruth's eyes looked so wide Ruby almost laughed. Ruth said, "Of all the things I thought you might tell me, this was the very last." She brought their refilled coffee cups back to the table.

Ruby said, "I didn't know exactly how to break it to you. I sure didn't mean to be a copycat."

"Oh, you silly girl." Ruth shook her head. "I just can't believe we're both pregnant at the same time. I think this is great."

Ruby frowned. "Well, it is, and it isn't."

Ruth said, "I take it you don't feel ready to have a baby."

Tears coursed down Ruby's cheek. "I'm just so scared. We haven't been married a year, and I'm already pregnant. It never occurred to me that would happen."

Ruth said, "Well, there is this little thing called birth control. I assumed you'd heard of it."

"Thanks, but maybe you should have mentioned that to my young husband. Did I tell you he lied to me about his age? I thought he was two weeks and two days younger than me. On his birthday I discovered it's a year, two weeks, and two days."

Ruth frowned. "So, you're putting together a case for him? He's too young to understand birth control?"

Ruby blew out a breath. "Well, it seems to me that's something he should have thought about."

Ruth started to reply but Ruby put up her hand. "Do I need to remind you, yet again, how I only came from the farm two years ago? I never had that sort of conversation with my mother. Meanwhile, my sweet husband has been a sophisticated city boy his entire life. How would I have known to suggest such a thing?"

"You make a good point. Still, I must also tell you it's way past time to be worrying about contraception. What are you going to do about it?"

Ruby sat still for a few moments. She said, "Did I ever tell you how many times my mother was pregnant and didn't end up having a baby?"

"You alluded to it. Is that what you're thinking?"

"Good Lord, no!"

"Sweetie," Ruth said. "The world is a rough place sometimes—especially for women and children. Women have only recently been allowed to vote."

"Are you saying my mother did the right thing?"

"No, I personally think it's a terrible thing to do. But I also know starving isn't a pleasant thing either."

Ruth reached over and took one of Ruby's hands in hers. "Sweet girl, why don't you talk to Jimmy about this? See what he says. You'll never know if you don't have a conversation about it."

Ruby raised her head and wiped her tears. "I know, and I understand. I just don't look forward to this."

When Ruby left Ruth's house, she felt so tired. This discussion with Jimmy was necessary, and she obviously had to tell him soon.

Suddenly, for the first time since they met, Ruby felt unclear about her husband's opinions and beliefs.

Chapter 89

Mid November 1938

By the end of the day, there seemed to be a consensus. It was the weekend after Ruby's talk with Ruth about being pregnant. The family congregated at Pauline's house for a discussion. Ruby's emotions were drained, and her brain felt weighted down with arguments. Most of the people in her life—at least the people who were most involved with the outcome—had now been told about the pregnancy. Apparently, her next job was to do whatever they said.

Some were adamant about the solution, and others seemed more ambivalent. One person helpfully made an appointment for her with a doctor who "did those sorts of procedures." Ruby's mother-in-law offered to accompany her. The only person who was absolutely sure, without any doubt at all, that Ruby should continue the pregnancy was Grammaw Honea.

"Listen to me, Ruby Ellen. This is your life, your future, and your child. Right now, you are the only one who can make this decision. You are the one carrying life. If you choose to get rid of it, that's going to be on you. If you choose to keep it, that's also going to be on you."

Ruby's face had been wet with tears for what seemed like hours as these discussions wore on. Jimmy's father wasn't there, and Ruby felt grateful for that. However, Ruby's mother seemed adamant about the solution. They were all seated around Pauline's dining room table for the discussion.

Jimma wasted no words. "Ruby, I don't know why you're making such a big thing about this. Women all over the world do this when they need to. You must know by now that I had to take care of these things on my own over the years."

All Ruby could say was, "Yes, Mamma. I know, but I never liked knowing." She felt the tears starting again.

During the long afternoon, Jimmy sat quietly unless he was outside having a cigarette. He seemed to remove himself from the equation. When she told him about the baby that morning, he first grinned and seemed happy. But as the day went on and the rest of the family gathered to chime in, he withdrew into himself. Ruby had never seen him do that, but it occurred to her it was probably a pattern he'd adopted for protection. He must have seen a lot of discord within the family during his young life. As the oldest, he had the most experience with the arguments and his parents' problems.

Pauline also seemed unusually quiet. But Jimma spoke emphatically about the need to not become parents while they were still so young and without funds to support a family.

By the end of that day, Ruby felt a huge burden on her shoulders. She also felt angry that so many people seemed to think they had control of her body. She was tired of listening to the on-going discussions about the life unfolding inside her body—a part of her and a part of Jimmy.

On the day of the appointment with the "special" doctor, Pauline offered to go with Ruby. She said Ruby should not be alone at such a time, and most everyone agreed. That morning, just as they were leaving, Grammaw Honea made her last statement on the subject.

"If you go through with this, you'll never know that little human. You'll never see her or him grow up. You'll always wonder what it would have been like. That's something you can't ever take back."

Those last words from Grammaw Honea kept replaying over and over in her mind. When they got to the doctor's office, the nurse took her into the room for the procedure and showed her where to put her street clothes. The nurse seemed to have a permanent case of the "chatties" and talked nonstop. She handed Ruby a gown, then helped her onto the table. When the doctor came in, Chatty Cathy patted Ruby on the knee and took her place beside the tray of instruments the doctor would use.

By this time, Ruby's pulse was running like a freight train. The doctor pumped up the blood pressure cuff and let out a low whistle.

"Mrs. Smith, you seem very agitated," he said.

In her mind, Ruby felt like saying, "No, shit, Sherlock!" Instead, she attempted to bring her breathing into a normal range.

After several minutes, the doctor seemed satisfied with her reading. He said, "I need you to tell me, before we start this. Have you been coerced into having this procedure?"

Ruby started to answer, but when she opened her mouth, she couldn't speak. Instead, tears washed down her face so fast she couldn't stop them. The doctor looked directly into her eyes for the first time.

"Do you want this pregnancy terminated?"

He watched her a few seconds, reached for some tissues, and handed them to her. She grabbed them, blew her nose, and sat up on the table. "I definitely do not want this procedure."

"Okay," the doctor said. He stood, pushed his stool back from the table and replaced the footstool to help Ruby get down.

"Was it your idea to come here?" the doctor asked as he reached for the doorknob.

"No," she said. "The family thought I should—well, except for one of them."

The doctor looked down at the floor for a few seconds, then raised his head and said, "I'm glad you are a strong, healthy young woman. I'm betting that the one relative who was the exception is smarter than all the rest."

Chapter 90

Late 1938

The Nazis, under the leadership of Adolph Hitler, continued their barbarous treatment of Jews. Many countries felt compassion for the people being murdered, delegitimized, and forced into "labor camps", but most leaders pleaded inability to take on more immigrants at that time. The few countries who took people in did the best they could, but overall, it seemed the world in general wanted to bury their heads and hope another world war would not happen during their lifetime.

Ruby and Jimmy were becoming nervous about the possibility of war. Now that they were expecting a baby, scary things going on in the world became more intimidating. They tried to understand how one crazed man like Adolph Hitler could succeed in his conquests so easily.

Ruby continued working at the Coffee Shop, but she also kept her monthly doctor appointments to make sure things were going well. Back then, there were only "old wives' tales" predicting the sex of the unborn child. It seemed everyone she knew had an iron-clad way to help her learn about the child-to-be.

The first person was Lizzie at the Coffee Shop.

"Girl," Lizzie said, "I've been predicting the sex of babies since I was twelve. Take off your wedding ring."

"What does that have to do with anything?" Ruby frowned as she twisted the ring loose from her finger.

Lizzie handed her a piece of string. "Put the ring on this string and let it swing over your right palm."

Ruby indulged her friend and did as she was told. "Okay, it's swinging. What does this mean?"

Lizzie said, "It's a boy. You're gonna have a boy."

"How can you tell that?"

"Because it went straight, you know, back and forth. That means you're having a boy."

"And you know this how?"

"All the women in my family have used it."

Ruby nodded. "Hmm. What happens if it doesn't swing back and forth?"

"Well, if it doesn't go back and forth, it goes in a circle. Then that means it's a girl."

"How many of them think that's true?"

Lizzie frowned. "It might not work for everybody, but we've had lots of boys in our family."

A customer suggested a different test. If the mother craves sweet things, it will be a girl. If they want sour things, it will be a boy. Ruby promised she'd try it, but the truth was she turned out to crave both sweet and sour things all during her pregnancy.

The final authority on the subject would come from Grammaw Honea, as Ruby always believed it would. But it would take a few more months before that test could be attempted. It had to do with where the "bump" in her belly would place itself. If the bump was higher, it would be a girl. A boy would be the result of a bump located lower in the abdomen.

Only time would tell.

Chapter 91

The Year of the Rabbit – 1939

The first half of 1939 filled the air waves with continuing news and reports about countries around the world fighting off German troops or deciding (instead) to join with the invaders. The United States stayed 'neutral.' This deadly dance kept the stock market in shambles. People living in Europe wondered if the United States would ever join the fight against Nazism.

Meanwhile, on the other side of the world, other countries were watching the steady movements of the Emperor of Japan. China seemed to be the main focus of the forces of Japan, and the U.S. was a 'friend' of China. No official help was sent, but many U.S. citizens felt the need to speak on China's behalf or offer their services to help.

At the same time, Ruby and Jimmy made plans for the birth of their first child. In the spring they moved back to Ruby's 1600 South Lake Street address. They now had a different apartment there with a bit more room and more storage for the baby stuff they would need.

Jimmy worked at the Coffee Shop until right after their first anniversary on April 1, 1939. He now had a salary of $20 per week, but he hoped his father might agree to raise it again after the baby came. There were some discussions—some of which were not very productive—and Jimmy decided it was time to move on and find work someplace else. In many ways the young man felt constrained and not fully appreciated by Smitty. In later life he would learn that fathers and sons often had difficult relationships, but at this moment in time, Jimmy needed to be seen as an adult. Unfortunately, his father still thought of him as a 'kid.' It would be many years later that he realized his attitudes toward his oldest son had created a sort of 'breech' in their relationship.

That relationship had never been 'close.' Gregory K. Smith had worked hard to become a naturalized, dedicated American citizen. That meant long hours when he worked for someone else, and even more long hours when he bought the Paris Coffee Shop in 1930. His boys didn't see much of their father back then. In Greece fathers showed their caring by working hard to feed and clothe their children. Their mother and grandmother were the adults who raised them, disciplined them, fed them, and loved them. Smitty loved them in his own way, but it was a gruff, 'manly' sort of affection. After the divorce he became almost a stranger to his children.

Jimmy had been closer to his father since he started work at the Coffee Shop. Jimmy's brother Paul now worked there part-time. Smitty would get to know his next oldest son. As each boy grew older, they seemed to naturally drift more towards their father. But for Jimmy, it was time to move on.

He found a job at the Texas Hotel in downtown Fort Worth. It paid $60 a month to start, and he hoped to move up and make more before very long. His job was planning parties and banquets in the restaurant area. He also hired the workers for that area.

By this time, Ruby felt very ready to have this baby. Now mid-April, she hoped the doctor was right about the delivery happening in early June. With the weather becoming 'summery', the heat index crept up like it always did this time of year. Ruby hadn't thought she could be more uncomfortable, but nature would show her otherwise.

On Thursday evening, June 1, 1939, the sun didn't set until 7:32 p.m. Around that time, Ruby experienced the first tiny signs that she might be starting the birthing process. The maximum temperature that day had been 89 degrees, and with the hint of rain in the air, the humidity seemed off the charts. Ruby turned on all the fans, trying to stay as cool as possible. It became more obvious her pregnancy would soon produce the waited-for event.

Since Jimmy's working hours were often late into the evening, Pauline had decided she would monitor Ruby's progress in case she needed help. On Thursday evening around 9:00 p.m., Ruby used the landlady's phone to call her mother-in-law. She told Pauline she was pretty sure her water had broken, and Pauline went into action. She phoned Jimmy at the Texas Hotel, and she called a cab to take her to Ruby and Jimmy's apartment. She asked him to wait while she went upstairs to get Ruby, along with the pre-packed suitcase of items she'd need for her stay in the hospital.

At first Ruby was stunned to learn that giving birth in a hospital meant a likely stay for at least five days. She had seen her mother give birth several times, never in a hospital of course, but it never occurred to any of the women out in the country that they needed a five-day rest after childbirth. This was one of the other differences Ruby noticed about city life.

Ruby's doctor advised her to check in to St. Joseph's Hospital, and he would join her when the delivery was more imminent. So, Ruby spent the wee hours of Friday morning either fitfully dozing off or experiencing the escalating pain associated with giving birth. More than once, Ruby felt in awe of her mother, her mother-in-law, and her grandmother for all the times those women, themselves, had been where Ruby was, right in that moment. They had all told her she would forget the pain once the child was born. She hung on to that promise and begged for it to be over soon.

Things got more urgent about 4:30 a.m., and Dr. Crawford magically appeared at Ruby's bedside. By this time, she was deep into the experience and doing everything the nurses were telling her to do. She found (to her delight) the pain lessened each time she let out a really loud yell. At 5:00 a.m. they wheeled her into the delivery room, but she was so busy with the wave of super-duper birthing pains that she barely noticed being moved.

Finally, at 5:33 a.m., shortly after official sunrise at 5:21 a.m. on this Friday morning, June 2, 1939, the baby made her appearance. As soon as the tiny bundle let out her first cry, Ruby joined her new daughter, with tears flowing freely. It had been a strange sort of exhilaration giving birth. Ruby felt relief her baby girl was healthy, and she felt pride in the accomplishment of giving birth.

She also felt sure that if men had been given the job of birthing children, the world would never have been populated.

$\mathcal{P}art$ $\mathcal{T}hree$

$\mathcal{C}hapter$ 92

Naming the Baby—As Told by the Baby

Five days after my birth, they brought me home from the hospital with a raging case of Impetigo, acquired while still in the nursery at St. Joseph's hospital. The next couple of weeks tried the patience and humor of anyone coming close to me.

In 1939, without the treatments of the 21st Century, people did the best they could to keep the patient comfortable and treat the sores with a soothing salve. The blisters created by this staphylococcus disease were uncomfortable on anyone, but newborn babies were especially difficult to treat. I was no exception.

It's not surprising that I do not remember my bout with Impetigo, but my mother spoke of it many times over the years. She said I cried vigorously each time anyone tried to 'doctor' the skin where the lesions erupted. Texas in June is really hot, and hot weather is particularly difficult for Impetigo patients.

It's a wonder my mother didn't give me away to the elves.

In those days expectant parents didn't have scientific evidence about which gender their child would be. So, they usually picked out two names: one for a girl, and another for a boy. Often it was the mother who chose the female name, and the father supplied the name for a boy. People in those days seemed influenced by celebrity names, the names of their ancestors, or a name which had caught their attention right before or during the pregnancy. As for me, my mother explained (much later in life) that I had been named 'Patricia' because that was Miss America's name in 1939.

But it turns out Patricia Donnelly didn't become Miss America until September 9, 1939. I was already three months old by then, so obviously that wasn't the source.

I really dodged a bullet by not being a boy. Gaylord Ravenal was the handsome, charming gambler played by Allan Jones in the 1936 movie 'Show Boat,' a particular favorite of my dad. Had I been a male child, my young father would have named me 'Gaylord Ravenal Smith.'

I've often thanked God for being a girl.

Chapter 93

The New Smith Baby

Word travels when a new baby arrives. This is especially true when it marks the beginning of a new generation.

On the 'Smith' side of the family, Grammaw Honea, Pauline, Gregory, and Jimmy's four brothers became a "different generation" with the birth of the new baby. Pauline was now a grandmother, and since she was only 39 years old, the new designation caused her a bit of consternation. Smitty didn't feel all that ready to become a grandfather either, but he took it in stride. Grammaw Honea had lived long enough (and through many more hardships than the younger family members) so she was the most accepting. What she and her siblings endured in life during the 1870s and 80s was eons away from how people lived and gave birth in 1939. Being born in a hospital, with access to doctors and medicines, and having more conveniences than anyone in her generation would ever have imagined, made her appreciate and understand progress. She wasn't so concerned about being old. At that time Grammaw Honea was 68 years old. Her father had died at 49 and her mother at 50. She felt blessed to still be on God's green earth at her age.

There was another positive aspect to the baby girl. Grammaw Honea had raised three children of her own (two girls and one boy) and she had assisted her daughter Pauline with raising her five boys. Grammaw believed it would be a nice change to help raise a little girl.

On Ruby's side of the family, things were different. First, her mother was not the oldest child. Jimma was 42 and although this was her first grandchild, there were many children on the Palmer side of the family. Ruby's father's family (the Scotts) had even more young children. Ruby soon realized her baby would be closer to Jimmy's family than to hers.

Shortly after the birth, Jimmy left his job at the Texas Hotel. It became clear to him he needed new and better opportunities for the sake of his young family. He decided on self-employment and started a Coin Machine business. He purchased a variety of machines, convinced merchants to let him install them in their businesses, and he serviced the machines with products. Some of them dispensed novelty objects while others offered the customer confectionary goodies (such as candy, chewing gum, breath mints, or other treats.)

With his new business, he earned anywhere from $25 per week and up. Having a wife, a new baby, and his very own business venture, made him feel like a fully grown man. It was a bit more than two months until his 19th birthday, and he glowed with pride at what he'd managed in such a short time.

Ruby worked part-time, and she and Ruth Nance took turns watching each other's children. Ruth had given birth to her daughter, Linda Ruth, on May 6, 1939. The two little babies were introduced to each other, and their mothers delighted in taking turns caring for them.

During all of 1939, the shadow of war loomed over the United States. On September 1, 1939, Hitler's armed forces invaded Poland, their neighbor to the east. On September 2, Britain's Prime Minister, Neville Chamberlain, sent an ultimatum to Germany to withdraw those troops from Poland or risk a second world war. On September 3, 1939, Germany ignored the British ultimatum and Britain and France declared war on the people of the Third Reich.

On that same day, a British ship, carrying 1,103 passengers, was sunk by a German U-Boat. Among those passengers were 300 Americans, but President Franklin Delano Roosevelt refused Britain and France's plea to join them in defeating Hitler. Roosevelt faced another election in 1940, and he felt the American people wanted to remain neutral in the European conflict.

Earlier in the summer, on June 2, 1939, a ship of 907 Jewish refugees was denied entry into Cuba. The German ship St. Louis was told to return the refugees to Germany. The captain had his crew spread information to their passengers that the United States had given them permission to doc in New York Harbor. He feared most of his passengers would commit suicide unless they had hope of entry into another country. But eventually, Great Britain, France, Belgium, and the Netherlands each admitted a percentage of the passengers, when the ship reached Europe in mid-June. Many of the passengers obtained immigration visas and left for the United States prior to the German invasion of Western Europe in May 1940. Unfortunately, at least 254 of the passengers from that ship were eventually murdered in the Holocaust.

On New Year's Eve 1939, Joseph Goebbels delivered a six-page rant about the success of Germany's fight to regain what their country had lost in The Great War. It was a rambling, incoherent screed 'suggesting Germany's complete innocence (and avoiding any mention of the German-Soviet treaty), and it made no predictions for the coming year, other than it would be a hard one.'

Some Americans firmly believed the United States should stay out of this mess, but others saw a future they believed wouldn't allow that.

And it wasn't only Hitler and his rampages through Europe. Japan had become a major force in its part of the world. Those who studied previous history, and those who read extensively about current situations, became increasingly alarmed.

They believed, eventually, the United States would be forced into this war.

Chapter 94

The Shadow of Things to Come

In 1939, Jimmy joined the Texas National Guard. Most of his friends and co-workers were convinced a new war would be inevitable. He believed his job history of supervising and being responsible for other workers was something the Army needed.

Now that he was his own boss, he had the freedom to attend Guard meetings and be involved in weekend maneuvers. His business gave him more opportunities to meet people, engage with them, and gain their confidence and respect. That could also be useful in years to come.

In September 1940, Jimmy joined the regular Army. He was now 20 years old. He had attained the rank of Sergeant during his guard membership, and that transferred over to the U.S. Army. He was sent to Camp Bowie, Texas.

By now, the baby was fifteen months old, and Ruby went back to work full time. Jimma wasn't available to babysit. She had a job (with room and board and a small salary) to care for an elderly woman. It was a good arrangement for Jimma.

Pauline and Grammaw Honea took care of the baby some of the time, and sometimes Ruby made baby-sitting arrangements with friends like Ruth Nance. Jimmy traveled back to Fort Worth occasionally to see his family.

In May 1941 Jimmy received a medical discharge from the Army. He had developed a chronic stomach problem which would trouble him periodically the rest of his life. The Army didn't think he should be in a combat unit with this medical condition. He remained in the Army Reserves. At the time of discharge, Jimmy was a Sergeant Grade IV. He did a tour of duty as Mess Sgt., Motor Sgt., Duty Sgt., and Personnel Sgt. That background gave him even more confidence in his ability to lead and manage people. He felt lucky to have received such training.

He went back to Fort Worth and found another job.

Chapter 95

1941 New Adventures

In May, Jimmy found work at the Biltmore Cab Company. He used his off time, and found a dream job in July.

Architectural and engineering company, Wyatt C. Hedrick, in Fort Worth, hired him as an apprentice, with the goal of becoming a full-fledged architectural draftsman. He learned skills and worked that job until October 1941 when he found an even better position.

Over the years, people realized Jimmy had a great deal of native intelligence, caught on quickly, and was eager to learn. He did not have the education required for these jobs, but he surpassed all their expectations.

Jimmy's new job required his family to move to Gatesville, Texas in the fall of 1941. He was Assistant Real Estate Project Manager for the U.S. Engineer. His job was to help procure land for a U.S. Government military base—Fort Hood. The starting salary was high enough that Ruby didn't need to work. She could take care of their child and their home.

Ruby wasn't nearly as shy as she had been. The sixteen-year-old girl who ran away to Fort Worth was a far cry from the more mature woman she was at 22. She met lots of new people who would only know her as an adult. These people didn't know how frightened she'd been her first year in Fort Worth. They wouldn't know—unless she told them—that she grew up on a farm and didn't finish high school. They couldn't know how hard she worked to be a different kind of woman than she was on that hot summer day in May 1936.

Jimmy started his new job at 21. He wasn't a 'kid' anymore. He enjoyed the camaraderie of his fellow workers and soon found he was a good host. Their small garage apartment became the Saturday night place to be when his boss and fellow employees, along with their wives, wanted to relax and have a few drinks. Though Gatesville was 'dry', other counties weren't. Those Saturday night get-togethers never had a problem procuring their beverages from a 'wet' county.

Christmas was just around the corner one Sunday, when Ruby and Jimmy had finished breakfast and were listening to the radio. H. V. Kaltenborn interrupted the regular program. The U.S. Naval Base in Honolulu had been attacked by Japanese bombers. Eight U.S. battleships were damaged and four had been sunk. The attack targeted and sank three cruisers, three destroyers, an antiaircraft ship and one minelayer. The USS Arizona sunk with 1,177 men on board that day.

On Monday, December 8, 1941, Franklin D. Roosevelt gave his famous speech to the U.S. Congress, saying that a state of war now existed between the United States and the Empire of Japan.

And just like that, all the speculation, discussions, and arguments were finished. The Emperor of Japan had declared war on the people of the United States of America. The U.S. had now reciprocated by declaring war on Japan, and, for good measure, declared war on Germany as well.

World War II—as predicted and feared—had begun.

Chapter 96

World Wars I & II – Who Were the Players?

It's never just "one" thing which sets off a war. Alliances made and broken over centuries may ultimately start it, but there are always grievances which can't be tolerated any longer. The Great War is an example.

Germany and Austria-Hungary needed to punish their enemies. Their excuse to proceed happened on June 28, 1914, in Sarajevo, Bosnia, with the assassination of Archduke Franz Ferdinand, heir to the Austro-Hungarian Empire, and his wife, Sophie. The assassin was a Serbian, and Serbia was in the alliance of the enemies of the German and Austro-Hungarian factions. Serbia appealed to Russia for assistance and didn't receive it. As feared, on July 28, 1914, Austria-Hungry declared war on Serbia. The Great War had begun.

During that conflict, Germany, Austria-Hungry, Bulgaria, and the Ottoman Empire (the Central Powers) fought against Great Britain, France, Russia, Italy, Romania, Serbia, Canada, Japan, and the United States (The Allied Powers). The Allied Powers claimed victory in November 1918. Russia had already dropped out because the Bolshevik takeover had assassinated the Czar and drained the Russian treasury. Russia had already suffered war casualties reaching almost 5,000,000 dead, missing, or taken prisoners. Germany agreed not to invade Russia, so the two countries signed the Treaty of Brest-Litovsk, which officially ended Russian participation in The Great War.

Adolph Hitler came to power in the 1930s, and he wanted to punish the entire world for the defeat suffered by Germany in the Great War. Russia (now The Soviet Union) felt complacent in their friendship with Germany because of the signed treaty in early 1918. The USSR, for the most part, turned away from the events happening in Europe because of Hitler's takeover.

When Germany took over Poland, the USSR not only allowed it but helped Germany defeat the country. As their reward, the USSR took half of Poland. Then, in 1939 Hitler and Stalin announced they had agreed on a "non-aggression pact" between their two countries. This "agreement" lasted from 1939 until June 1941. During that time Stalin provided a great deal of support to Germany.

History sources tell us the fighting in 1939 was so intense and disbursed around the world that it became known as World War II.

Then The Great War of 1914 to 1918 became (retroactively) World War I.

Stalin was warned that Hitler planned to invade the Soviet Union. But Stalin didn't believe it. Hitler invaded the USSR in June 1941, causing Stalin to now seek alliances with the Allies.

After the attack on Pearl Harbor, the U.S. officially entered combat with the Allies: Great Britain, Australia, Belgium, Bolivia, Brazil, Canada, China, Denmark, Greece, Mexico, The Netherlands, New Zealand, Norway, Poland, South Africa, Yugoslavia, and the USSR. The Axis nations were Germany, Italy, and Japan. Later they were joined by Hungary and Spain.

The rest of the world remained "neutral."

Now, back to our story.

Chapter 97

1943

Jimmy Smith continued working with the U.S. Department of Engineering in Gatesville, TX. Now that the United States had officially committed to the war, it became even more important to get Fort Hood built and ready for occupancy. Ruby continued taking care of the home front and providing any help she could for their small community. She felt gratitude that Jimmy was home, helping the war effort in his own way, and not being sent into battle.

In July 1943, nineteen months after Pearl Harbor, Ruby's snug life took another blow. The U.S. Government wanted to send Jimmy to Alaska. The panic Ruby felt now would be just one more test of courage in her young life.

On the surface, his job would be overseeing security of the ALCAN Highway being constructed at that time. He would still be employed by the War Department, U.S. Engineers. The thrill of this assignment—going to the territory of Alaska—excited Jimmy more than anything he'd ever done. He had his 23rd birthday in August, and he could hardly believe his good luck. Alaska was the last untamed territory belonging to the United States and was more than twice the size of Texas. It wouldn't become a state for several more years, and that only increased his excitement. Stories of panning for gold, hunting big game, and spending time in that huge, wild place had tweaked Jimmy's interest for years. Now he would go there—not in the vivid dreams of a young boy—but as young man.

Ruby's 24th birthday in August gave her vastly different thoughts about this change. She and her daughter would return to Fort Worth because she had both friends and relatives there. Most important, she could go back to work—probably at the Coffee Shop. Patricia was now four years old, and it should be easy to find someone who could care for her while Ruby worked. But what would happen to her relatively new marriage? She couldn't help feeling pangs of jealousy, watching Jimmy's excitement at being on his own in Alaska.

She made up her mind to stay calm—at least for now. They could get help moving clothing and linens back to Fort Worth. She would look for a furnished apartment and make sure she had a job. She would spend her free time writing interesting, romantic letters to her absent husband. She would make the best of the situation.

What else could she do?

Chapter 98

Summer 1943 - You Do What Ya Gotta Do

The preliminary plans Ruby made before leaving Gatesville that summer of 1943 fell by the wayside when they returned to Fort Worth. Jimmy left for Alaska almost immediately. Ruby's idea of finding a furnished apartment proved undoable. She reluctantly agreed to move in with Jimmy's mother and grandmother.

Pauline and Grammaw Honea were thrilled to have four-year-old Patricia with them. They happily agreed to take care of her. Ruby was welcomed back to the Paris Coffee Shop. Even though many of the men in Fort Worth had gone off to war, there were still plenty of people who had to eat every day.

Those living alone looked forward to having a daily meal at the Coffee Shop, served by a friendly, efficient waitress. Food rationing was in force, and families had to be frugal with their Ration Books. Because restaurants had more flexibility with rationing requirements, people chose eating out to save ration stamps. The American people understood the need for strict rationing of food. Troops overseas needed to be fed. Nobody begrudged the food being sent to our men and boys fighting this war. Everyone understood and pitched in to help. The goodness and strength of the American people inspired everyone to help the war effort.

On Ruby's 24th birthday, August 12, 1943, she bought a brand-new mahogany bedroom set. It was the first furniture she ever bought, and she would keep it for many years. If you watched a movie from the 1940s, it was furniture you might see. She made payments on her purchase for the next year.

Pauline offered the "front room" of her home to Ruby and Pat. There were two front doors: one for a 'living room' (the front room) and one for a 'bedroom'.

Pauline's three sons and Gramma lived with her. Before the war was over, two of the boys would move out. She understood it was important for Ruby, having a private place for herself and her child. Both women made a big effort to avoid contention with each other. But eventually Pauline had a mother's worry about her oldest son, and the young woman he had married. From Ruby's standpoint, she felt unwanted pressure to be something she was not. Her childhood experiences with a volatile stepfather, who frequently beat her and treated her as an unwanted child, made her somewhat wary of people.

When she ran away from the farm, Ruby vowed to not let anyone put her down or treat her with disrespect. She still suffered from lack of a normal relationship with a father figure. She didn't understand why Pauline made snarky remarks, or why she seemed jealous when Jimmy paid more attention to Ruby. An unbiased observer would have understood immediately. Pauline was jealous.

As for Pauline, she had married young, produced five sons in a matter of eight years, and ended up being divorced. She also never had a father figure to love her. When Pauline and Gregory divorced, she was left to raise five boys. Fortunately for her, Gregory continued to support Pauline, the boys, and his mother-in-law.

Chapter 99

Moving Right Along

Grigorios Konstantin Acikis emigrated from Greece to the USA in 1915. The Ottoman Empire had sway over all of Greece and huge swaths of land throughout Europe, Africa, and parts of Asia. The Great War raged, and people died in droves every day. These people had no hope for a decent life. The 16-year-old boy stepped off the ship *Themistocles* when it docked in New York, and he began his journey to become an American citizen. He ended up in Fort Worth, Texas.

He found work in restaurants and in 1918 he married Pauline Larason, a young woman with an ethnic background of a mostly "Heinz 57" variety. She was part English and Dutch, with a tincture of Irish. In the 1920s, Grigorios started the process of becoming a U.S. citizen, which was finalized around 1926. After that, his name was officially what he'd been calling himself all that time: Gregory K. Smith. He started working at the Paris Coffee Shop in 1926 and bought it from Vic Paris in 1930.

From 1920 until 1928, his wife, Pauline, gave birth to five sons. Soon after the last birth, Pauline announced she was finished having babies. Gregory still loved her, and she apparently still loved him, but for Pauline the price was too steep. They divorced sometime after 1930.

I never asked anyone (and wouldn't have had the nerve anyway) why they simply didn't use birth control.

Gregory searched for a Greek girl this time. She would likely be more compatible and perhaps not mind having several children. On March 9, 1940, he married a beautiful woman, Artemis Pavles, the Greek girl of his dreams. At that time, she was 23 years old. He (if you believe he was born in 1899 as I do) was just short of his 41st birthday. In February 1942, Art gave birth to Gregory Nicholas Smith. In August 1943, she gave birth to Michael Gregory Smith. Michael would, eventually, take his father's place running the Paris Coffee Shop in 1965 after Gregory was diagnosed with Parkinson's disease.

Michael was born on the same day Ruby's mahogany furniture was delivered—not that it has anything to do with the story. It's just that Ruby always remarked she remembered the day she bought the furniture because it was the same day as Mike's birth. I heard that story more times than I can count. I use it here to keep both important and trivial information flowing.

Now you know how Ruby so easily kept dates in her head.

Chapter 100

On The Home Front – 1940s

It had been five years since that day Jimmy brought Ruby to Sunday dinner and his four brothers were formally introduced to her. Not only had Jimmy graduated to adult status, so had his brothers.

Brother Paul, next oldest, volunteered on November 16, 1940, very shortly after his 18th birthday. He served overseas from July 15, 1942, until July 16, 1944. He was wounded in battle in Italy, and he wrote a letter to the *Fort Worth Press*, asking them to send a photographer to his mother's home. He wanted a photograph of his mother, his grandmother, and his only niece, Pat. The Press decided this would be a nice local-hero article, and they complied. They not only took the photo of those three family members, but wrote a nice, back-home story featuring the escapades of Paul, the wounded war hero, lying in a hospital bed, hoping for pictures from home.

Paul was attached to the "Black Scorpion Squadron," and the men in that group earned unit citations five times. One was for shooting down 87 German planes on Palm Sunday, 1943.

Jimmy's next-in-line brother, Bill, was categorized as 4-F. Bill had worn thick glasses starting as a small boy. He certainly couldn't pass the eye exam for service in the military. Bill stayed at home and helped his mother and grandmother. Bill worked in a service station across the street from the Coffee Shop. His love of cars as a little boy made this job a natural for him.

Bob, born in February 1926, enlisted in the Army as a Private in January 1945. He was almost 19 at the time and was quickly sent to southern France for a short while. That left the youngest son, David, at home.

David had his 17th birthday in early January 1945. Both David and Bob were 6 feet, 3 inches, and considerably taller than their other three brothers. Most people assumed they were older than they were. For that reason, David figured he could "sneak" his way into the service.

At some point during early 1945, he convinced the Merchant Marines to sign him up, claiming to be eighteen. He had just passed his seventeenth birthday, but apparently, they didn't require a birth certificate. That branch of the service might have been desperate for recruits at the time because the Merchant Marines in World War II were vital to the outcome of that war. They provided critical logistical support, carrying personnel, supplies, and equipment needed by the combined Allies to defeat the Axis powers. The weight of the supplies needed to support just one soldier for only one full year was between 7 to 15 tons. Considering how many troops were involved, that's a staggering number of supplies.

The Merchant Marines constituted one of the most significant contributions made by any nation to the eventual winning of the Second World War. They also suffered staggering losses of ships, supplies, and personnel before that win arrived.

Young Thomas David Smith, fortunately, survived and returned to his family unscathed.

Chapter 101

1944 – The Reunion Trip

In early 1944, Ruby took a train trip to Minneapolis, Minnesota. At first, she found the train ride exciting, but something else excited her more. Jimmy would be there to meet her. She enjoyed the train—up to a point—but after a couple of days, she was more than ready to reach her destination, see her husband, and spend a few quiet days together.

This could be called a "furlough" for Jimmy, and it was easier to have Ruby meet him in Minneapolis rather than have him return all the way to Fort Worth. Of course, there were other reasons. The military didn't want a lot of attention on what Jimmy's job was in Alaska. By keeping this reunion to just him and his wife, there was little risk and no explanations to friends and relatives in Fort Worth.

It wasn't unusual during World War II for the government to have secrets from its citizens. While that sounds a bit like an old movie, with spies lurking in the shadows, waiting to pounce on the hero, it's accurate. If I wrote this as a novel, I might have something like that boiling in the plot.

We can assume it comes down to tried and true logistics. Young married man, separated from his wife in the middle of the war, needs a bit of recreation. Send his wife to meet him halfway, both parties renew their normal lives for a couple of days, then it's back to work for the guy, the wife goes back happy, no harm, no foul—well, except for just one tiny thing.

Picture this: We already know this young man has dreamed of a life of adventure since he was at least 14. Then, at age 17, he gets married, settles down, and tries multiple ways of making a living. At 18, his first child is born. None of that scratches the itch of adventure.

Then comes the big break. Act two in young man's life has put him in the wild, untamed land, where he looks like someone with an important job. He's tasked with protection, investigation (of sorts) and keeping an eye out for saboteurs and spies. It could be said he's a government agent. The guy is now only 23 years old.

Part of the reason for bringing his young wife up to Minneapolis to reconnect with him is so that he can prepare her for a possible change of plans. It won't be easy, but Jimmy is sure he can sell the idea.

He wants her to agree to him signing on for another fourteen months, after the original tour of fourteen months.

So, how do you think Ruby will respond?

Chapter 102

What Were You Thinking?

As the oldest of his mother's five boys, Jimmy had expected and received positive outcomes when he made requests. His mother adored him, his father was extremely proud of him, and his grandmother had always cheered him on. He had a beautiful wife who believed he was the greatest, and he felt confident he would gain her approval for whatever he wanted to do.

Life was about to dump rain on his parade.

The first two days were wonderful. Ruby was happy to be with him. She was interested in him showing her the city. On the third day, he decided to bring up his great news about serving another fourteen months.

He made reservations at a fancy restaurant and asked for the small corner table. He would explain how much he was needed—how important it was.

Dinner was delicious, and Ruby seemed content. He cleared his throat and commenced his planned surprise. He set his cigarette in the ashtray and played with the book of matches. He explained the importance of taking another year in Alaska and described the issues.

When he realized Ruby had not responded, he stopped talking and looked at her for the first time since starting his story. He hadn't expected what he saw. She sat across from him with a look on her face he didn't understand. Ruby had not spoken, and Jimmy began to wonder if she ever would. He should have known better.

"Do you have any concept. . ." Ruby's green eyes flashed, and her voice pierced him. The smile he'd plastered on his face slipped away like a melted ice cream cone on a hot summer day. He made his best effort to pay attention to what she now said.

". . . and your mother made some remark to me about my not being understanding enough for all you were going through. If you think, for one minute, I'm going to live another fourteen months with your family, you have another think coming. You either come back when this tour is over, or I will take our daughter and go someplace where we are appreciated."

Jimmy felt a cold, clammy chill run up his spine. His plan had crashed and burned. He had to think fast.

"Let's not decide now. Maybe if you sleep on it . . . "

Ruby pushed back from the table. "Sleep will not change my mind. Either stick to our original plan, or you can stay up here for the rest of your life if you want."

She grabbed her handbag and started for the door. Jimmy beckoned the waiter, handed him cash for their bill, and hurried to catch up with his wife.

Jimmy had just taken a step toward maturity. He might not be there, but he was on his way. He wanted to turn things around, so he had to speak fast.

"Okay, I won't take the assignment."

A street photographer snapped a photo of the handsome couple. He handed Jimmy a ticket to retrieve the printed picture at their hotel the following day.

The next morning, he retrieved the photo taken of himself and Ruby after last night's dinner. The look on her face in that photo would always remind him to never again try putting one over on Ruby Ellen.

Chapter 103

The Aftermath

Ruby returned from her brief stay in Minneapolis with a new sense of her own ability. She felt new strength to face challenges and stand up for herself when needed.

It wasn't just about speaking out for what she wanted. Her entire life had been molded to comply with orders from her elders. That's not unusual for children, but when young girls become young women, they aren't seen as behaving properly when they want to challenge or disagree with something. Until that point, Ruby had been a "compliant" wife. The announcement of Jimmy's intention to extend his time in Alaska had come as a shock and disappointment. In the moment he told her about it, she saw something in his face and manner which troubled her. He apparently wasn't missing her, their child, or their life together. How does a young wife accept that her husband would rather stay away from them for another year?

Ruby had deliberately trained herself to remember his absence would only be a bit more than a year. She had consoled herself during the long, lonely nights, thinking he was missing her as much as she missed him. If he could even think about extending this separation, she believed he wasn't as eager to be together as she was. Just knowing that caused an ache in her heart—one which would take time and love to heal.

She decided not to let on at home that her trip was anything but wonderful. She described to Pauline and Grammaw Honea the lovely hotel, the elegant dining room, and the thrill of being in a large city.

A few days after Ruby returned, Ruth invited her over for dinner to hear all about her trip. That's when Ruby let out her dismay and tears.

Dub was in the living room listening to a series of mystery programs he enjoyed on the radio. So, while Ruby helped Ruth with the dishes, she told her the story.

When Ruth turned off the water after rinsing the last dish, she wiped her hands on her apron. "How about another cup of coffee, my friend?"

"That sounds good to me."

Ruth filled their cups, still on the kitchen table, and sat down beside her friend. "There's something you should understand about men. When they are as young as Jimmy is, and when the two of you decided to marry before he was eighteen . . ."

Ruby interrupted. "I know, I know, I should have asked, or maybe even discussed it with his mother or father. But it never occurred to me he wasn't the same age as me. He told me he was. How was I supposed to know he lied about it?"

Ruth grinned and reached over to pat Ruby on the hand. "It's okay. I'm not criticizing you. You couldn't have known how much longer it takes men to become grownups, and I have a theory about that. I've rarely met a man under the age of 25 who didn't still have a lot of learning to do. I think it's because of nature's timetable."

Ruby looked puzzled. "I'm not sure what that means."

"Well, think about it. Most girls start having their periods between the ages of 12 and 14. Boys that age *might* physically be able to father children, but I don't think that's the average. Somewhere in there, nature meant for the males to be older and wiser. They were supposed to have learned how to hunt, bring home the buffalo, and have the strength to keep a family fed.

"I think these things have gotten sort of screwed up in the last fifty or so years. These days I'm not seeing that many 17-year-old boys who have the sense it takes to even care for themselves."

Ruby shook her head. "Well, we certainly have enough young American men fighting and dying, in the Pacific and in Europe. What about them?"

"I suspect those young men have grown up much faster than their contemporaries here at home. Fighting a war turns boys into men, but it doesn't change biology. In the past, people died, on average, somewhere in their forties. Now, most live into their sixties. Since the life span is increasing, I think young people are taking longer to 'grow up'."

Ruby sipped the last of her coffee. "Once again, you've taught me what I didn't know I needed. Why are you so darned smart?"

Ruth grinned. "I've been married twice. From my own experience, I can see the difference between young and mature. One day you will too."

Although Ruby didn't hold out hope, she said, "I guess we'll have to wait and see."

The two women finished their discussion just in time to join Dub in the living room. He grinned at them as they entered.

"Have a seat, ladies. "Inner Sanctum Mystery" is about to start. Dub's delighted grin raised Ruby's mood from life's problems and lightened her spirit. Hearing that squeaking door produced on this radio program let everyone know they were in for a scary mystery. It was a perfect way to top off Ruby's day.

An hour later, she said goodbye to her friends and walked to the bus stop. While she waited, she pondered what Ruth had said about how boys grew into men. She remembered what a wonderful man her grandfather was. The way he treated his wife and children made Ruby feel warm and safe. Her stepfather, on the other hand, had made her life miserable.

Ruby supposed it must be something she needed to study more before she would understand what made men the creatures they were.

Chapter 104

The War Drags On

When Ruby and Pat first moved into the house on East Maddox, Ruby had convinced herself the war wouldn't last very long. She optimistically believed life might soon become normal again. But as the months slipped by, reports from the overseas reporters on the radio, and the newsreels shown at the movies, made her wonder if normal would ever return.

Thanks to the wisdom of her friend Ruth Nance, Ruby's hurt feelings about Jimmy wanting to stay in Alaska longer than planned, had diminished much sooner than she had expected. She did miss him, and she still wasn't happy about the need to live with her mother-in-law. But she now realized that her situation was much better than many women of her age and in her circumstances.

It soon became clear to her that his plea to extend his stay in Alaska had nothing to do with her. The letters he wrote always expressed his love and how much he missed being with her. But he also wrote about how different it was being in that huge, wild country. She could almost feel his excitement when he described going fishing with some of his buddies. He'd never had the opportunity for things like that as a little kid unless his Uncle Ed took him. Jimmy's father was too busy working. He never spent much time with any of his first set of children.

Ruby wisely decided to make her letters to him about what was happening at home. She told him about the movie she'd seen that week, or some picnic she'd gone on with her friends. She even talked about Jimmy's brothers—especially those who were still at home.

Then one day she discovered an interesting thing at the music store where she sometimes bought records. It was a small recording studio, and for just fifty cents she could record both sides of a record and have it mailed to Jimmy. This was wonderful. It would give her little girl a chance to sing to her daddy. Ruby believed the child had lost the memory of her father. She coached her to sing *You Are My Sunshine* and then say "hello" to her Daddy.

As for Ruby, she wanted him to hear her voice and think of being with her. Toward the end of her side, she sang *Danny Boy* for him. It was a song they both enjoyed.

After making the recording Ruby decided to send him a letter each day if possible. She noticed that in his letters to her, he seemed more interested in what was going on at home now than he had before their trip to Minneapolis. She felt a sense of regaining something she thought she had lost. Because of that, the remaining time of his temporary assignment seemed to slip by faster.

Maybe when he returned, the war would be over for Ruby.

Chapter 105

What's Happening with the War in 1944?

The citizens of the United States went about their business as best they could during The War. For one thing, thousands of US citizens were now working in wartime industries.

In Fort Worth, Texas, swarms of women worked at Consolidated—an airplane factory turning out bombers daily. Many of these women became rivetters because there weren't enough able-bodied men available to do the jobs. One of those rivetters was Ruby's mother, Jimma Parnell. Jimma 'changed' her birthdate to meet qualifications for this well-paid job. When she realized she was too old, she simply shaved off four years of her age and got the job.

Daily radio broadcasts and newsreels at the movies kept the average American informed about The War. At that time, it seemed everyone had a vested interest in all the effort being done at home, and how the bravery and incredible fighting skills of the American soldiers and sailors seemed to be making a difference. As it turned out, 1944 would stand out as an important milestone in the efforts of the Allied military leaders and troops under their command. As you read some of these highlights, you'll get a sense of how engaged everyone was, and how they hung on to any words of progress and encouragement they could find:

January 16, 1944 - Dwight D. Eisenhower becomes Commanding General, U.S. Forces, European Theater.

February 19, 1944 - Leipzig, Germany is bombed for two straight nights, the beginning of a bombing campaign against German industrial cities by Allied bombers.

March 13, 1944 - On Bougainville, Japanese troops end the failed assault on American forces at Hill 700.

May 6, 1944 - Heavy Allied bombings of the Continent in preparation for D-Day

May 15, 1944 - Allied leaders King George VI, Winston Churchill, Dwight D. Eisenhower, George S. Patton, and others met for the final joint briefing in London.

June 5, 1944 - Operation Overlord commences when more than 1,000 British bombers drop 5,000 tons of bombs on German gun batteries on the Normandy coast in preparation for D-Day.

June 6, 1944 - D-Day begins with 155,000 Allied troops hitting the beaches of Normandy and pushing inland in the largest amphibious military operation in history.

July 20, 1944 - The Plot is carried out by Col. Claus von Stauffenberg in a failed attempt to assassinate Hitler.

July 24, 1944 – U/S. takes Tinian Island, the base from which the atomic bombers will depart.

August 22, 1944 - Hitler issued the first of several orders to the German commander of Paris to destroy the city.

August 25, 1944 - Paris is liberated; De Gaulle makes a triumphant speech at the hotel de la Ville. August 31, 1944 - American forces turn over the government of France to Free French troops.

January 25, 1945 – Victory of The Battle of the Bulge

The Battle of the Bulge claimed more than 100,000 casualties over almost six weeks. The Allies headed for Berlin. Hearing the reports of victory of this terrible battle gave Americans something to cheer about—and it wasn't a minute too soon.

Chapter 106

Everyday Life on the Home Front – Spring 1944

Ruby and her daughter enjoyed playing records on the record player she found on sale one day. Many of the records they owned were "gifts" from the owner of the Jukebox company who had a machine installed at the Paris Coffee Shop. The vendor came by once a week to bring new records for the jukebox, and often to replace popular records which had been played so much they were not as crisp and clear. That vendor always offered Ruby the old and out-of-date records being replaced.

Ruby spent much of her time working, and some of it visiting with friends and her family members living in Fort Worth. At some point between 1930 and 1940, Ruby's grandparents had moved away from the farm around Somervell County, Texas, and bought a small home on the western edge of Fort Worth. Ruby's mother, Jimma, also bought a home on the same road but about two blocks south of the Palmers. It was very close to her work at Consolidated, and much easier for her to travel back and forth.

It's interesting to think about what people had at their disposal back in those times. By today's standards, it wasn't much. Simply getting from place to place often presented difficulty. Buses were the primary transportation for the great majority of the people in a city.

Many may not realize that no new cars were being manufactured during World War II. All the car manufacturers had been commandeered by the Federal government to produce vehicles for the military. And it wasn't just automobiles. Tanks, personnel carriers, all sorts of war-related items were desperately needed, not only for the US troops, but for our allies. The US had more and better factories than many of our partner countries.

As you might imagine, old cars were kept running years beyond the time which would have seemed reasonable. Auto mechanics had no difficulty finding a job at one of the many "service" stations. Back then, these businesses not only sold gasoline, but their most important function was to keep old cars running and serviceable for their owners. It wasn't unusual back then to occasionally see a female mechanic.

The times and the war being fought had a major impact on women. Because so many men were overseas, fighting the enemy, women discovered they could do much of the work men had always done. It wasn't just a boon to those women. It was the tiniest seed being planted—one that started a revolution of sorts. Now people became aware that women were capable of so much more than the world had imagined.

And the awakening of those women caused them to reevaluate their place in that world.

Chapter 107

The Adventurer Returns

In September 1944, Ruby welcomed Jimmy home from the wilds of Alaska. Now they needed a place to live—the sooner the better.

Ruby came up with a plan, and even her mother-in-law agreed. Ruby and Jimmy would rent a hotel room until they could find a place to live. Their daughter would stay with her two grandmothers.

The next day, he and Ruby arrived at Pauline's to see his little girl. When he left, she had just turned four. She was now passed her 5th birthday. She had seen pictures of her father during his absence, but now she didn't recognize him. It would take time and patience.

Many other soldiers and sailors returned home only to find their younger children no longer remembered them.

There was an upside to Jimmy being gone for fourteen months—living in Alaska at the government's expense. He saved almost all his salary, so he could put a down payment on a house. He and Ruby wasted no time locating a home they could afford.

In 1943, a new development west of Fort Worth located in River Oaks had built a group of homes to accommodate the hundreds of workers at Consolidated. The homes were small but nice, offering two bedrooms, one bathroom, a living room, dining area, and kitchen. It also included a one-car garage. It had a good-sized front yard and a spacious backyard. The price was $3,000.00. Jimmy's savings made the modest down payment, with reasonable monthly mortgage payments. There was enough savings left over to furnish the house. For the first time Ruby had a home which was truly hers.

The young family moved into their new home in 1944, just before winter set in. They had bus service about half a mile away, and they made good use of it for several years. Ruby continued working at the Coffee Shop, but Jimmy needed to find his next employment opportunity. Fortunately, he already had a plan.

He had always looked up to his Uncle Ed. Hugh Edward Chapple was Chief of Detectives at the Fort Worth Police Department. The second day Jimmy was back in Fort Worth, he visited his uncle at the Police Department. When Jimmy walked out of the facility, he had filled out an application. With his recent government service in Alaska, he was hired two weeks later as a patrolman for the Fort Worth Police Department. Thomas J. Smith was a young man on his way.

At 24 years of age, he couldn't have predicted his future success.

Chapter 108

War News in 1945

The year 1945 was full of news. The first shocking event was the death of President Franklin Delano Roosevelt. He died of a cerebral hemorrhage on April 12, 1945. His election for a fourth term had been in November 1944, and his fourth inauguration was on January 20, 1945. He had been president since 1933. Many Americans couldn't remember living under any other president.

Whether you loved him or hated him, everyone in the United States was stunned and frightened. Roosevelt's leadership through World War II had given the citizens the courage to keep on working and supporting our overseas troops. He had been the leader the United States needed. Roosevelt and Churchill were the two heads of state which heaven granted to a nervous world. Those two men were able to keep Joseph Stalin from making things worse than they already were.

Strangely, probably fewer than ten percent of U.S. citizens had any idea who the vice president was, or how capable he would be in this sudden ascendence to power. He took the oath of office several hours later, still in a state of shock. Harry S. Truman later told reporters, "I don't know if you fellas ever had a load of hay fall on you, but when they told me what happened yesterday, I felt like the moon, the stars and all the planets had fallen on me."

Seventeen days later, on April 30, 1945, Adolph Hitler committed suicide in his underground bunker in Berlin. He and his new wife, Eva Braun, swallowed cyanide capsules. Just to be sure, Hitler shot himself in the head. The staff living inside the bunker gathered the bodies and burned them in the garden atop the bunker. Major problem handled for the entire world.

On May 8, 1945, German forces surrendered to the Allied Forces. Germany was turned over to the Allies and carved up. The war—in Europe at least—was over.

But not everywhere. Japan was still fighting in the Pacific, and they had no idea what was about to happen. Harry Truman had finally been briefed on the Manhattan Project on April 24, 1945. Learning about the secret development of an atomic bomb being assembled by physicists in New Mexico was a stunning revelation to him.

On July 16, 1945, the Los Alamos scientists traveled to Alamogordo to test the bomb. It was detonated at the White Sands, NM proving grounds and deemed a success. J. Robert Oppenheimer, the director of the laboratory, watched from a bunker. At the time, he remembered a line from Hindu scripture, *Bhagavad-Gita*: "Now I am become Death, the destroyer of worlds."

It was up to U.S. President Harry Truman to decide whether to use this new, devasting weapon on the people of Japan to end the war.

The Potsdam conference was a meeting of the Allies to discuss the future of post-war Germany. During that conference, the United States called for the unconditional surrender of Japan. The Potsdam Declaration was issued on July 26, 1945. The U.S., Great Britain, and the Republic of China argued that Japan's position was useless. The document's final sentence stated: "The alternative for Japan is prompt and utter destruction." There was no mention of the atomic bomb.

On July 29, 1945, Japan rejected the declaration.

On August 6, 1945, the first atomic bomb was dropped on the city of Hiroshima. The destruction was huge, but Japan remained defiant and refused to surrender. The fighting continued.

On August 9, 1945, the city of Nagasaki was destroyed with the second and last atomic bomb in the United States arsenal. After much discussion and internal dissent, Japan agreed to surrender.

On September 2, 1945, in Tokyo Bay, 250 Allied warships lay at anchor. The flags of the U.S., Britain, the Soviet Union, and China fluttered above the deck of the battleship Missouri. Japanese Foreign Minister Mamoru Shigemitsu signed on behalf of the Japanese government. Supreme Allied Commander Douglas MacArthur accepted the surrender and signed the document.

What had been a gray, cloudy sky during the ceremony, dissolved into brilliant sunshine at the conclusion of the signing. Nature must have appreciated the occasion – the end of the most devastating war in human history.

Chapter 109

1945 to 1949

World War II was finished, and Ruby Ellen Scott Smith was happy. She wasn't rich—far from it. But she had a nice home, a husband, a daughter, and youthful energy.

On June 2, 1945, Patricia had her sixth birthday. First grade would begin the day after Labor Day.

Castleberry Elementary School was overcrowded. The uptick of population in the school district due to the war work being done at Consolidated caused the school the go on a split schedule. The early shift was at 8:00 a.m. and ended at Noon. The second shift commenced at 1:00 p.m. and lasted until 5:00 p.m. Patricia's first grade class was in the second shift.

In 1945, Ruby met one of her neighbors across the street. Gertie Weisberg had a son named Michael and a husband named Joe. Gertie offered to have Patricia come to their house when Ruby and Jimmy were working. That immediately became a big help to Ruby, and she and Gertie remained fast friends for many years.

Meanwhile, Jimmy's career as a Fort Worth Police Officer brought him frequent newspaper mention. From now on, he was called either T.J. Smith, or Thomas J. Smith. In those days, reporters spent a lot of time checking the police blotters for reports of crimes. They almost always included the names of the officers who had made the arrests or who had answered the call. Patrolman T.J. Smith became a frequent name.

His first big newspaper coverage came when he shot a man who had murdered someone in Indiana, was on the run with his fellow criminal, and who was about to shoot Jimmy's partner, Marshall McMahan. This newspaper splash happened on April 1, 1946, just seven months after he joined the force. The front page sported large photos of the police car with two bullet holes in the right-side rear window. The photographer had Jimmy sit in the drivers' seat, gun drawn and pointed toward the backseat window. The night of the shooting, Jimmy, while keeping an eye on his partner who was confronting the two criminals, saw one of the men pull out a gun. Jimmy shot through the closed window, wounding the criminal with the gun.

The Star-Telegram announced on January 7, 1947, that Patrolman T. J. Smith had been promoted to the rank of Sergeant.

On August 12, 1949, Ruby celebrated her 30th birthday. On that day, she got her own photo in the newspaper, sharing publicity with the Fort Worth Zoo's most famous elephant—Queen Tut. It turned out the Queen shared Ruby's birthday. Someone mentioned that fact to the newspaper, and a reporter and photographer thought it would be a good human-interest story. Ruby rushed down to the Forest Park Zoo, and the Star-Telegram photographer caught a shot of Ruby eating a peanut, while Queen Tut looked on expectantly. Ruby finally shared her peanut stash with Queen Tut, and the two parted company, never to meet again.

They say elephants have remarkable memories. It would be interesting to know if Queen Tut remembered Ruby. I know Ruby always remembered the Queen.

Chapter 110

The Past Returns

When Ruby left home in May 1936, she had no idea Jimma would leave Joe Parnell just a month later. After struggling with some health problems Jimma went on to work several jobs to support herself in Fort Worth. During the years between 1936 and 1943, she managed to save some money from her efforts, including her painting. However, her windfall job as a "Rosie the Riveter" at Consolidated's airplane factory was her best-paying work.

During those years away from Johnsville, Jimma often returned to visit her children. She made sure they were doing well living with their father. She still had no interest in returning to her husband, who had always tried to control her ability to earn money. The constant arguing and angry accusations were things she no longer wanted in her life.

Occasionally Ruby also visited her childhood home to see her siblings. Since Joe no longer had any control over her, he wasn't as angry and mean as he had been when she was a child. She felt quite capable of preventing any of Joe's past behavior.

In 1944, Ruby was surprised to learn that Joe and the younger children had left the farm. When he moved in with Jimma in the house she'd purchased the year before, Ruby realized he must have learned Jimma's wartime job paid well. Why continue being a farmer who couldn't earn enough to feed himself and his children. They were, after all, still a married couple. It must have been obvious to him that she would take care of him and the remaining two children.

Ruby decided it was Jimma and Joe's problem. As the saying went, "She had no dog in that fight."

The "new" Joe Parnell wanted to help Jimma, so he offered to enlarge her small home. He built another bedroom, installed an indoor bathroom, and made some useful improvements. Ruby was impressed by his skills and enthusiasm in helping upgrade Jimma's home. Ruby decided she would allow her daughter to meet Joe.

Margaret and Rhonda, Ruby's two youngest sisters, were in their early teens. Jimma's home was within a short walking distance from Castleberry Elementary School. It was 1945, and Patricia was in first grade there. Her two young aunts were in Castleberry's eighth grade class. That year they often took her home with them and cared for her on days Ruby needed help. Patricia was introduced to Joe, but she didn't see him often.

Time went by quickly for Ruby. By 1946, Joe and Jimma had parted again. They were still married, but still couldn't get along. Margaret and Rhonda were out on their own now. He moved into a small apartment several miles away and learned how to use the Fort Worth bus system to get around town.

One day in late October 1947, Joe paid a visit to Ruby and Patricia at their home on Byrd Drive. As they talked, Ruby noticed how old and frail Joe had become. She realized she now almost felt sorry for him. He'd been so cocky when she was a little girl, and a tiny part of her felt almost jubilant about his current situation. But a larger part of her felt sad that such a strong, active man had lost so much. She walked outside with him when he left and watched as he reached the top of the hill. He turned around and waved at her and Patricia. They waved back, and he slowly disappeared over the hill. It was the last time Ruby saw him.

On Tuesday, January 13, 1948, Joe Parnell suffered a heart attack and died in Fort Worth. He would be buried in Johnsville, Erath County, on Saturday. Ruby made the decision that she and Patricia would attend the funeral.

The night before the trip to Johnsville, Ruby ironed the dress she planned to wear the next morning. While doing so, she saw her tears falling on the dress she'd just ironed. She'd been fighting a headache all day, and she'd taken some aspirin. As she ironed, she felt overwhelmed with sadness. The man she had feared and hated as a child was dead. Why did she feel so sad? As her tears continued to fall, she felt a hard lump growing in her throat. It became almost impossible to swallow, and she became panicky.

She tried to analyze what was happening to her and got the idea it must be the aspirin she'd taken. She had never felt so frightened and hadn't experienced such a reaction to simply crying.

Her daughter watched her and said, "Mommy, why are you crying?"

Ruby simply said, "I feel sad, and that aspirin I took gave me a lump in my throat. It's hard to swallow. I'll be okay when the aspirin wears off."

The next day was cold and cloudy—perfect weather for a funeral. Ruby drove their family car down to Johnsville with only Jimma and Patricia as her passengers. It was a typical country funeral in a small Texas town. The little church was filled, and the ladies had prepared food for the reception afterwards. They lowered the coffin into the prepared grave, and the mourners filed out of the cemetery.

Joe Parnell was dead. He'd gone the way of all flesh, and if she could believe the preacher's impassioned words at the service, Joe would now be with Jesus. Eventually, as the years went by, she tried to forgive her stepfather for the things he'd done—or thought about doing. For many years, Ruby would experience the lump in her throat, and she always insisted taking aspirin was the cause. Even when she stopped taking aspirin, the lump occasionally returned. For years she felt trapped between feelings of sadness for the way her stepfather ended up, and her feelings of anger against him for what he had done to her.

Forgiveness can take a very long time.

Part Four

Chapter 111

Everything Changes—Nothing Stays the Same

In the late 1940s Ruby thought her life was settled and her future would flow along as usual. Life always surprises.

She looked back on her last few years and marveled at how far she had come. She remembered her initial shyness the first months she lived in Fort Worth. With the help of friends, she grew more confident over the years and felt good about herself and her life.

She still worked occasionally at the Paris Coffee Shop, but she also spent time working at other restaurants. Her skills, her efficiency, and her personality made her an ideal restaurant employee. She worked at Leslie's Chicken Shack some of the time, and ended up snagging a job at Jonnie Monaghan's Real Hickory Smoked Bar-B-Q. It was at 702 Jacksboro Highway in Fort Worth in the late 1940s and early 1950s. While working there she made enough in tips and salary to purchase a brand-new spinet piano for her daughter. Both she and Patricia started taking piano lessons in 1948.

One day her friend Gertie Weisberg, who lived across the street from them, asked her if she'd like to try modeling. Because Gertie's husband, Joe, was a photographer, he often received assignments which included finding models.

"I've never been a model," Ruby said. "What would I have to do?"

Gertie grinned. "Joe took on a job for a magazine. They need a couple of young, beautiful ladies to pose on bicycles. Joe wondered if you'd be interested. I said I'd ask."

Ruby frowned. "Why me?"

"Well," Gertie said, "Joe says you'd be a knock-out for this job, and he hoped you'd have a friend or relative who is also gorgeous and can fill the second slot."

"I'll think it over and let you know," Ruby said. "I'll see if I can get Jimmy's cousin, Betty Jean. She's eighteen years old and a beautiful blonde."

By the end of the week, Ruby had invited Betty Jean to join her in this unexpected adventure. The photo shoot went well, and when the magazine came out, both women were proud to have been included. For Ruby, who had spent her teenage years deflecting insults her from stepfather, it was a long-awaited verification that other people saw her as beautiful and poised.

In 1949, the citizens of Fort Worth (thanks to station WBAP-TV) became some of the first television watchers in that part of the country. Jimmy, Ruby, and Patricia visited friends who had a set, and within a couple of weeks, Jimmy made sure they had one. They tried out several sets before they decided to purchase a console consisting of an AM-FM radio, a three-speed record player, and a twelve-inch TV screen. At the time, there was only what they called a "Test Pattern" during the early part of the day and early afternoon. After school let out, Hopalong Cassidy would ride across the small television screens on his beautiful white stallion to the delight of all the children (and many of their parents.)

Ruby had been impressed with her table radio years ago. Owning a piece of furniture which included not only the radio, but a record player, and the miracle of television was mind boggling. It was a beautiful piece of furniture and the family's entertainment hub for many years.

In January 1950, Jimmy received a plum assignment. He was being sent to the FBI National Academy in Quantico, Virginia, to attend a three-month school especially designed for police officers from all over the country. The Fort Worth Police Department would reap the benefit of this highly regarded training. Upon return from the session, Jimmy would oversee training for new Fort Worth police officers.

Ruby was invited to attend the graduation event in Washington, D.C. In April, she and several wives from other police forces in Texas, Oklahoma, and Kansas, traveled by train for the event.

The wives were treated to tours in Washington and Virginia, and tours of the FBI, including the shooting range. FBI agents were on hand to explain about the various firearms they had used over the years. One of those was a Thompson submachine gun.

There were about 25 ladies on the tour that day. When the Special Agent who was explaining the various firearms asked if any of the ladies would like to have a try at shooting the Thompson, nobody spoke up.

He turned to Ruby and said, "How about the lady from Texas?"

As a kid on the farm, Ruby knew how to handle a shotgun, but she was interested in how this larger, grander firearm would operate. So, she stepped forward and let the agent show her how to hold it and focus on the target. Ruby lined up her sights and shot a barrage of bullseyes with the Thompson.

The ladies were awed by Ruby's abilities. One little old lady who had come to see her son graduate, sidled up to Ruby. She had a look of admiration and awe on her face when she asked, "Do you practice often?"

Ruby beamed and said, "No, not really."

For the rest of the celebrations, Ruby's prowess with the Thompson submachine gun was the talk of the crowd.

Chapter 112

1950

When new decades begin people sometimes straddle the past, knowing the future may or may not be a good thing. It's tantalizing to ponder on exciting possibilities and perhaps upheavals which might occur. Most people find the courage to press ahead and not invite trouble. In the end, we accept whatever we get and move on. For the Smith family, the 1950s would upend their lives.

When Jimmy and Ruby returned from Washington, D.C., she could hardly wait to tell Ruth all about it. On her next day off, she stopped by Ruth's house for coffee and a chance to chat.

"It was so amazing," Ruby said. "I actually walked through the house where George and Martha Washington lived. The entire estate was huge, and both George and Martha are buried there on the grounds. It was like seeing history up close. When we studied the American Revolution in school, I never dreamed I'd see Mount Vernon."

Ruth smiled as she listed to her young friend. "You've had some amazing things going on the past few years. I remember when we first met how shy you were, and how much more you wanted to learn. It seems to me you are well on your way."

"I know," Ruby said. "I'm still trying to believe I really toured the FBI and met J. Edgar Hoover."

"Not to change the subject, but how are your relatives doing these days? Didn't you tell me something about your grandmother being ill?"

Ruby sighed. "She's had a few health issues. I heard she had fallen and broke her hip. You know, she'll be 80 in May."

"I remember your telling me that earlier. How about your grandfather?"

"He's a tough old bird. I suspect he'll outlive Granny. I plan to go visit them this weekend."

But Ruby didn't make it until a week later. By that time, her grandmother had suffered a stroke. Ruby had a sick sensation in her stomach. Her precious grandparents were suddenly so old and frail. Where had the time gone?

Ruby's beloved grandmother, Ellen Missouri Coleman Palmer, died on June 16, 1950, at her home in the River Oaks section of Fort Worth. Ruby joined her mother, all her mother's brothers and sisters, and her own siblings at the funeral. Everyone agreed this was a bitter pill for the entire family. Now they all pledged to keep an eye on J.R. He would continue to live alone in the house he had shared with Ellen.

On Sunday, June 25, 1950, Grammaw Honea fell and broke her hip. On that same day, the North Korean People's Army poured across the 38th parallel between North Korea and South Korea. That boundary had been established between the Soviet-backed Democratic People's Republic of Korea to the north and the pro-Western Republic of Korea to the south. Suddenly a new war had flared up. It had been slightly less than five years since the end of World War II. There was no appetite for this new war. In fact, rather than call it a war it was dubbed "The Korean Conflict."

Before long, more and more countries volunteered to help South Korea hold on to their country. Military personnel from the United States, who had put away their uniforms after the war in Europe and Japan, dug them out again and made the trip to South Korea. New untested soldiers were added to the mix. Many countries heeded the call. No one wanted communism to overrun the free people of South Korea.

In September 1950, because of the Korean Conflict, the FBI put out a call for more agents. During times of war, many more agents were needed to protect national security. At the start of the Korean Conflict, the qualifications for service as a Special Agent of the FBI required either a law degree, or a degree as a certified public accountant. The FBI was in a crisis and couldn't find qualified candidates. Therefore, they waived the qualifications and went back over the list of law enforcement officers who had, within the past year, been trained at the National Academy at the FBI. The top students were contacted and offered a position as a Special Agent of the FBI. One of those phone calls went to Fort Worth Police Sergeant Thomas J. Smith.

It was as though God, himself, had looked down and granted this rare gift to Jimmy Smith. When he told Ruby about it, she was happy for him. Then it began to sink in that if Jimmy joined the FBI, their little family would most likely be sent to another part of the country. It took all the talking Jimmy could manage to convince Ruby they would have a better life if he took this job. Jimmy would immediately resign from the Fort Worth Police Department and return to the FBI Academy to receive extra training. It would take six weeks more training to become a Special Agent.

That meant Ruby had to oversee selling their house in River Oaks, packing up their belongings, hiring a moving company, taking Patricia out of school, and being ready to go wherever this new job would take them. Ruby had never—even in her wildest dreams—concocted such a scenario. Yet here it was, so she stepped up and took charge.

Jimmy returned from his final training the first week in October 1950. He brought with him the news that his assignment would be San Diego, California. They needed a reliable automobile for Ruby to drive from Fort Worth to San Diego. They visited the Chevrolet dealer in Fort Worth, where they purchased a brand new 1950 Chevrolet Bel Air two-door hardtop. The color was chartreus, with a black top. The total price? $1,741.00. They traded in their old clunker, which lowered the price minimally, and not a moment too soon. As the mechanic at the dealership drove the old Mercury coupe to the back of the lot, the clutch fell out. Score one for Jimmy. He left that same day for his new assignment in San Diego.

Ruby had already put their house on the market. Now, she would keep working until it sold—she hoped before the end of the year.

On October 11, 1950, Celia Ullom Larason Honea died as the result of complications from the hip fracture. Ruby felt sadder than she expected. The old woman had taught Ruby many things, and Ruby had become very fond of this frail, tiny woman. Her funeral was held at the end of the week. Her daughter, Pauline, was now alone.

When Pauline and Gregory Smith divorced, Grammaw Honea moved in with Pauline and the boys to help with their care. At that time, Jimmy was 10, and the youngest boy, David, was only two. Gregory agreed to continue making the house payments and would give Pauline a monthly support check as long as Grammaw Honea lived. When Grammaw Honea died, Pauline would sell her house.

Ruby had learned to drive four years earlier and only drove short trips on the highway. This trip would be a major challenge. At the same time, Pauline realized she was now able to help Ruby with the driving to California. Serendipity.

The first week in December, the house on Byrd Drive was sold. The movers came two weeks later, and Ruby and Patricia packed up the clothes they would need for the trip. They left on December 21, 1950, the last day of school and the start of Christmas vacation. After the new year, Patricia would be enrolled in California.

Jimmy found an apartment for his family in La Jolla, California, a suburb just north of San Diego. One of the FBI agents there had taken Jimmy under his wing to show him around and suggest an area close to an excellent elementary school. With luck, their furniture would arrive shortly after Christmas. Things seemed to be going well.

The three travelers arrived in San Diego without incident late Sunday evening, December 23, 1950. Jimmy had been living in a hotel room, and he rented an additional room for Patricia and his mother to share. The next morning Ruby, Pauline, and Patricia got their first glimpse of California. In the bright, warm sunshine, they saw trees blooming, huge, thick stalks of ice grass, and a profusion of flowers unheard of in Texas winters. When they left Fort Worth, the skies were grey, cloudy, and cold. All the vegetation had gone into hibernation or just given up. Seeing the profusion of color and plant life in California was a Christmas treat.

It was also the beginning of a new kind of life.

Chapter 113

Goodbye Texas – Hello California

The week between Christmas 1950 and New Year's Day 1951 didn't play out as expected. The furniture which left Fort Worth in mid-December had yet to arrive in La Jolla. They moved into the empty apartment and relied on the "kindness of strangers" for cots, a card table, and some folding chairs. Pauline returned home to Texas right after Christmas.

The apartment complex featured a host of buildings, each accommodating four apartments: two upstairs, and two downstairs. The Smith family apartment was on the second floor. The view of the Pacific was breathtaking, and Ruby loved watching the sunset on her balcony.

After the furniture arrived, Ruby met some of the people Jimmy already knew. The agent who had suggested the apartment was Special Agent Ray Suran. He and his wife, Janet, had a daughter, Cathy. She was Patricia's age. They were both in the sixth grade at La Jolla Elementary. The two girls became fast friends.

Ruby didn't need to work outside the home now. The apartment complex had tennis courts, so Ruby bought a tennis racket and practiced. Jimmy introduced her to several agents and their wives.

Before long, Ruby became friends with three of the FBI ladies. She thought back to her days on the farm and all the dreams she'd had over the years. Her reality now was already more than she'd ever dreamed.

Two of the FBI families belonged to a beautiful church in La Jolla—St. James by the Sea. Even the name delighted Ruby. She thought she and Patricia should see how this church might fit them. Ruby had never known any Episcopalians, and she had never been a regular church attendee, but she decided she wanted to become one. New confirmation classes were just beginning, so Ruby and Patricia enrolled. Six weeks later, on the first Sunday in May 1951, mother and daughter were confirmed as Episcopalians.

Ruby felt a major shift happening in their lives. She realized living far away from their relatives would bring her immediate family unit together tighter than it had ever been. Jimmy was happier than she'd ever seen him, and she glowed with pride in his accomplishments. Ruby realized she now had confidence to expand her own talents.

For the first time, she felt eager to try new things. She bought a portable Singer sewing machine and made slipcovers for their living room furniture, drapes for their windows, and experimented with new recipes she found. She loved the view of the ocean when she opened the drapes each morning. They went down to the beach every weekend. They explored the area and learned new things.

If Ruby's decision to run away from the farm and go to Fort Worth had been important, she now realized the move to La Jolla was even more fulfilling and significant for her. The fear she'd wrestled with when they moved from Texas had taught her an important lesson. She had all she needed to handle new things and different locations.

But more than that, she enjoyed the challenge.

Chapter 114

1951

There was a noticeable difference between the ongoing war in Korea and World War II. Although the U.S. wanted to stop the spread of communism, the fighting this time was in just one area of the world. While there were always concerns about what the Soviet Union might unleash on humanity, the situation in Korea was not the same as the destruction caused in Europe in World War II. Even so, it was bad enough to be putting troops through the sausage grinder of war, and families were concerned about their sons and daughters in peril.

In May 1951, Jimmy received notice of a transfer to Albuquerque, New Mexico. This time they made sure their furniture wouldn't be delayed. They would rent an apartment close to downtown and use the summer to find a house to buy.

On Friday, June 22 the furniture was loaded and headed for Albuquerque. Jimmy, Ruby, and Patricia took their last look at the beautiful, balmy Pacific shore. That night they rested their heads in a motel in Blythe, California where the temperature was close to 100 °. The next day they traveled through the Arizona desert by way of Flagstaff. Jimmy was required to call in to the FBI periodically during the trip. He stopped at the Sheriff's office in Flagstaff to make the call. Ruby and Pat waited in the car in the shade of the mountain trees. They hoped Albuquerque would be as temperate as Flagstaff. That night, they stopped in Gallup, New Mexico and registered at a hotel featuring photos of movie stars who had slept there. Portraits of John Wayne and other stars hung on the walls. Who knew New Mexico had a thriving film industry?

Next morning, June 24, 1951, Ruby was anxious to end this trip. In 1950 very few cars had air conditioning, and June had been hotter than usual. After three long, hot hours on the road, they drove over the top of a hill, and Albuquerque came into view. The mountain backdrop of the city was a lovely bluish-purple.

A short ten miles brought them to the edge of West Central Avenue (also known as Route 66.) The Texas Ann Motel sported a huge sign with a Longhorn steer. The snow-topped letters at the bottom of the sign promised the weary travelers air conditioning. It couldn't have come at a better time. The temperature on the neon sign at the bank showed 99°.

Welcome to the Land of Enchantment.

Chapter 115

The Albuquerque Adventure – And Beyond

Until Ruby found herself living in La Jolla, she'd never encountered many differences in major life experiences. Texas was big, but her entire life had been spent no more than 100 miles from where she was born. California was an entirely new atmosphere, not only in climate and scenery, but in dozens of other ways. Living in Albuquerque, New Mexico would bring another brand-new set of experiences, culture, food, and attitudes.

The population in Albuquerque in 1950 was 96,815, compared to the 1940 census of 35,449. Much of the increase came from World War II. On that June day in 1951 when they arrived, Ruby was almost 32 years old. The previous year's move taught her to enjoy the different places and people she would meet. She found herself excited about the possibilities in front of her.

They found a nice apartment close to downtown. Jimmy could take the bus to his office each day, and Ruby and Patricia could use the car to look for houses.

They spent about seven weeks in the apartment. During that time, they met several of their neighbors, and became good friends with the manager and his family. Apparently, the Smith family had the only television set in the entire complex. They discovered Albuquerque had only one television station, and it broadcast for only three hours each evening. The kids in the area came to sit on the Smith's front porch and peek through their screen door to watch whatever might be broadcast that night.

Each day, Ruby scoured the real estate section of the Albuquerque Tribune for possible homes for sale. She checked them out and reported back to Jimmy each evening. Before long, Ruby discovered a firm who was building homes in a new addition about nine miles from downtown. They went to see them and found one already under construction. They bought it. Ruby had the pleasure of choosing paint colors for the rooms and picking out the carpet. However, there was one major problem. No telephone lines where available that far out of Albuquerque, and there wouldn't be any for at least a year. They moved in on Jimmy's 31st birthday, August 28, 1951. One year later, the telephone company had added more lines, and the Smith's had a phone. Only one bad thing: they were on a twelve-party line.

Lots of new and amazing things happened during those years. For example, the U.S withdrew from the Korean War in 1953. There was a ceasefire and armistice agreement bringing the conflict to end, but since the armistice wasn't signed by all, the war, after more than 72 years, is "technically" still in progress. Many prisoners on both sides were returned; many weren't. Even today, the subject is complex.

President Harry Truman, who never in his wildest dreams thought he'd be president of the United States, finished his eighth year in that office in January 1953, when former General Dwight David Eisenhower became the 34th President. There were so many historic things, both good and bad, going on in the 1950s. One was the explosion of television across the nation.

When Ruby and Jimmy bought their television set in 1949, the number of programs being shown was relatively small. Moving to California had expanded their access to TV entertainment beyond expectation. Their move to Albuquerque saw almost non-existent television programing. But by 1953, two more stations opened, and the wide world of TV in Albuquerque caught up.

For Ruby, there was an event far more important in the 1950s: she presented Jimmy with a son on October 24, 1953. After two years of trying to have another child, Ruby found a doctor who took care of a problem, which allowed her to have another pregnancy. David Marshall Smith became the focus of the household, and a major lifestyle change for the Smith family.

In January 1954, Ruby learned that her grandfather, J.R. Palmer, had died only two months prior to his 84th birthday. She had visited with him in Fort Worth the last time they were there on vacation. Both her grandparents had been so important to her, and both were now gone. Ruby felt a huge hole in her heart, but she would always be thankful they had been in her life.

In 1956, the family moved into a newly constructed, larger home in Albuquerque. From that time on, Ruby and Jimmy always chose a home under construction so they could have things just the way they wanted. In 1959, shortly after their daughter married, they sold that home and bought another new home under construction.

Ruby had been donating time to St. Mark's on-the-Mesa Episcopal Church since they arrived in Albuquerque. She was a member of the Altar Guild and very active with the group. Eventually, Jimmy decided to become a member of the church, and he took classes to become a Lay Reader.

In 1958, Ruby and Jimmy would celebrate their 20th wedding anniversary on April 1. They decided they wanted to renew their vows with another ceremony. They even bought each other gold wedding bands for the occasion, and they invited friends and neighbors to attend their reception afterwards at their home that day.

Their son, David, was not yet five years old. He had heard his mother, father, and sister discussing the event, and the preparations for it. Ruby was embarrassed when one of her neighbors stopped by a few days before the event. It seems David had gone through the neighborhood telling everyone his mother and father were getting married on April 1. Ruby's friend, Claudine Thomas, remarked that when David knocked on the door to tell her about it, she said, "It's about damn time!"

The celebration was a huge success, and David's four-and-a-half-year-old telling of it became a treasured family story.

Pat (as she was now called) had graduated from high school in Albuquerque in 1957 and went to work at the telephone company. She married in 1958 and became a stenographer in 1959 at the FBI office in Albuquerque. When Pat discovered in early 1960 that she was expecting a baby, Ruby volunteered to take care of the child so Pat could go back to work.

But as it often happens, Ruby's plans were derailed.

Chapter 116

The Call of the Ocean

One Saturday morning in May 1960, Pat was working a week-end shift at the FBI and intercepted a teletype message for her father. The message said Jimmy was to report to The Army Language School in Monterrey, California. Pat immediately called her parents to report this surprise transfer. Jimmy was not surprised, but he hadn't warned Ruby. He was ordered to report to the Language School in June to begin his forty-seven weeks of training in the Albanian language. Ruby, Jimmy, and six-year-old David would be pulling up stakes and moving.

Ruby felt blindsided. They had lived in Albuquerque since 1951, made many friends, loved the climate, and Ruby was reluctant to leave her daughter. The only saving grace was they would be living by the Pacific. She worried about missing her grandchild's birth in October. Jimmy gave his assurance she could return to Albuquerque by train to help their daughter through the first two weeks after the baby came.

In June, Jimmy left to begin his classes. Once again, he left Ruby to sell the house, pack up the furniture, and follow him to Monterrey. She got it all done by her 41st birthday in August. She and David flew to Monterrey to join Jimmy. He had rented a lovely house in Pacific Grove, just half a block from the beach. The wonderful California weather and the sound of the ocean would sooth Ruby's disappointment leaving her daughter and the unborn grandchild.

Jimmy celebrated his 40th birthday that same month. Time flew faster than they expected. Ruby decided to enjoy their time in California and hope their next assignment would be just as lovely.

When Ruby and David arrived in Monterrey, they found that Jimmy's choice of a new car this time was a VW convertible. For Ruby it was fun to drive and fuel efficient. She happily tooled around Pacific Grove during their less-than-a-year assignment.

Ruby met her granddaughter, Paula Lynn, right after the child's birth in October 1960. Ruby rode the train from Monterrey to Albuquerque, arriving the day Pat and the new baby came home from the hospital. She stayed two weeks to help her daughter ease into her new situation. It was a tradition Ruby wanted to uphold as a grandmother.

At Christmas break, Ruby, Jimmy, and seven-year-old David hopped into the VW to make the 1,000-mile trip from Monterrey to

Albuquerque. It was important to spend the holiday with their daughter's family because it would likely be the last for a long time.

After Christmas they drove home and in March 1961 made one short trip from Monterrey to Los Angeles to visit Jimmy's brother Bob and his family. After that last trip, Ruby suggested they needed a larger automobile before embarking on another long trip. Shortly before Jimmy graduated, they purchased a new, powder blue Ford Falcon.

In May, Jimmy received orders for his next office. As he had expected, they would be heading for the New York City office of the FBI. At first Ruby felt excited.

It wouldn't take long to burst that bubble.

Chapter 117

A Texas Girl Confined in New York – 1961 to 1964

Anyone who has spent time in Texas, or any other southwestern state, understands big blue skies, lots of space to breathe, and friendly people. Ruby Ellen Scott Smith was that sort of woman. She could have been the cover model for a country girl, born and raised with lots of space to roam. The people she had met during the past eleven years in California and New Mexico were mostly friendly, down-home types, who would give you the shirt off their back, if you needed it. This was the atmosphere she knew and understood. Now she was about to meet her Waterloo.

Jimmy graduated from the Army Language School fluent in Albanian. He could now hold conversations with natives of that country who were mostly concentrated on the East Coast. They had escaped their home country, which was still behind the Iron Curtain. The FBI needed a liaison such as Jimmy to interact with these refugees. The Smith family once again packed up their belongings and furniture. It would be sent to a new residence in New York City—as soon as they could find a suitable apartment, in a good school district.

The Smith family piled into their new Ford Falcon and headed first from Monterrey to Albuquerque, where they would spend a few days with their daughter and her family. Then they would push on to New York City.

If you've never been to New York City, you might not understand that it's actually five different boroughs, all clustered together, to make one big city. They are, in alphabetical order, the Bronx, Brooklyn, Manhattan, Queens, and Staten Island. The census in 1960 showed the sum total of all those boroughs was a staggering 15,563,968 souls. They cover about 319 square miles. One could hardly call it the wide-open spaces.

Ruby and Jimmy found an apartment in Flushing, Queens, New York. It was in a thirteen-story building, and they would be living on the twelfth floor. In all Ruby's years of moving around, this sort of apartment living was radically different from her other experiences. The building teemed with people. They came and went all the time. If you left your apartment, you found yourself surrounded by strangers. The Smiths lived in that same apartment from 1961 until September 1964.

At first, Ruby busied herself with fixing up their new home. She introduced herself and David to other neighbors. David would be eight years old in October, and Ruby hoped he could get to know children who would also be in the third grade when school started.

From the beginning, Ruby noticed the people in New York were—on average—not especially friendly. In all her other living places, she quickly met and became friends with several other women. Now, she frequently found herself being ignored or snubbed. It took her a few weeks and meeting some friendly people to understand that because most New Yorkers had been in that area all their lives, privacy was important to them. To Ruby, that didn't explain the rude, snide comments they made.

Because the population was so dense, most New Yorkers tried to ignore other people. Everywhere you went, it seemed there were always crowds of people who did their best to pretend you weren't there. And yet, life seemed to go on. It just wasn't the kind of life Ruby had experienced prior to arriving there.

What she never understood were the people who, even though they hadn't met her, made fun of her accent, or her clothing, or just her as a person. The friendliness and acceptance she'd found all her life, in Texas, California, or New Mexico, was the norm to her. In New York, she felt completely out of her element.

David made a few friends, and fortunately he didn't seem as unhappy as Ruby. Jimmy was gone a lot. Just getting to the FBI office and returning home at night took more than an hour. In other places they lived, it had been a matter of minutes.

In the summer of 1963 Ruby convinced Jimmy to take some vacation time and they took the train to Albuquerque to visit with their daughter's family. While they were in Albuquerque, Jimmy received a call saying he needed to fly to Washington, D.C. That left Ruby and David to return to New York by train a couple of weeks later. They enjoyed the trip.

Ruby acknowledged there were some good times in New York. Several different relatives made the long trip to visit them. They were able to take David (and a few of their relatives) to the 1964 World's Fair in Flushing. Often on Sundays, Jimmy would drive them into Manhattan to see the sites. Jimmy loved the city and took every opportunity to check out all the interesting stores and buildings.

One day they visited the Empire State Building. As they rode up in the elevator to experience the view at the top, Ruby suddenly remembered the day in May 1931, when she'd listed to the radio broadcast at Granny and Grandpa Palmer's house. That was the day she heard them describe this amazing building as it first opened to the public.

Where had the time gone? In so many ways, it seemed like yesterday, but when she looked down from the top, she felt the first chill of something she would experience more often as time relentlessly clicked by.

It stops for no one. And even more intriguing, it moves faster the longer you live. She shuddered at the sudden insight. From this day forward, she tried to remember the gift of time, given to all of us, every day of our lives.

Chapter 118

The Loss of Innocence

Ruby and David returned to New York City from Albuquerque by train in the summer of 1963. David would have his tenth birthday in October.

By November 1963, Ruby seemed as settled as she would ever be in New York. She busied herself making Christmas lists for her family. But Thanksgiving would happen first. She and Jimmy enjoyed preparing turkey with all the trimmings. That year they had invited friends to join them for Thanksgiving dinner.

On Friday, November 22, 1963, Ruby was making her grocery list. Her TV was tuned to CBS, broadcasting "As the World Turns." She was almost finished when she heard an announcer interrupt the program and say that President John F. Kennedy had just been shot in Dallas, Texas.

Ruby thought that couldn't be true. She hadn't voted for the man in 1960, but she had come to admire him more than she would have imagined. Ruby was 44 now and it was the first time she'd seen a president close to her own age. She could identify with him.

Walter Cronkite appeared on the screen in the New York City CBS studios. He announced President Kennedy died at Parkland Hospital at 1:00 p.m., Central Standard Time (2:00 p.m. Eastern Time.)

Ruby remembered the day Franklin Delano Roosevelt had died in April 1944 in Warm Springs, Georgia. This was far worse. In 1944 people didn't have television to show the events happening. Now, almost everybody had access to 24/7 broadcasts. For the next four days, nothing else was on. Ruby's grocery list didn't get finished until the following Tuesday because she was glued, along with everyone else, to the unfolding of a major disaster.

When Lee Harvey Oswald was arrested and charged with killing not only the President, but also a Dallas Police Officer, Ruby felt sick that this young man had grown up in Fort Worth. When Oswald was shot as they transferred him, Ruby initially didn't believe it. Then word came that Oswald had died in the same Emergency Room at Parkland Hospital.

Ruby Ellen Smith was never particularly fond of her name. She considered changing it often. When she saw Lee Harvey Oswald gunned down by a man using the name Jack "Ruby", she disliked her name even more. She feared hearing others talk about this deranged individual and relating his name to hers.

Eventually, she learned that Jack Ruby's last name at birth had been Rubenstein. He changed that to "Ruby" in 1947—probably in an attempt to become a different person. As time went by, Ruby Ellen decided she would ignore this sleezy, angry little man who had stolen her name.

Years later Ruby sensed that the assassination of President Kennedy created some sort of "shift" in the universe. She pondered all the subsequent troubles the country endured in the rest of the 1960s. It occurred to her that once the hand of evil is released into the world, it's very hard to cleanse.

Chapter 119

Lessons Learned in the Sixties

When they first moved into their apartment in Flushing, NY, Ruby got on the waiting list for a Garden Apartment. Vacancies didn't often happen and there was a long line of residents on the waiting list. She was surprised in the early fall of 1964, when one of these apartments became available. Ruby quickly arranged to have their furniture moved. She hoped the new apartment, in a smaller building, would make life better.

Unfortunately, they only lived there four weeks. Jimmy received orders to report to headquarters in Washington in November 1964. He would be working in the Intelligence Division—his absolute dream job.

Ruby arranged for movers to take away their furniture. Thankfully, Jimmy drove the Falcon back from Washington, picked up Ruby and David in New York, and took them to Lanham, Maryland. He had rented an apartment for them, and their furniture was on its way. Ruby couldn't have been happier.

David was enrolled in school, and Ruby once again put her "home" in order. She loved Maryland. There were dozens of small towns surrounding Washington, D.C., and they were the sort of places where she felt at home. When spring came, Ruby felt almost reborn. There were trees, flowers, grass—all the things she had missed in New York. In Maryland, she made friends almost immediately. Nobody made fun of her accent, and the people were friendly.

On Valentine's Day, 1965, Ruby and Jimmy signed the contract to buy a new home under construction. It was in a new portion of Bowie, Maryland, where the Levitt Company was building an entire community of new homes. Ruby and Jimmy picked out the largest lot in the group. Both were eager to plant a garden, have cookouts in the backyard, and all the other things they had missed during their time in New York.

The floor plan they chose was a two-story colonial-style home, with three bedrooms, two and a half baths, living room, separate dining room, and a big kitchen with breakfast/family room. It was the most beautiful home Ruby could remember.

In June 1971, David graduated from high school in Bowie, and several relatives attended the ceremony. Pat, Sam, and Paula had arrived, as had Pauleen, and one of David's cousins, Vivian.

Sadly, a month before David's graduation, word came that Jimmy's father, Gregory K. Smith had died. At the age of 72, Smitty had succumbed to the ravages of Parkinson's disease. His youngest son, twenty-one-year-old Michael, had stepped in to manage the Paris Coffee Shop in 1965 when Smitty first became ill.

When his father died, Mike was 27. He maintained the family's historic and popular restaurant until he decided to sell the business and retire, at 76, in 2020. The family business, the Paris Coffee Shop, purchased by Gregory K. Smith in 1930, would be remodeled, and reopened with the same, familiar name in 2022.

But it would never be the same to those of us left in the Smith family, and other people in Fort Worth.

Chapter 120

Time Marches On

In 1972, Ruby and Jimmy made plans to visit family in Kansas, New Mexico, and Texas. They departed Maryland on April 27 and arrived in Kansas City on April 28 to visit Ruby's cousin Curtis Kemp and his family. Next, they drove for two days, arriving in Albuquerque on Sunday evening April 30 at their daughter, Pat's home.

Very early Tuesday morning, May 2, the phone rang. It was FBI Headquarters in Washington asking for Jimmy. He took the call, hung up, and announced they must immediately return to Washington, D.C.

J. Edgar Hoover had died in his sleep. His housekeeper went to check on him that morning when he hadn't come down for breakfast. She immediately notified the FBI, and the executive group under Mr. Hoover agreed Tom Smith should immediately return to Washington to take charge of Mr. Hoover's personal files.

Ruby and Jimmy quickly repacked their suitcases, jumped into their 1972 Chevy Caprice and headed straight back to Maryland. So much for their final leg of the vacation to Texas.

Hoover's body was taken to the Capitol Rotunda to rest under the dome. It was a rare exception of the individuals who were normally given that honor. But J. Edgar Hoover was as iconic as any politician or military officer who had rested in that honored place.

Hoover had been director of the FBI from May 10, 1924, when he was 29 years old, until May 2, 1972, when he was 77. He had taken the Bureau from its early days, when it was called the Bureau of Investigation, then the Department of Investigation, up through the Great Depression and beyond. On July 1, 1935, it became the FBI—the Federal Bureau of Investigation.

L. Patrick Gray was appointed acting director on May 3, 1972. Since Jimmy was Chief of Research in the Intelligence Division, Mr. Gray asked him for help to understand the various departments and issues. Gray had a rough term as Acting Director and was replaced less than a year later. William D. Ruckelshaus became Acting Director on April 30, 1973. Clarence M. Kelly arrived July 9, 1973, to serve as the new Director of the FBI. Tom Smith accompanied Mr. Kelly to testify at several Congressional Hearings during 1973-1974.

Maybe someday there'll be a book all about Jimmy, aka, Thomas J. (Tom) Smith. It could be very interesting if it wasn't constrained from discussing most of his entire FBI career.

Chapter 121
Retirement

In early 1974 Ruby was only 54. She realized something many other wives in her age group had already faced. It could be a difficult discussion between a husband and wife because each partner would be affected. Jimmy had begun thinking about retirement.

Not many of today's women could understand or appreciate the "pickle" Ruby found herself in. After he became an FBI agent in late 1950, she didn't work outside the home again except for small forays when she wanted to get out of the house for a change. Today's younger women can't imagine society in the 20th Century. Women Ruby's age, if they were married to a typical working man, had spent their years managing the home. Wives cared for the children, maintained the house, did the shopping, meal planning, cooking, laundry, and oftentimes gardening. These wives understood their lives would be upended when their husbands retired from their daily job.

In 1974, Ruby and Jimmy had been married 36 years. The last 24 years of that time he was at work every weekday except for holidays and vacations at the FBI. When he became an agent, he was often gone more than a 9 to 5 routine. A wife develops a certain pattern when the husband is at work. When that stops, you must wonder how much your own life will change.

FBI agents were eligible to retire after twenty years of service and/or 55 years of age. Jimmy had been at the Bureau for twenty-four years. In the summer of 1974, he had his 54th birthday. The stars were in alignment.

Ruby knew the past two years had been difficult for him. The death of J. Edgar Hoover brought a series of temporary directors. Watergate happened. Washington D.C. was in the grip of scandal. The FBI was being vilified daily, and morale suffered. Tom Smith turned in his papers and retired as of October 4, 1974. He retired as Deputy Assistant Director for Domestic Intelligence.

For the next seven months, Ruby and Jimmy basked in doing whatever they wanted. For the first time in their lives, they didn't need to work, and weren't concerned about money.

In May 1975, Ruby started talking about moving. She was tired of the Washington D.C. area. David had moved into his own apartment. He wanted to stay in Maryland.

Ruby and Jimmy longed to get back to their roots—or at least a comfortable setting. They agreed it came down to Fort Worth or

Albuquerque. How to choose?

Pat took advantage of the situation and composed a comprehensive three-page letter to her parents. She explained in detail why she thought they should choose to live in Albuquerque. One of the major reasons was so they could get to know their only granddaughter, and she could get to know them. After reading it, Ruby and Jimmy were convinced.

They drove to Albuquerque in June and looked for a house. They found one—under construction of course—and signed the contract. It would be ready around the first part of September.

They returned to Maryland and prepared to sell the house. The move to Albuquerque would be in September. Now all they must do was find a buyer.

They couldn't know how surprisingly that would play out.

Chapter 122

Connections

Over the years Ruby and Jimmy made a long list of friends. Some were from their early days in Fort Worth, such as Ruth and Dub Nance, Jody and Dub Mahanay, and Gertie and Joe Weisberg. They treasured Ray and Janet Suran, and Jerome and Virginia Wright from La Jolla, and almost more friends than they could list from Albuquerque. One friend they met in Albuquerque was a young man named Graham Van Note.

Ruby and Jimmy first met him in 1956 when he was 19 years old. He was on temporary assignment from the Navy at Sandia Base in Albuquerque for Special Weapons Training, put on by the Unified Training Command. When the course ended, he would board the aircraft carrier USS Kearsarge for a year-long cruise in the Pacific.

During his six months in Albuquerque, he became a part of the Smith family. He helped Jimmy rototill the backyard and plant grass, and they spent hours talking about subjects which interested them both. He and Ruby became fast friends, and she saw him as one of her kids.

When he was released from the Navy in 1959, he returned to Albuquerque and stayed briefly with the Smiths. He attended the University of New Mexico and took on a part-time job as Night Security Clerk at the Albuquerque FBI field office. After obtaining his degree, he became an FBI Agent. During all those years, Graham stayed in contact with Ruby and Jimmy, wherever they were stationed, even after he was married.

In early August 1975, the FBI transferred him to Headquarters in Washington, D.C. He would need to be there by the first part of September. He already knew Ruby and Jimmy were planning to move, and he contacted them about buying their house. He and his wife and daughter had visited the Smith's over the years and were familiar with the house and the neighborhood. It seemed like a serendipitous solution for everyone.

On the appointed day, the movers showed up to take the Smith furniture out of the Bowie house. On that same day, the movers carrying the Van Note's furniture also showed up to put furniture into that same house.

By the end of the day, the Smith's furniture was on its way to New Mexico, and Ruby and Jimmy bid a fond farewell to Maryland.

Chapter 123

Christmas 1975 in New Mexico

This book is supposed to be about Ruby's life. Things pertaining to her many relatives are shown to explain how they fit into Ruby's life.

For example, it was mentioned that Ruby's daughter, Pat, was married in 1958. This young man's name was Sam. He was a new police officer, one of the things Pat admired about him. They had a daughter, Paula, and everyone assumed they would grow old together.

On June 1, 1973, Pat and Sam divorced. Sam went to California for his summer Coast Guard assignment. Pat started a new job and moved into an apartment in Albuquerque where she and Paula planned to live.

On August 25, 1973, Pat married Phil, a much older man, and they set up their newly married life. After that, things got complicated—especially for Paula, who was 12 going on 13.

Sam remarried that same year, and Paula went back and forth between the two households. In 1974 she moved in permanently with Sam and his wife, Julie.

In 1975 Pat's husband, Phil, was temporarily on assignment in Germantown, Maryland, for Sandia Corporation. When Phil was given that assignment in early August, he spent the first couple of weeks with Ruby and Jimmy at their home in Maryland. After that, he was able to find a small apartment in Germantown until his assignment was over the following year.

Ruby and Jimmy arrived in Albuquerque in early September 1975 and stayed at Pat's house until their furniture arrived. They were delighted with their new home, and they quickly reconnected with many of the friends they had left behind in 1960. Jimmy especially wanted to become involved with the Society of Former Special Agents of the FBI. Many of the agents he'd worked with in Albuquerque in the 1950s were also now retired and part of that group.

Ruby made lots of new friends in their new neighborhood, and renewed friendships with ladies she'd known years before. She enjoyed decorating the new house. They once again had a huge backyard, and Jimmy couldn't wait to plant his lawns.

When David turned 22 in October 1975, Ruby was sad because that was the first birthday she hadn't been with him. She also knew they couldn't really afford to bring him to Albuquerque for Christmas.

Phil was still working in Germantown, and he planned to come back to Albuquerque for Christmas. David and Pat talked on the phone and arranged for Phil and David to get tickets for the same flight. Pat would pick them up late in the evening of December 23.

The next morning (Christmas Eve), Pat called Ruby and told her she and Phil were bringing over a surprise gift. She asked Ruby and Jimmy to sit where they couldn't see her placing the gift under the tree. David sat in front of the tree, and Pat put a Christmas bow on his head. When Ruby and Jimmy came around the corner and saw their son, Jimmy had a huge grin on his face, and Ruby dissolved into tears of joy. Their precious boy was "home" for Christmas after all.

After that, they made sure to bring David to Albuquerque for Christmas every year. He usually arrived a day or two before Christmas Eve and returned home a day before New Year's Eve.

A few years later, that schedule had to be revamped. He still visited but on a different schedule.

Chapter 124

What Do I Do for the Rest of My Life?

Moving your entire household from one state to another can take a long time. It's not just the actual moving as much as it is creating the home atmosphere. After all the furniture was properly arranged, new curtains sewn and hung at the windows, and new pieces replacing old furniture, there was the planting the front and back lawns and deciding on trees and flowers. The process took about a year, and when Ruby looked around her cozy new home, she proclaimed it finished.

She had celebrated her 57th birthday in August, and she was still young enough to want activities. Both her children were grown and on their own. Her husband was happily reestablishing old friendships and taking on new activities with them. Now that he was retired, he seemed to have lots of things to do.

During that time Ruby decided to volunteer at the Bernalillo County Medical Center Hospital in the gift shop. She found it satisfying—at first. Then her thoughts moved on to other things. What should she do with the rest of her life?

In February 1977 they took a trip back to Maryland to visit David and their friends still in that area. On the way back to Albuquerque, they stopped for lunch at a charming combination restaurant and gift shop in Virginia. After lunch Ruby visited the gift shop area and spied something she absolutely could not resist: a beautiful, antique reproduction doll. It was a boy doll, about sixteen inches in height, dressed in old fashion clothing. He wore gold wool tweed knickers, and jacket, lace-up shoes with brown stockings, a white shirt, a black bow tie, and a jaunty brown cap. His bisque face had a happy smile, and his name was Gladdie.

He cost $125.00, and Ruby decided she had to have him.

She spent the 1800-mile trip back to Albuquerque holding Gladdie in her lap. As the miles rolled by, her thoughts turned to the woman who had made this beautiful doll. It hadn't occurred to her until that moment that there were people out there creating these beautiful reproduction dolls. By the time their car drove into the driveway in Albuquerque, Ruby had made up her mind what her next big project would be.

Ruby Ellen Scott Smith would—come Hell or high water—find someone to teach her how to make beautiful dolls like Gladdie.

Chapter 125

And The Artistry Begins

Even as a small child, Ruby had determination and purpose. It's likely those attributes were the very things which angered her stepfather. Over the years, Ruby learned how to utilize these traits to her best advantage, and in 1977 that's how she began her dream career.

She never thought of herself as an artist. She didn't paint pictures like her mother or Aunt Ina, she didn't make ceramics like Aunt Margie, and she assumed she didn't have talent along those lines. But when she bought the sewing machine in 1951, she realized she was adept at sewing. For the next few years, she happily sewed curtains for each new home, and tackled other projects with good outcomes. She made several outfits for her daughter, and a few for herself, too.

When the idea came to her about becoming a doll maker, she reasoned that with the proper tools and someone to help her get started, she might become pretty good at it. She thought it would become a fun hobby to keep her entertained, while her husband pursued his own activities. Once her decision was made, she focused on finding a mentor. Soon, she met the perfect person to get her started.

She found a woman who made bisque dolls. Ruby picked out a photo of a doll she wanted to create. The doll maker gave Ruby a crash course, showing her how to pour the slip into molds for the head, body, arms, and legs. Next Ruby purchased the greenware parts for a doll she liked from this woman. The doll maker then showed her how to clean and buff the greenware with pieces of nylon hosiery. The teacher had a kiln, and she explained how the buffed greenware pieces would need to be fired. Ruby took the pieces home to buff. The next day, she returned to have her doll pieces fired. Her teacher showed her how to oil them before painting.

Ruby worked three days, carefully painting each part of that doll, making it as beautiful as she could. She returned to the doll maker's home to have the doll pieces fired one more time to set the painting. After that, the lady showed her how to string the pieces into a complete doll.

Now she was really hooked. She purchased Mildred Seeley's book, *How to Make Reproduction Dolls for Fun & Profit*. The book had dozens of photos of Antique Reproduction Dolls, and Ruby decided to have the Doll Maker pour the parts for each doll Ruby wanted to make. Ruby ran the Doll Maker ragged over the next several months by purchasing the greenware pieces for dozens of Antique Reproduction Dolls.

It soon became evident that Ruby needed her own equipment and supplies. She spent so much time driving back and forth to the Doll Maker, it became expensive and time consuming. Jimmy pointed out they would be way ahead of the game if he just bought Ruby her own set of molds and her own kiln to fire the greenware pieces. It had to be less expensive than constantly running to the Doll Maker for pouring and firing of all the dolls Ruby planned to make.

Once that happened, Ruby was truly in business—although she didn't think of it that way. To her, it was simply a new hobby, albeit an expensive one. Without ever thinking about it, Ruby became a doll expert. The dolls she made were exquisite, and she started sewing the clothes for them herself. Sometimes she still bought outfits she didn't want to tackle sewing, but over time, she did most of the sewing of the clothes. Eventually she acquired close to a thousand molds for doll making.

Within the first year, people began asking to buy some of the dolls she had made. That surprised her, but she agreed to sell some of them. Eventually she took orders for making dolls. People would see the dolls in her collection, and they would select the doll they wanted Ruby to make. Then she would pour the molds, buff the greenware, and fire the painted pieces in her new kiln. Life became so much easier.

Ruby took dozens of classes, both locally, and in other states. She became so successful she conducted classes for other people. She was now a full-time doll maker, and she couldn't have been happier. She went to numerous doll shows, sometimes in other states. She became well known and her dolls were in demand.

Over the years, Ruby sold large numbers of the dolls she made. Eventually she became a judge at some of the doll shows and State Fair events. She also won many blue ribbons when she entered competitions.

For several years, Ruby's doll sales were $10,000 a year. She had a tax ID and a local Business License. One year when Jimmy was doing their taxes, he informed her she was making about fifty cents an hour with all her doll making. But making money was never the point. She never stopped trying to improve her techniques.

One of her best ideas came when she decided to make composition bodies for her dolls rather than the heavy, more breakable bisque bodies. The arms and legs she made continued to be bisque, because that was the way antique dolls had always been done.

Jimmy came up with the idea that he could help her by taking on the making of the composition bodies. In addition, he started playing around with paints and created a set of paints to be used for tinting the bisque doll faces, arms, and legs. He even advertised in doll magazines to sell his paints to other doll makers.

Ruby was surprised and pleased when Jimmy started accompanying her to doll shows and events. He would pack boxes of dolls in the car for her and wheel them out on a cart to the doll event when they got there. He helped her by filling out sales slips when dolls were purchased, and he took care of her state sales tax reports.

Ruby couldn't have been more surprised or happy about her husband's eventual interest in her doll business. When she thought back to their early days of marriage, no one, especially her, would have predicted this massive change in her husband. But then when she thought about that 17-year-old boy she married in 1938, and the man he had become along the way, she felt warm, proud, and happy for the way things turned out.

These were their golden years, giving her the gift of his love, support, and attention. That was something she cherished more than anything.

Chapter 126

The Intermediate Years

From her beginning in the business of doll making in 1977 to the time she decided she could no longer keep up the pace, more than 20 years passed. During all those years Ruby enjoyed entertaining friends and relatives from all over the country. She loved preparing special meals for friends and relatives, and she loved having them come to their home.

By the beginning of the 1980s, guests were impressed with the huge collection of both antique dolls, and the antique reproduction dolls Ruby had made for herself. One wall in the dining room had floor to ceiling glass cabinets showcasing her work. In the living room there were two huge oak cabinets displaying her collection of antique dolls. There were dolls standing by the window, sitting in chairs, and a life-sized doll in the foyer. Anyone coming to the front door would see a blonde, five-foot, five-inch creature dressed in an antique white dress from the early 1900s. One unintended consequence was it scared away those who approached the open door in the summertime.

In the early 1980s, Ruby's daughter Pat married again, but it didn't last long enough to matter. Ruby and Jimmy worried about both their children and hoped both would be happily married by now.

In the spring of 1985, Pat had been renting an apartment for almost six months. She had purchased a townhouse under construction. It was supposed to be finished by July, but construction wasn't moving as fast as promised. When another lease became due on the apartment, Ruby and Jimmy suggested Pat put her furniture in storage and move in with them until the new townhouse was ready.

At the end of May, Pat moved in with her parents. By this time Pat was about to have her 46th birthday. Ruby and Jimmy would be 66 and 65, respectively, in August. It was the first time they had lived together as a family since Pat married that first time in 1958. But this time, David was on his own, and it was just the original three members of Ruby and Jimmy's family.

When the townhouse was finished it was the middle of September. Ruby knew Pat was anxious to finally move into the new place, but Ruby found herself experiencing the same feelings of loss she'd had back in 1958 when Pat married and left home.

Both Ruby and Jimmy helped their daughter on moving day. When things were finally in place for her to spend that first night in her new home, Pat had one last dinner at her parents' house. When she left that evening, both Ruby and Jimmy experienced, once again, the "empty nest" syndrome. Ruby cried, and Jimmy hugged her sympathetically.

At least they were living in the same town with their daughter and granddaughter. David was still 2,000 miles away.

Chapter 127

Mid 80s to Mid 90s – Happily Ever After

In Ruby's world she wanted "happily ever after" for everybody. She had vowed when she married, it would be forever. In the grand scheme of things, she was right on track. Still, she worried about her children's future.

Ruby was thrilled when, in late 1985, Pat renewed an acquaintance with her high school sweetheart. Ruby and Jimmy were ecstatic about this development, although Pat tried to temper their enthusiasm. She had decided she wasn't very good at marriage and would therefore remain single. But someone else was involved in this equation - her high school sweetheart, Don Wood.

It took six months, but finally in March 1986, he wore her down. Don proposed marriage and Pat finally accepted. The wedding would be in July 1986, the same day as Don's 30th high school reunion that evening. Ruby was pleased because she had always thought Don was "such a nice boy!" Ruby decided their reception after the Saturday morning nuptials would be at her house. She got busy with the planning, and for one last time, Jimmy gave away his daughter, in the same church where she'd married the first time—with the same minister.

In 1988, Ruby and Jimmy's 50th wedding anniversary was approaching. They decided to host a big party for friends and relatives. Since April 1 was Good Friday that year, they decided to host the party on Saturday, April 9, 1988. Dozens of people drove or flew into Albuquerque from all over the county to honor them. The guest list included old friends and all the relatives. Their son David came and visited several days. Ruby selected a beautiful pink dress for the occasion. Pat's stepdaughter, Carrie, was in town, and helped Ruby select it. She told Carrie that day that this was the dress she wanted to be buried in. It was a magnificent gathering and celebration, one Ruby and Jimmy would remember always.

Now they turned their attention to David. It took time, but in 1991 when he was 37, he popped the question. He married his lovely fiancée, Fran on March 21, 1991. Ruby and Jimmy drove back to Maryland for the wedding, and Pat, Don, and Paula flew there to attend. It was a lovely wedding, with a sit-down dinner afterwards. At last, both their children were happily married.

Christmas, 1996, was the first time David wasn't with them on Christmas Eve. Instead, he and his new bride arrived on the day after Christmas. Fran had never been to New Mexico, and Ruby and Jimmy had a lovely reception to introduce their new daughter-in-law to their friends.

Now they could enjoy their remaining years. But, just like many other people in their 70s, they hadn't worried about future medical events.

Chapter 128

Healthcare and Aging

In the 1980s when Ruby was in her 60s, she underwent hip replacement on her right hip. At that time, Jimmy was in excellent health and took good care of her during her recovery.

In the 1990s, Ruby required replacement surgery on her left hip. This time, she spent a couple of weeks in the hospital's Rehabilitation Center. Apparently, the medical community thought older people needed more time and assistance healing from hip surgery. Jimmy brought her things from home, visited her twice a day, and after discharge, took care of her needs at home.

Jimmy was an excellent cook. When he retired, he took over most of the cooking. He handled things at home when Ruby was discharged from the hospital. Some of their friends and neighbors also helped out when needed. At this time, both Ruby and Jimmy were in their late 70s.

People change as they age, of course, and Ruby and Jimmy were in their 80s in the year 2000. Jimmy seemed to slowly be losing some of his cognitive function. It was almost unnoticeable at first, but as time when by, he changed. Immediate family members noticed. He was still very active, continued doing most of the cooking and grocery shopping. He always prepared the Thanksgiving and Christmas Eve dinner.

When September 11, 2001, happened, everybody in America seemed glued to their television sets. The awful sight of the collapse of the Twin Towers in New York City was heartbreaking for everyone watching. Strangely, Jimmy, who had loved his time working in New York City, seemed unfazed. He sat in front of the television set, without comment, apparent concern, or paying much attention. Normally he would have been engaged in discussions. Instead, his brain didn't react to the horror.

On a cold, winter day in January 2002, Jimmy slipped on the ice and fell. His head hit the sidewalk, but it didn't bleed, and he brushed off the incident. Things seemed the same as usual. Ruby and Jimmy even bought a brand-new Honda sedan that month. Jimmy still drove some of the time, but Ruby took over more often. His personality was slightly different. He smiled a lot, but he didn't talk much. Ruby tried her best to ignore what was happening. Her husband had already been given an MRI and was evaluated by their family doctor. That doctor assumed he had Alzheimer's, but no treatment or other tests were done.

Late in the evening of March 20, 2002, Ruby called Pat. Jimmy had fallen in the bathtub, and Ruby wasn't strong enough to help him out. Pat and Don rushed over, and Don was able to pull Jimmy out of the tub. He didn't seem at all upset about it.

Next morning, March 21, Ruby called again. Jimmy had spent most of the night sleeping on the floor because he had rolled off the bed. Ruby needed help getting him up. Pat told her to call 9-1-1, then rushed over to do what she could. She arrived at the same time the EMTs did. They said he needed to go to the hospital. Ruby accompanied Jimmy in the ambulance while Pat followed them in her own car.

In 2002, there were precious few neurosurgeons in New Mexico. There was one in Santa Fe, but everyone hoped to keep Jimmy in Albuquerque.

By the end of the day, Thursday, March 21, 2002, Jimmy was taken to three different hospitals. At the University of New Mexico teaching hospital, they found the neurosurgeon they needed. Surgery started almost immediately on Jimmy's 81-year-old brain.

Jimmy's surgery took about four hours. Ruby and Pat were able to see him as soon as he returned from the recovery room. He was awake and they breathed a sigh of relief.

As luck would have it, March 21, 2002, was also the 10th Wedding Anniversary for, David and his wife, Fran. Ruby stayed in touch with them several times that day to report how things were going for his dad. David would fly to Albuquerque to see his father. He arrived the next day and visited him every day before he had to return home to manage his business.

The doctors said there had been a brain bleed, and they believed it was now under control. Time would tell, but the overall impression from the medical people was that Jimmy's brain wasn't going to get back to normal. The diagnosis of Alzheimer's was very likely incorrect, but they weren't sure and couldn't diagnose anything else. Obviously, the brain bleed was the most recent problem, but they couldn't know what else would happen.

When it was time for release from the hospital, Jimmy was admitted to a rehab facility. There he would receive physical therapy and other treatment with the hope he could eventually return home.

Both Ruby and Pat visited him every day, but they couldn't see any improvement. He still couldn't walk, and he talked very little.

When April 1, 2002, came along, it was Ruby and Jimmy's 64th wedding anniversary. Pat decided it was important for Ruby to receive an anniversary card signed by Jimmy. She purchased a suitable one and took it to the rehab facility so Jimmy could sign it. Pat felt unsure how much Jimmy really understood during this time. She coaxed him to write "Love, Jimmy." He took the pen she gave him and instead wrote his own, loving message to his wife—"All My Love, Jimmy."

On that day, he didn't need his daughter's input.

After three weeks in rehab, the manager of the facility informed Ruby that Jimmy—because of his insurance coverage—could only stay there for 30 days. The deadline was fast approaching, he hadn't improved, and he wouldn't be allowed to go home. The manager recommended Ruby find a long-term care facility for him. Ruby and Pat would inspect the recommended facilities after the weekend.

In all the years they had been married, Jimmy had been the one steering the ship. His work always dictated where they would live, and what things they would do.

Now Ruby was supposed to come up with a facility where her husband would likely be confined for the rest of his life.

Chapter 129

How Do You Say "Goodbye?"

On Friday, April 19, Jimmy was taken to a hospital to remove a minor cyst on his leg. He would be returned to the rehab facility toward the end of the day. Ruby stayed with him at the hospital until 5:00 p.m., and Pat arrived right after her mother left. Jimmy was awake and doing fine, and a nurse showed Pat the incision from the procedure. Jimmy seemed to be in no pain, but he wasn't very talkative. He was scheduled to return to rehab within a few minutes so Pat hugged her dad, and said, "I love you, Papa."

Jimmy hadn't smiled or shown any emotion. His wooden response was simply, "I know."

On Saturday, April 20, Ruby and Pat planned to attend a Doll Club event in the early afternoon. They stopped by the rehab facility to check on Jimmy but he was sleeping. They went to their event and after it ended a few hours later, they stopped by again to check on him. He still slept.

On Saturday night at 11:00 p.m., Ruby called Pat to tell her the rehab was transporting Jimmy back to the University Hospital where he'd had the brain surgery. He had slept all day, and the rehab employees worried he might need hospital care.

Ruby, Pat and Don arrived at the hospital and Jimmy was still sleeping. The nurses explained the brain bleed was back, and it would take another brain surgery to stop the bleeding. Ruby was asked to make the decision, and it wasn't easy.

Another surgery would temporarily stop the bleeding, but the doctors thought it would likely happen again in a couple of weeks. They believed his condition was terminal, and that surgery wouldn't prevent the inevitable. The idea of another surgery was rejected.

From Midnight Saturday until 7:00 a.m. Sunday morning, Ruby, Pat, and Don sat in Jimmy's room. Ruby and Pat sat at his bedside, touching him, and Don semi-slept in a chair in the corner. Ruby frequently talked to him as she held his hand. She told him it was okay if he needed to leave.

At 7:00 a.m. Sunday morning, April 21, 2002, the day nurse came in to take Jimmy's vitals. She encouraged the family to go home and rest after their long vigil. She told Ruby she would call if anything changed.

They decided to stop by the rehab facility and retrieve Jimmy's belongings. Pat went in to gather up his things, while Don and Ruby waited outside in the car. Just as Pat finished packing, Don came in. Ruby had received the call on her cell phone. Jimmy had died at 7:20 a.m., Sunday, April 21, 2002. He was 81 years old.

As they should have expected, Thomas J. (Jimmy) Smith chose his own time to go.

Chapter 130

Life without Jimmy

The funeral was on Wednesday, April 24, 2002. A large crowd attended, including his brothers Paul, Bob, David, and his half-brother Michael. Nieces and nephews and many old friends were there, as were members of the many organizations where he was a member. Dozens of people came to Ruby and Jimmy's home after the internment. David arrived a day before the event and stayed an extra two days after.

Ruby held up well after her husband's death. Jimmy's illness had happened in a series of small bits over the past year and a half. It had given her time to accept the eventual loss. Deep down inside the survival part of her brain, she adapted to being alone again.

She was almost 83 now. She thought of her situation as a new chapter. She attended a small Episcopal church each Sunday and enjoyed the camaraderie of the group. She made new friends and felt a kinship with widowed friends. They lunched and went to events together.

Ruby flew to Maryland a few times to see David and Fran, and she even took some automobile trips with a couple of her doll friends. Her garden was another joy for her, and she sat out on her cozy covered patio every day in spring, summer, and even fall. She kept bird seed in huge plastic cans to supply multiple bird feeders each day. A series of bright blue Scrub Jays found that Ruby was a pushover. She kept a full-sized garbage can full of shelled, unsalted, peanuts. She sat out on the patio in her vivid blue robe. It attracted the Scrub Jays, and they hopped up on her lap to get the peanuts.

Holidays were special. Decorating the Christmas tree was important. Thanksgiving dinners, birthday dinners, and all the other family dinners kept Ruby active and happy. Out of town friends and relatives continued visiting, and she loved having the company.

A few months before her 90th birthday, Ruby confided to Pat that she had some concerns about her bills. She discovered she'd paid one twice, and that bothered her. Ruby decided it would be safer if Pat paid her bills from this point on, and Pat agreed.

In mid-summer, Ruby once again developed a problem with her left hip. Pat took her to the orthopedic doctor who had done the surgery on it. X-Rays showed her previous hip surgery had "come apart." The thigh bone was detached, and Ruby needed reconstructive surgery with a specific orthopedic surgeon. Pat made an appointment for an evaluation.

Ruby looked forward to her 90th Birthday party. Pat took care of the food, drink, and decorations, and Ruby called all her friends, inviting them to celebrate with her on August 12, 2009, at her home.

It was a big success. Ruby sat in her rocking chair and guests took turns talking with her. A huge cake with her name on it, ice cream, and old-fashioned red punch topped off the event. Lots of photos were made, and Ruby was a happy woman. At 90 she felt good, with the exception of her hip problem. Once that was fixed, she reasoned things would improve.

About five weeks later, a night-time emergency would bring the house of cards tumbling down.

Chapter 131

Independence Isn't Always What It's Cracked up To Be

One night in mid-September 2009, Ruby attempted to get out of bed around 1:00 a.m. to use the bathroom. She discovered she couldn't walk. The leg with the dangling thigh bone had apparently repositioned itself, leaving her unable to walk on her own. She called her next-door neighbors. This young couple had become close friends—especially after Jimmy's death. They had helped her with various things over the years, and they immediately grabbed their key and went to check on Ruby.

When they realized the situation couldn't be easily handled, they called Pat and Don, who immediately dressed and drove to Ruby's house. The decision was made to call 9-1-1, and within minutes the paramedics arrived and determined Ruby needed more help than they could give.

Anyone who has had the experience of being taken to the ER in the middle of the night knows how this goes. Pat explained to the doctors about Ruby's pending reattachment surgery. It was scheduled for early October, but in the meantime, Ruby needed constant care. There was no way she could go back home until after that surgery.

It turned out that an elderly person in Ruby's condition could not be admitted to an assisted living facility until the patient had spent three days in a hospital. Fortunately, the hospital found a room for her. During those required three days, the helpful staff found an assisted living group who had room to care for Ruby until her scheduled surgery.

After her three-day hospital stay, Ruby was moved to an assisted living facility very close to Pat and Don's home. It seemed like an answer to prayer, solving the situation.

Unfortunately, Ruby didn't see it that way.

Chapter 132

September 2009 - What Happens When Our Brain "Shifts"?

From the time Ruby Ellen Scott Smith became a teenager, she had done her best to remain in control of her destiny. She was bright, energetic, and had a sturdy body which knew hard work. Her self-administered emancipation at age 16 in 1936 had taught her she had to maintain authority over herself. She was proud of how she had managed her life all these years, and she wasn't about to let strangers step in and tell her what to do at age 90.

The night they transferred her from Presbyterian Hospital to The Montebello assisted living and rehab facility, Ruby's personality began to change. She wanted to go home. She immediately hated what was happening as they wheeled her into the room she would use temporarily. It was as though she couldn't think rationally. When Pat and Don tried to explain that she needed to be there because she couldn't even get to the bathroom on her own, she became enraged. People in Texas would have called it "pitching a hissy fit."

When anger didn't get her anywhere, Ruby cried. Unfortunately, that didn't change things. This is where she would receive nursing care, and it would be in a place designed to help people with problems getting around.

Within a few days, Ruby calmed down—at least for the time being. Pat visited her every day, and some of her friends came to see her, too. That helped a lot, and her angry outbursts diminished significantly.

Montebello had facilities for transporting their patients to doctor or hospital appointments. This was a huge help—especially for Pat. Transporting her mother in the family car in her debilitated condition wouldn't have worked.

Finally, the day arrived for the surgery. By now, Ruby was in a better mood. She'd undergone hip surgery twice already. How bad could it be the third time?

When you're 90 years old it can be pretty bad.

Chapter 133

October 2009 - Putting It Together

The surgery date was October 13, 2009. The surgery and recovery room time lasted about five hours. She was taken to her room in the early evening.

After a few days, the hospital transferred her to their Rehab Facility at Kaseman Hospital. There she would start physical therapy. The doctor who did the surgery said that after rehab at Kaseman, she needed seven months to heal. She would be returned to Montebello where they could continue the rehab work. She wouldn't be allowed to walk at all during that time. She could only "put a toe" down. She could transfer from the wheelchair to the bed or other chair by using just her right foot and lightly balancing with her left toe. The same technique would be used for the bathroom.

Ruby's mental state took a nosedive during her stay at Kaseman Rehab.

Three weeks later she returned to Montebello. The first few weeks she was alone. Thanksgiving came, and Pat, Don, Paula, and her husband, Danny, brought Thanksgiving dinner to Ruby. Around December she gained a nice roommate, and they got along well. On Christmas Eve, Pat, Don, Paula and Danny prepared the traditional Christmas Eve dinner and present opening. They could bring Ruby to her home for only four hours, but even that short time lifted her spirits.

Finally, the seven-month rehabilitation confinement at Montebello ended. In April 2010, Ruby returned to her beloved home. She would, however, need outside help each day, twice a day.

The first day was a rough one. Ruby didn't like the first woman the caregiver company sent and became highly emotional. Ruby's minister came by and was able to calm her. The homecare company found two new women who would take turns—one (Carvella) would be there Monday through Friday, and the other (Rose) would take over on Saturdays and Sundays. Ruby became very fond of both women. Each day one of them arrived at 8:00 a.m. to fix breakfast for her, and then help her shower. They also did laundry, and other chores. They then prepared her lunch, and left at 1:00 p.m. In the evenings, they arrived at 4:00 p.m., prepared dinner for Ruby, did any chores needed, and got her ready for bed. Then they left at 8:00 p.m. each evening.

Ruby loved to have her hair done every week. Pat took her to the beauty shop on Tuesdays at 1:30; right after her caregiver left the first shift. Ruby had a walker now, and she could even stroll through the Farmers' Market.

Holidays and birthdays were always at Ruby's house. Whichever caregiver was on duty that day would join the fun. They became an essential part of the family.

David continued flying to Albuquerque each year to have a belated Christmas with Ruby. It always filled her with joy when her precious son arrived for his yearly visit.

From the time Jimmy died in April 2002, until Ruby's hip problem surfaced in September 2009, she managed her life, finances, and took care of her home and garden. Because she had always been a rather independent woman, she managed those seven years well.

The hip surgery in 2009 and her subsequent stay in rehab until April 2010 was less than pleasant for her. Returning home when she did gave her back part of that freedom she craved.

Sadly, it lasted slightly less than three years.

Chapter 134

New Challenges

In late January 2013 Ruby developed pneumonia. At first it seemed to be a simple chest cold. But one Monday morning, Ruby's weekday caregiver, Carvella, called Pat and said she thought Ruby should be seen at the Emergency Room. Her coughing seemed worse than before.

Pat met Carvella and Ruby at the Emergency Room. Several hours later physicians decided Ruby should be transported by ambulance to the downtown Presbyterian Hospital. There she would be treated for pneumonia. By now, Ruby was 93, and though she was a sturdy woman, she had already been through pneumonia twice in the past twelve years. Another bout at her age wasn't good.

When time for that hospital discharge came around, Presbyterian was reluctant to send Ruby back to her home with the partial care she'd been receiving since 2010. Instead, they determined she should once again return to Montebello to undergo inhalation therapy. The doctors there would then decide whether her strength was good enough to be in her home again with part-time care.

After eight weeks of therapy and evaluation, the doctors told Pat and Don that Ruby's mental ability had declined and wouldn't permit part-time care. They refused to release her until arrangements were made for Ruby's entry into an assisted living facility.

Oh, and by the way, they needed her out of there in two days.

The search was on for a place where Ruby could be happy. It was a tall order because Pat and Don knew Ruby wouldn't really be happy unless she could return to her own home.

Money was one issue. If Ruby had been a wealthy woman, she could have returned to her home with 24/7 care, and all would have been wonderful. While Jimmy had arranged for her to receive a larger monthly annuity if he predeceased her, it still wouldn't be enough to pay for that sort of care. Going home wasn't on the table.

Carefree Living was a well-maintained facility which had cared for Don's mother, Marie, before she died. They employed nurses and caregivers, and they were well-suited for the job. It was close by, reasonably priced, and the employees there were kind and experienced. Fortunately, they had one private room available. Pat and Don quickly grabbed it and prayed Ruby would settle in and be comfortable.

Chapter 135

Ruby's Home Away From Home

Pat dreaded telling her mother she couldn't return to her own home. Home meant so much to Ruby, but they had reached that moment when it simply couldn't happen. Surprisingly, Ruby didn't have the intense reaction which Pat had feared.

They got Ruby settled in her new living space. In the next few days, Pat brought most of Ruby's clothing from her closet at home. They brought the necklaces, pins, and earrings her mother was fond of wearing, and also brought several of her favorite dolls. All the caregivers were impressed with Ruby's artistry in creating those beautiful dolls.

Ruby requested a TV set for her room, and that helped her feel more comfortable. She could watch the news and favorite programs when she wanted. She had a comfortable reclining chair and she soon discovered she could take great "catnaps" in it. By this time, she only got around with the help of a walker. But she was free to go from her room to the dining room or to the recreational area. In nice weather, she could sit outside on the covered patio.

The staff found ways to keep their residents engaged. They played bingo and other games each week, they participated in arts and crafts activities, and about once a week they invited a musician to entertain the group. They even had "chair" exercising sessions. Meals were served at tables for four residents. Ruby made friends with many of the ladies.

Carefree Living put on a Cinco de Mayo celebration every year on May 5. Friends and relatives of the residents were invited to participate and sit with their loved one. The food was always outstanding, and brightly costumed Mexican dancers entertained.

When Ruby's birthday came along, Pat and Don would arrange to bring her to their house for the event. They invited other friends and relatives and Ruby enjoyed that.

For Christmas that first year, Pat and her friend Joan Taitte put up the Christmas tree at Ruby's house. On Christmas Eve, Don and Paula's husband Danny picked up Ruby and brought her back to her house to enjoy Christmas Eve dinner and the traditional Christmas Eve event of opening the presents. Pat always gifted Ruby with at least one sweater which featured a beautiful red cardinal.

David would sometimes be in a position to fly to Albuquerque right after Christmas to visit his mom. He would sleep on Pat and Don's living room sofa during those visits. Ruby was always so grateful to see her beloved son.

Ruby continued to enjoy birthdays, Thanksgivings, and Christmases at Pat's house. Paula and Danny and other old friends often participated. Ruby was delighted to have these parties.

By this time her hearing was pretty bad, so she often misheard what folks were saying, which made for lots of laughter when she repeated what she thought they said. She hated wearing the hearing aids and would take them out after a short time. She said it felt like she had chewing gum in her ears. The caregivers at Carefree Living struggled to keep track of Ruby's hearing aids.

Pat and Don took Ruby to dental appointments, doctor's visits, and audiology appointments. She seemed to enjoy going for a drive. Many of her friends also visited her at Carefree Living. Pat usually visited her each week.

When Ruby became a resident of Carefree Living, she used her walker to get around the facility. By late 2017, she could no longer walk and was confined to a wheelchair. Her memory continued to worsen and sometimes she thought Pat was her sister.

Pat and Don learned that people in Ruby's situation were allowed to enter hospice care for six months at a time. A doctor could recommend hospice and the patient would have access to a visiting doctor, a visiting nurse, a hospital bed, wheelchair, and a visiting social worker. The patient could go off of hospice and return to the program whenever the situation warranted it. All of this was available to patients on Social Security.

Ruby went on hospice for two, six-month terms. She was removed from the Hospice program for a short while, but it became obvious she still needed it. She simply wasn't improving now. At age 98, improvement wasn't in the cards.

On Wednesday, April 4, 2018, Carefree Living determined Ruby needed to go back on the hospice program. Pat went to meet the hospice representative to sign paperwork for putting Ruby back on the program. When Pat arrived, she was stunned to see her mother in the back room where people who had difficulty feeding themselves ate.

Ruby was hunched over the plate, not eating, and didn't seem aware of anything around her. Pat went over to talk to her, and Ruby didn't seem to know Pat was there. This was a dramatic change in her situation.

As Pat signed the paperwork, she looked over and saw her mother now feeding herself. She hoped this signified that perhaps Ruby had simply been napping previously.

On Sunday morning, April 8, 2018, at around 8:00 a.m., Pat and Don were having their usual Sunday breakfast. The phone rang and the caller ID advertised it was Carefree Living. Carefree Living often called to ask questions, or advise they needed something for Ruby. Pat answered the phone, and the voice at the other end asked if this was Ruby's daughter? It was a new voice, probably an attendant who worked the night shift and was ready to leave for the day.

Pat confirmed that she was Ruby's daughter. This lady—obviously anxious to get it done quickly—simply said, "She died."

Ruby entered Carefree Living in March 2013. She died on April 8, 2018, on her mother's 122nd birthday.

Chapter 136

Sometimes Things Come Full Circle

Ruby Ellen Scott Smith left her earthly body and joined her husband on Sunday morning, April 8, 2018. It often seems that people on the verge of crossing over have the ability to "decide" when they will make the transition. As it happens, April 8 was the birth date of Ruby's mother, Jimma. Did some part of Ruby's brain decide to leave life on that date? Was there an important reason? Was it just an interesting coincidence?

I think it's intriguing to contemplate these things, but many people might think otherwise. Perhaps someday we'll all finally learn the answers to so many of life's questions. If she really did "pick" her time for leaving this earth, perhaps she also timed it to be close to her beloved Jimmy's date of death on April 21, 2002. Ruby's funeral was set for Friday, April 20, 2018.

Ruby and Jimmy's son David flew to Albuquerque for the funeral. He arrived on Wednesday, April 18, in time for the Visitation at the mortuary Thursday evening. Many of Ruby's friends, and even friends of her daughter and granddaughter came by to offer their condolences. There were lots of flowers, and Ruby wore the beautiful pink dress she'd worn for her big 50th anniversary party in 1988.

Ruby outlived most of her relatives. Two of her nephews from Texas attended the service, but their parents were no longer alive. All of Ruby's sisters and four of Jimmy's brothers predeceased her. Many of Ruby and Jimmy's good friends also passed away ahead of her. Even most of Ruby's wonderful doll club friends were already gone to their reward.

Ruby Ellen Scott Smith packed a lot of living into her 98-almost-99-years of living. She knew misery and wonderful happiness. She endured poverty and gained plenty. She lived through tumultuous times and wonderful experiences. She found courage to leave a bad situation and make a better life for herself.

She loved her family, but especially the family she made for herself. She inspired her children to do their best and take responsibility for themselves. She made hundreds of friends through her lifetime and kept in touch with most of them throughout their lives. She was admired and respected by many more people than she would ever have imagined.

And much to her surprise, she really was an artist. The proof is in the beautiful dolls she made for herself, and for so many people.

I hope she knows how much she meant to those who knew and loved her, and how very, very special she was.

Epilogue

By the onset of my 50s, I realized how much Ruby Ellen Scott Smith had overcome in her life journey. Her young years had a lot of trauma and unhappiness. She worked hard to create a good life for herself. She loved to read and had a vast library to prove it. Music warmed her soul. She played records or CDs most of her adult life.

She was a prolific gardener. Starting in the 1950s, she planted gardens in every home they owned. She also had a love of birds and maintained feeding stations for all of them well into her 90s.

One of her favorite birds was the Cardinal. She'd seen them all her life in Texas and Maryland. New Mexico doesn't have them in our area. When she returned to New Mexico later in life, she started receiving Cardinal-themed gifts from her friends. They gave her refrigerator magnets, coasters, napkins, earrings—all featuring Cardinals.

Not long after she died, I received mental "suggestions" to write a book about her life. At first, I dismissed the idea. Then one day my mind started exploring the possibility. I would write about her life and the historic events happening in those years. I believed telling her story might help 21st century people understand what 19th and 20th century people endured all those many years ago.

I started the project, but it was slow and sporadic. Then messages started coming to me in the form of catalogs containing Cardinal-themed items.

For years, I've been a catalog junky. Long ago I sent off for a dozen or so, and those requests gave birth to dozens more. During the years before Mom died, I don't recall ever wanting to buy something with a Cardinal on it.

About a year after she passed, an eruption of catalogs appeared in my mailbox. Almost every other page featured clothing, towels, pillows, and decorative items with Cardinals on them. There was, jewelry, tablecloths, and Christmas tree ornaments. It became a running joke every mail delivery.

One day, my husband said, "Your mother is sending you a message to get back to work on her book." So, I took his advice and went back to work.

The catalogues still come. Unfortunately, one of the downsides is the number of items I've now purchased with a Cardinal prominently featured. I'm sure my mother is gleefully laughing. Now that Raising Ruby is finished, I pray the onslaught stops.

Acknowledgements

I can't imagine being a writer without the assistance of the many people who helped me on this project.

Without my wonderful husband, Don, this would not have happened. He has encouraged me from the moment the idea came. He keeps the world out of my way while I struggle with what to say. (Oh, good grief! I'm waxing poetic now!) The next supporter was my beautiful daughter, Paula. She, too, is a writer and understands the challenges. My brother, David Smith, owner of U-Photo.com, worked on photographs for me to use. He also reminded me of significant events for the book. I'm thrilled with the cover he's crafted for our mother's book.

Because I wanted accurate history, I called on several people for help. My knowledgeable cousin, Cecelia Smith Gilbreath, sent me history books about Fort Worth and looked up records from the past. She cheered me on and helped me believe I could do it. She helped me remember important events concerning our family members.

My second history helper would be Linda Barrett at the Fort Worth Public Library. She always responded to the many questions I emailed to her, and she provided accurate information. She was especially helpful with facts about the Casa Mañana celebration in 1937 and 1938. I hope she enjoys the finished product.

I've had wonderful exchanges with Mylinda Rosen, whose grandmother was Ruth Nance, my mother's best friend and the one who helped her get settled in her new home in Fort Worth.

Because most of this book was written during the shutdowns of the COVID pandemic, I didn't have the opportunity to get feedback from my writers critique group. But one of those ladies, Ruthie Francis, patiently allowed me to read each new chapter to her over the telephone. That helped immensely. Another fantastic and well-published author helped me with editing Part One. Thanks to Jane Lindskold for taking the time to make things better.

And last, but definitely not least, Mike Orenduff, managing editor at Aakenbaaken & Kent, was excited about my plunge into a biographical project. He encouraged me and waited patiently for it to be completed. Without his enthusiasm, I might still be slugging it out. Thanks, Mike, and to all your helpers at A&K.

Finally, my mother, Ruby Ellen Scott Smith, was a woman of many talents, and one who lived through some bad times and some really wonderful ones. I hope she knows how much I admired and loved her. Her strength and persistence was a huge model for me growing up.